Art & Ardor

Art & Ardor

ESSAYS BY

Cynthia Ozick

1 9 83

Alfred A. Knopf New York

THIS IS A BORZOI BOOK
PUBLISHED BY ALFRED A. KNOPF, INC.

Grateful acknowledgment is made to the following for permission to reprint from previously published material:

The Jewish Publication Society of America: *Remembering Maurice Samuel* which is copyrighted by and used through the courtesy of The Jewish Publication Society of America.

The New York Times Company: *The Loose, Drifting Material of Life*, originally published as a review of *The Diary of Virginia Woolf, Vol. 1* © 1977 by The New York Times Company. *I. B. Singer's Book of Creation*, originally published as *Collected Stories of Isaac Bashevis Singer* © 1982 by The New York Times Company. *The Fourth Sparrow: The Magisterial Reach of Gershom Scholem*, originally published as *Slouching Towards Smyrna* © 1974 by The New York Times Company. Reprinted by permission.

Some of the essays in this collection were originally published in the following: *Commentary, Confrontation, Judaism, Midstream, Mademoiselle, Moment, Ms., The New Republic, The New York Review of Books, The New York Times, Partisan Review,* and *Salmagundi.*

LIBRARY OF CONGRESS CATALOGING IN PUBLICATION DATA
Ozick, Cynthia.
Art & ardor.
I. Title. II. Title: Art and ardor.
PS3565.Z5A9 1983   809   82-49191
ISBN 0-394-53082-9

Manufactured in the United States of America
Published May 17, 1983
Second Printing, July 1983

FOR ROBERT A. GOTTLIEB

esteem and love

Contents

Foreword

I have a conscientious and responsible friend, a professor and a scholar, and also a reputable literary critic; in her heart she is a secret playwright. She wants to make things up: characters, settings, dialogues, plots. So far she has not allowed herself to begin: she is too conscientious, too responsible. Instead, she concentrates, in sober prose, on literary and historical subjects. She knows that make-believe is frivolity. She will not permit herself a descent, however alluring, into the region of the trivial. She is a writer of essays.

My own predicament is opposite. I never meant to write essays. Only once have I ever written a piece of nonfiction on purpose and for its own sake, self-propelled. The desire came on me spontaneously, long ago, just after reading George Orwell's "Such, Such Were the Joys . . . ," a memoir of Orwell's melancholy childhood in an English boarding school. I was then somewhere in the middle of seven fruitless years given over to the writing of a novel that was never completed. The abandoned novel was called *Mercy, Pity, Peace, and Love,* a line from Blake; I have always regretted the loss of those rich words. The essay-written-for-its-own-sake *did* get finished, however, and even published (never mind in what mutilated and fragmented form), and though my own childhood was as far from an English boarding school as can be imagined, the essay's theme was Orwell's: school injustice and school humiliation. For more than twenty years, the essay and the novel have shared a cardboard box in some unremembered attic corner.

If all this carries with it an elegiac air, it is because I learn from it that volition is not always the robust master of Self we expect it to be. What we think we are surely going to do, we don't do; and what we never intended to do, we may one day notice that we have done, and done, and done. Consequently, except for the drive—once —to mimic Orwell (and who can mimic Orwell?), I see, after two decades of never intending it, that I have written over one hundred essays—some in the form of articles or fugitive pieces; others to serve a public occasion (a talk at a conference, for instance); three or four, out of political necessity, as forays into advocacy journalism ("artists and writers," Chekhov said, "should engage themselves in politics only enough to protect themselves from politics"); the rest an outgrowth of reading and reviewing. (Reading to save one's life is almost always private.) Of these hundred and more, all were instigated or invited. The stimulus was inevitably external. But if "invited" has the sound of welcome, that is by and large a misrepresentation of struggle and scramble. Most of the hundred were written catch-as-catch-can, out of unashamed print-lust, in the absence of what is usually called a "platform." They were written on quicksand, without a place to stand: no regularly supportive periodical, no professorship, no body of learning, no assurance, no early mark made for oneself; every start a new start; walking round a thought—an assigned, appointed, prescribed, imposed thought—as if it had dropped from the sky in need of pristine examination. The hundred were mainly written as spurs pressed hard in the dark, in response to an occasional summons from a chance voice. What was that summons? Print; and the sure knowledge that print is often chance.

All the same, essays seem a deviation, a diversion: the region of the trivial, no matter how momentous the subject. We can speculate why. Essays summarize. They do not invent. In undertaking the writing of an essay (or article, or "piece," and most particularly in journalism), I know beforehand what I think. I see the end, it is all the while uncompromisingly, inflexibly, in sight, and my task is to traverse the space between. The risks are small. The way is predictable. It is a journey of obligation within borders, not an adventure. But in beginning a story I know nothing at all: surely not where I am going, and hardly at all how to get there. In a story, one cannot guess what lies at the close of the sentence, much less any wider goal or climax or resolution. Yet the resolution always miraculously rises to organize itself and everything around it. Fiction is all discovery; discovery plotted—fallen into, rather—by character: first the writer's, and only then the characters'. Even failure is worthwhile —so much has been dared: scaling an edge to find out something "new," "true"—inherent, immanent, encoded—that was unsuspected at the start, and by the end seems both ingenious and right. No essay carrying its bundle of information, subject matter, "field," theme, argument, intent, no essay carrying its armful of context, point of view, explicit history and explicit culture, can equal that. Essays know too much.

Except sometimes. Knowledge is not made out of knowledge. Knowledge swims up from invention and imagination—from ardor —and sometimes even an essay can invent, burn, guess, try out, dig up, hurtle forward, succumb to that flood of sign and nuance that adds up to intuition, disclosure, discovery. The only nonfiction worth writing—at least for me—lacks the summarizing gift, is heir to nothing, and sets out with empty pockets from scratch. Sensibility (or intellect, or susceptibility) is most provoked when most deprived of scaffolding; then it has to knot sheets for the climb. A number of essays included here began without the freight of preconception. Whether or not they are serviceable or poor examples of thinking is something the reader will determine. But in the writing they felt, for the most part, as much scouted and discovered as stories themselves. And that, I think—in an era when the notion of belles-lettres is profoundly dead, and when the capacious idea of the person-of-letters who can take on a range of available forms is no more than a legendary glimmer—that can be the only justification for their having been written at all.

C. O.

Art & Ardor

Justice (Again) to Edith Wharton

Nearly forty years ago, Edmund Wilson wrote a little essay about an underrated American novelist and called it "Justice to Edith Wharton." She was in need of justice, he claimed, because "the more commonplace work of her later years had had the effect of dulling the reputation of her earlier and more serious work." During this last period—a stretch of about seventeen years, from (roughly) 1920 to her death in 1937—Edith Wharton's novels were best sellers, her short stories commanded thousands of dollars; but both in mode and motivation she remained, like so many others in the twenties and thirties, a nineteenth-century writer. She believed in portraying character, her characters displayed the higher values, her prose was a platform for her own views. In 1937, when Wilson undertook to invigorate her reputation, the machinery of nineteenth-century fiction was beginning to be judged not so much as the expression of a long tradition, or (as nowadays we seem to view it) as the exhausted practice of a moribund convention, but more bluntly as a failure of talent. Wilson accounted for that apparent failure in Edith Wharton by speculating on the psychological differences between male and female writers:

Essay published in *Commentary*, October 1976.

It is sometimes true of women writers—less often, I believe, of men
—that a manifestation of something like genius may be stimulated by
some exceptional emotional strain, but will disappear when the stimulus has passed. With a man, his professional, his artisan's life is likely
to persist and evolve as a partially independent organism through the
vicissitudes of his emotional experience. Henry James in a virtual
vacuum continued to possess and develop his *métier*. But Mrs. Wharton had no *métier* in this sense.

What sort of "justice" is this? A woman typically writes best when
her emotions are engaged; the barren female heart cannot seize the
writer's trade? Only a decade ago, such a declaration would have
been derided by old-fashioned feminists as a passing insolence. But
even the satiric reader, contending in one fashion or another with
this passage, would have been able, ten years ago, to pluck the
offending notion out as a lapse in the texture of a measured and
generally moderating mind.

No longer. Wilson's idea returns only to hold, and it holds nowhere so much as among the literary proponents of the current
women's movement: Wilson's lapse is exalted to precept. The idea
of Edith Wharton as a "woman writer" in need of constantly renewable internal stimuli, whose gifts are best sustained by "exceptional
emotional strain"—all this suits the newest doctrine of sexual exclu-
siveness in literature. Indeed, one of the outstanding tenets of this
doctrine embraces Wilson unrelentingly. "Rarely in the work now
being written by women," according to an article called "Toward
a Definition of the Female Sensibility,"

> does one feel the presence of writers genuinely penetrating their own
> experience, risking emotional humiliation and the facing-down of
> secret fears, unbearable wisdoms. . . . There are works, however,
> . . . in which one feels the heroic effort stirring,*

and there follow numerous examples of women writing well because
of the stimulus of some exceptional emotional strain.

Restitution, then (one supposes), is to come to Edith Wharton not
from the old-fashioned feminists, but from the newer sort, who

---

*Vivian Gornick, *The Village Voice*, May 31, 1973.

embrace the proposition that strong emotion in women, emotion uniquely female, is what will best nourish a female literature. What we are to look for next, it follows, is an ambitious new-feminist critical work studying Wharton's "vicissitudes of . . . emotional experience" and correlating the most fevered points with the most accomplished of the fictions.

Such a work, it turns out, more extensive and more supple than Wilson's pioneer brief would suggest, has just made its appearance: Ellen Moers's *Literary Women*. Like other new feminists, Moers believes that there is such an entity as the "history of women," that there are poetic images uniquely female, and even "landscapes charged with female privacy." She writes of "how much the freedom and tactile sensations of near-naked sea bathing has meant to modern women," and insists that a scene recounting the sensation of walking through a field of sea-like grass provides that "moment when Kate Chopin reveals herself most truly a woman writer." Edith Wharton's life—a buried life—ought, properly scrutinized, to feed such a set of sympathies, and to lure the attention of restitution. *Literary Women*, after all, is conceived of in part as a rescue volume, as a book of rehabilitation and justice: a number of writers, Moers explains, "came to life for me as women writers as they had not done before. Mrs. Gaskell and Anne Brontë had once bored me; Emily Dickinson was an irritating puzzle, as much as a genius; I could barely read Mary Shelley and Mrs. Browning. Reading them anew as women writers taught me how to get excited about these five, and others as well."

Others as well. But Edith Wharton is omitted from *Literary Women*. Her name appears only once, as an entry in an appendix. Only *The House of Mirth* is mentioned there, along with a reference, apparently by way of explanation of the larger omission, to the chapter on Edith Wharton in Alfred Kazin's *On Native Grounds*. Pursuing the citation, one discovers that Kazin, like Wilson, like the new feminists, speaks of "the need that drove her to literature." Whatever the need, it does not engage Moers; or Kazin. He advances the notion that "to Edith Wharton, whose very career as a novelist was the tenuous product of so many personal maladjustments, the novel became an involuted expression of self." Unlike the new feminists, Kazin will not celebrate this expression; it represents for him a "failure to fulfill herself in art." Wharton, he concludes, "remains not a great artist but an unusual American, one who brought the weight of her personal experience to bear upon a modern American literature to which she was spiritually alien."

Justice to Edith Wharton: where, then, is it to come from? Not taken seriously by the dominant criticism, purposefully ignored by the radical separatist criticism of the new feminists*—she represents an antagonism. The antagonism is not new. Wharton describes it herself in her memoir, *A Backward Glance:*

> My literary success puzzled and embarrassed my old friends far more than it impressed them, and in my own family it created a kind of constraint which increased with the years. None of my relations ever spoke to me of my books, either to praise or blame—they simply ignored them; and among the immense tribe of my cousins, though it included many with whom I was on terms of affectionate intimacy, the subject was avoided as if it were a kind of family disgrace, which might be condoned but could not be forgotten. Only one eccentric widowed cousin, living a life of lonely invalidism, turned to my novels for occasional distraction, and had the courage to tell me so.

She continues: "At first I felt this indifference acutely; but now I no longer cared, for my recognition as a writer had transformed my life."

So it is here—in this uplifting idea, "my life," this teleological and novelistic idea above all—that one will finally expect to look for Wharton's restitution "as a writer." The justice that criticism perversely fails to bring, biography will achieve.

Perhaps. The biography of a novelist contains a wonderful advantage: it accomplishes, when well executed, a kind of mimicry. A good biography is itself a kind of novel. Like the classic novel, a biography believes in the notion of "a life"—a life as a triumphal or tragic story with a shape, a story that begins at birth, moves on to a middle part, and ends with the death of the protagonist.

---

*Though, to be fair, I have heard of at least one new-feminist literature class that has studied *The House of Mirth*—evidently because it is so easy to interpret its heroine as the ideal victim.

Despite the reliable pervasiveness of birth and death, hardly any "real" life is like that. Most simply unfold, or less than that, dream-walk themselves out. The middle is missing. What governs is not pattern but drift. Most American lives, moreover, fail to recognize that they are sticks in a stream, and are conceived of as novels-of-progress, as purposeful *Bildungsromane* saturated with an unending hopefulness, with the notion of infinite improvement on the way toward a salubrious goal; the frontier continues to inhabit the American mentality unfailingly.

And most American biographies are written out of this same source and belief. A biography that is most like a novel is least like a life. Edith Wharton's life, though much of it was pursued outside of America, is an American life in this sense: that, despite certain disciplines, it was predicated on drift, and fell out, rather than fell into place. If other American lives, less free than hers, drift less luckily between the Scylla and Charybdis of obligation and crisis, hers drifted in a setting all horizon, in a perpetual noncircumstance clear of external necessity. She had to invent her own environment and its conditions, and while this may seem the reverse of rudderless-ness, what it signifies really is movement having to feign a destination. A life with a "shape" is occasioned by what is present in that life; drift grows out of what is absent. For Edith Wharton there was —outside the writing—no destination, and no obligation to get there. She had houses, she had wealth; she chose, rather than "had," friends. She had no family (she was estranged from her brothers, and we hear nothing further about the affectionate cousins), she had no husband (though she was married to one for more than half her life), she had no children. For a long time she resented and disliked children, and was obsessed by a love for small dogs. She was Henry James's ideal American heroine: she was indeed his very heiress of all the ages, she was "free," she was cultivated both in the conventional and the spiritual sense, she was gifted, acute, mobile; she appeared to be mistress of her destiny.

The destiny of such freedom is drift, and though her life was American in this, it was European in its resignation: she had no illusion that—outside the writing—she was doing more than "filling in." Her one moment of elevated and secure purpose occurred when, inspired by the model of Walt Whitman in the hospitals of the Civil War, she founded war relief agencies in France during the First World War. She supervised brilliantly: she supervised her friendships, her gardeners, her guests, the particulars of her dinner parties, her households; she even, to a degree, supervised the insurmountable Henry James—she took him for long rides in her car, she demanded hours in London and tea at Lamb House, she finagled with his publisher to provide him with a handsome advance (she herself was the secret philanthropist behind the scenes), she politicked to try and get him the Nobel Prize for Literature. She supervised and commanded, but since no one demanded anything of *her* (with a single exception, which, like the Gorgon's head, was not to be gazed at), she was captain, on an uncharted deep, of a ship without any imaginable port. She did everything on her own, to no real end; no one ever asked her to accommodate to any pressure of need, she had no obligations that she did not contrive or duty that she did not devise. Her necessities were self-imposed. Her tub went round and round in a sea of self-pleasing.

All this was outside the writing. One learns it from R. W. B. Lewis's prize-winning biography,* which is, like a posthumously uncovered Wharton novel, sustained by the idea of "a life." It has the fecund progression, the mastery of incident, the affectionate but balanced devotion to its protagonist, the power of suspenseful development, even the unraveling of a mysterious love story, that the "old" novel used to deliver—the novel before it became a self-referring "contemporary" art-object. In its own way it is a thesis novel: it is full of its intention to bring justice to Edith Wharton. A massive biography, almost by its weight, insists on the importance of its subject. Who would dare pass that writer by to whom a scholar-writer has dedicated, as Lewis has, nearly a decade of investigation and discovery? "They are among the handsomest achievements in our literature," he remarks of her major fictions. And adds: "I have wondered, with other admirers of Edith Wharton, whether her reputation might today stand even higher if she had been a man."

Edith Wharton: A Biography (Harper & Row, 1975). The prizes are the Pulitzer, the National Book Critics Circle Award, and Columbia University's Bancroft Prize.

If the last statement has overtones of the new feminism—glory but for the impediment of sex—the book does not. Lewis sets out to render the life of an artist, not of a "woman artist." Unexpectedly, though it is the artist he is after, what he succeeds chiefly in giving us is the life of a woman. The "chiefly" is no small thing: it is useful to have a documented narrative of an exceptional upper-class woman of a certain American period. Still, without romanticizing what is meant by the phrase "an artist's life," there is a difference between the biography of a writer and the mode of living of a narrow American class.

Can the life justify the writer then? Or, to put it otherwise, can biography take the place of literary judgment? Lewis's book is a straightforward "tale," not a critical biography. Nor is it "psychobiography": though it yields new and revealing information about Edith Wharton's sexual experience, it does not propose to illumine the hidden chambers of the writer's sentience—as, for example, Ruby V. Redinger's recent inquiry into George Eliot's relationship to her brother Isaac, with its hunches and conjectures, purports to do, or Quentin Bell's half-study, half-memoir of Virginia Woolf. Lewis has in common with these others the revelation of a secret. In the case of Quentin Bell, it is the exact extent of Virginia Woolf's insanity; in the volume on George Eliot, the secret is the dense burden of humiliation imposed by an adored brother more cruel and rigid than society itself. And in Lewis, the secret is an undreamed-of, now minutely disclosed, adulterous affair with a journalist. In all three accounts, the writer is on the whole not there. It is understandable that the writer is mainly absent for the psychobiographer; something else is being sought. It is even more understandable that the writer should be absent for a nephew-biographer, whose preoccupation is with confirming family stories.

But if, for Lewis, the writer is not there, it is not because he fails to look for her but because she is very nearly invisible. What, through luck and diligence, he causes to become visible is almost not the point, however unpredictable and startling his discoveries are. And they are two: the surprising place of Morton Fullerton in Edith Wharton's middle years, and the appearance of a candid manuscript, written in her seventies, describing, with the lyrical explicitness of an enraptured anatomist, a fictional incestuous coupling. The manuscript and the love affair are so contrary to the established Wharton legend of cold propriety that they go far to make us look again—but only at the woman, not at the writer.

The real secret in Lewis's biography is devoid of sex, lived or imagined, though its centerpiece is a bed; and it concerns not the woman but the writer. The secret is divulged on page 353, when Wharton is fifty-one, and occupies ten lines in a volume of nearly six hundred pages. The ten lines recount a perplexing incident—"a minor fit of hysterics." The occasion is mysterious: Edith Wharton and Bernard Berenson, touring the great cities and museums of Europe together, arrive at the Hotel Esplanade in Berlin. They check into their respective rooms, and Edith Wharton, ignoring the view of the city though she has never been there before, begins to rage

> because the bed in her hotel room was not properly situated; not until it had been moved to face the window did she settle down and begin to find Berlin "incomparable." Berenson thought this an absurd performance; but because Edith never harped upon the physical requirements of her literary life, he did not quite realize that she worked in bed every morning and therefore needed a bed which faced the light. It had been her practice for more than twenty years; and for a woman . . . who clung so tenaciously to her daily stint, the need was a serious one.

The fit and its moment pass; the ensuing paragraphs tell of German politics snubbed and German music imbibed—we are returned, in short, to the life of an upper-class American expatriate tourist, privileged to travel in the company of a renowned connoisseur. But the plangent moment—an outcry over the position of a bed—dominates the book: dominates what has gone before and what is to come, and recasts both. Either the biographer can stand up to this moment —the woman revealed *as writer*—or the book falls into the drifting ash of "a life."

It falls, but it is not the biographer's fault; or not his fault alone. Edith Wharton—as writer—is to blame. She put a veil over the bed that was her workplace, and screened away the real life that was lived in it. What moves like a long afterimage in the wake of reading Lewis is a procession of stately majesties: Edith Wharton always standing, always regal, always stiffly dressed and groomed, standing with her wonderfully vertical spine in the hall of one of her great houses, or in the drawing room of her Paris apartment, with her fine hand out to some equally resplendent guest, or in her gardens, not so much admiring her flowers as instructing or reprimanding the servants of her flowers; or else "motoring" through the dust of some picturesque lane in the French countryside, her chauffeur in peaked hat and leather goggles, like blinders, on a high seat in front of her, indistinguishable from the horse that still headed most vehicles on the road.

If this is the Wharton myth, she made it; she wove it daily. It winds itself out like a vivid movie, yet darkly; it leaves out the window-lit bed. What went on outside the bed does not account for what went on in it. She frequented literary salons, and on a smaller scale held them (after dinner, Henry James reading aloud in the library); she talked bookishly, and with fervor; she was an intellectual. But she was not the only brilliant woman of her time and status; all of that, in the biography of a writer, weighs little.

Visualize the bed: she used a writing board. Her breakfast was brought to her by Gross, the housekeeper, who almost alone was privy to this inmost secret of the bedchamber. (A secretary picked up the pages from the floor for typing.) Out of bed, she would have had to be, according to her code, properly dressed, and this meant stays. In bed, her body was free, and freed her pen.

There is a famous photograph of Edith Wharton seated at a desk; we know now, thanks to the "minor fit of hysterics" at the Hotel Esplanade, how the camera lies—even though it shows us everything we might want to know about a way of life. The time is in the 1890s, the writer is in her early thirties. The desk is vast, shining, with a gold-tooled leather top; at the rear of its far surface is a decorated rack holding half a dozen books, but these are pointless—not only because anyone using this desk would need an impossibly long reach, but because all the volumes are faced away from the writer, with their backs and titles to the open room. Two tall electrified candlestick-lamps (the wire drags awkwardly) stand sentinel over two smaller candlesticks; there is a single letter, already stamped; otherwise the desk is clear, except for a pair of nervous ringed hands fiddling with a bit of paper.

The hands belong to a young woman got up, to our eyes, as theatrically as some fanciful notion of royalty: she is plainly a lady of fashion, with a constricted waist and a constricting tall collar; her dress is of the whitest fabric, all eyeleted, embroidered, sashed; her hair is elaborately rolled and ringleted; an earring makes a white dot below the high dark eave of her hair; her back is straight, even as she leans forward with concentrated mouth and lost eyes, in the manner of a writer in trance. Mellifluous folds hide her feet; a lady has no legs. She is sitting on a graceful chair with whorled feet—rattan framed by the most beautiful carved and burnished wood. (A rattan chair with not a single hole? No one could ever have *worked* in such a chair; the photographer defrauds us—nothing more important than a letter will ever be written at this desk.) The Oriental carpet, with its curious and dense figures, is most explicitly in focus, and over the edge of it a tail of skirt spills, reflected white on a floor as sleek as polished glass. In the background, blurred to the camera's lens but instructive to ours: a broad-shouldered velvet chair, a marble bust on an ebony pedestal, a table with a huge porcelain sculpture, a lofty shut oak or walnut door. —In short, an "interior," reminding us that the woman at the unused desk has undertaken, as her first writing venture, a collaborative work called *The Decoration of Houses*.

There are other portraits in this vein, formal, posed, poised, "intellectual" (meaning the subject muses over a seeming letter or book), all jeweled clips and chokers and pearls in heavy rows, pendants, feathered hats, lapdogs, furs, statuesque burdens of flounced bosom and grand liquescent sleeve, queenly beyond our bourgeois imaginings. And the portraits of houses: multiple chimneys, balconies, cupolas, soaring Romanesque windows, immense stone staircases, summer awnings of palatial breadth, shaped ivy, topiary like oversized chess pieces, walks, vistas, clouds of flower beds.

What are we (putting aside Marxist thoughts) to make of this avalanche of privilege? It is not enough to say: money. The class she derived from never talked of money; the money was invisible, like the writing in bed, and just as secret, and just as indispensable. The "love of beauty," being part of class habit, does not explain it; perhaps the class habit does. It was the class habit that kept her on the move: the class habit that is restlessness and drift. She wore out houses and places, or else her spirit wore out in them: New York, Newport, Lenox—finally America. In France there was the Paris apartment in the Rue de Varenne, then a small estate in St. Brice-sous-Forêt, in the country north of Paris, then an old chateau in Hyères, on the warm Mediterranean coast. Three times in her life she supervised the total renovation of a colossal mansion and its grounds, in effect building and furnishing and landscaping from scratch; and once, in Lenox, she bought a piece of empty land and really did start from scratch, raising out of the earth an American palace called The Mount. All of this exacted from her the energy, attentiveness, and insatiable governing impulses of a corporation chief executive; or the head of a small state.

In an architectural lull, she would travel. All her life she traveled compulsively, early in her marriage with her husband, touring Europe from February to June, afterward with various male companions, with the sense, and with the propriety, of leading a retinue. Accumulating "scenes"—hotels, landscapes, seascapes, museums, villages, ruins—she saw all the fabled cities of Europe, the islands of the Aegean, Tunis, Algiers, Carthage, the Sahara.

And all the while she was surrounded by a crowd. Not simply while traveling: the crowd was part of the daily condition of her houses and possessions. She had a household staff consisting of maids ("housemaids" and "chambermaids"—there appears to be a difference), a chief gardener and several under-gardeners, cook, housekeeper, major-domo, chauffeur, personal maid, "traveling" maid, secretary, "general agent," footmen. (One of the latter, accompanying her to I Tatti, the Berenson villa in Italy, inconveniently fell in love with a Berenson maid, and had to be surrendered.) These "establishments," Lewis remarks, "gave her what her bountiful nature desired: an ordered life, a carefully tended beauty of surroundings, and above all, total privacy." The "above all" engenders skepticism. Privacy? Surveying that mob of servants, even imagining them crossing silent carpets on tiptoe, one takes the impression, inevitably, of a hive. Her solitude was the congested solitude of a monarch; she was never, like other solitary-minded American writers (one thinks of Poe, or of course Emily Dickinson, or even Scott Fitzgerald), completely alone in the house. But these hectic movements of the hive were what she required; perhaps she would not have known how to do without them. Chekhov could sit at a table in the middle of the din of a large impoverished family, ignoring voices and footsteps in order to concentrate on the scratch of his pen. Edith Wharton sat up in bed with her writing board, in the middle of the active business of a house claiming her attention, similarly shutting out the only family she had. A hired family, an invented one. When she learned that her older brother Freddy, living not far away in Paris, had suffered a stroke, she was "unresponsive"; but when Gross, her housekeeper of long standing, and Elise, her personal maid, both grew fatally ill within a short space, she wrote in her diary, "All my life goes with those two dying women."

Nicky Mariano, in her memoir of her life as secretary-companion to Berenson, recalls how Edith Wharton treated her with indifference—until one day, aboard a yacht near Naples, she happened to ask after Elise. She was at once dispatched to the cabin below to visit with the maid. "From then on I became aware of a complete change in Edith's manner to me. There was a warmth, a tone of intimacy that I had never heard before." And again, describing how Wharton "looked after her servants with affectionate zeal and took a lively interest in all their joys and sorrows," she produces another anecdote:

> I remember how once during one of our excursions with her, she was deeply hurt and angry when on leaving a villa near Siena after a prolonged visit she discovered that neither her maid nor her chauffeur had been asked into the house.

What is the effect on a writer of being always encircled by servants? What we are to draw from this is not so much the sadness of purchased affections, or even the parasitism (once, left without much help for a brief period, she was bewildered about her daily survival), but something more perplexing: the moment-by-moment influence of continuous lower-class companionship. Room ought to be given to considering this; it took room in Wharton's life: she was with her servants all the time, she was with her friends and peers only some of the time. E. M. Forster sought out the common people in the belief that too much education atrophies the senses; in life and in art he went after the lower orders because he thought them the embodiment of the spontaneous gods of nature. In theory, at least—perhaps it was only literary theory—Forster wanted to become "instinctual," and instinct was with the working class. But Edith Wharton kept her distance even as she drew close; she remained mistress always. It made her a kind of double exile. As an expatriate settled in France, she had cut herself off from any direct infusion of the American sensibility and the American language. Through her attachment to her servants, she became intimately bound to illiterate lives remote from her mentality, preoccupations, habitual perceptions—a second expatriation as deliberate as the more obvious one. Nor did her servants give her access to "ordinary" life (she was no Lady Chatterley, there was no gamekeeper for her)—no one is "ordinary" while standing before the monarch of the house. Still, she fussed over her army of hirelings; it was a way of inventing claims. For her servants she provided pensions; she instituted a trust fund as a private charity for three Belgian children; she sent regular checks to her sister-in-law, divorced from her brother a quarter of a century and therefore clearly not to be taken for family. For family, in short, she substituted claims indisputably of her own making. She could feel responsible for servants and acquired dependents as others feel responsible for parents, brothers, children: but there was a tether made of money, and the power-end of the tether was altogether in her hand. With servants, there is no murkiness—as there sometimes is in friendship—about who is beholden to whom.

With her friends it was more difficult to invent claims; friendship has a way of resisting purchase, and she had to resort to ruses. When she wanted to release Morton Fullerton from the entangling blackmail of his former French mistress, she arranged with Henry James to make it seem as if the money were coming impersonally from a publisher. Fullerton having been, however briefly, her lover, it was hardly possible to hand over one hundred pounds and call it a "pension"; the object was not so much to keep Fullerton's friendship free as to establish the illusion of such freedom. It was enough for the controlling end of the money tether to know the tether was there; and anyhow the tether had a witness and an accomplice. "Please consider," James wrote, entering into the plot, "that I will play my mechanical part in your magnificent combination with absolute piety, fidelity, and punctuality."

But when it was James himself who came to be on the receiving end of the golden tether, he thundered against the tug of opulence, and the friendship was for a while impaired. The occasion was a proposal for his seventieth birthday: Edith Wharton, enlisting about forty moneyed Americans, thought to raise "not less than $5000," the idea being "that he should choose a fine piece of old furniture, or something of the kind"—but to James it all smelled blatantly of charity, meddling, pity, and cash. Once he got wind of the plan he called it a "reckless and indiscreet undertaking," and announced in a cable that he was beginning "instant prohibitive action. Please express to individuals approached my horror. Money absolutely returned."

It was returned, but within a few months James was hooked anyhow on that same line—hooked like Morton Fullerton, without being aware of it. This time the accomplice was Charles Scribner, who forwarded to James a phoney "advance" of eight thousand dollars intended to see him through the writing of *The Ivory Tower* —but the money was taken out of Wharton's own advance, from another publisher, of fifteen thousand dollars. The reluctant agent of the scheme, far from celebrating "your magnificent combination," saw it rather as "our fell purpose." "I feel rather mean and caddish and must continue so to the end of my days," Charles Scribner grumbled. "Please never give me away." In part this sullenness may have been guilt over not having himself volunteered, as James's publisher, to keep a master artist free from money anxiety, but beyond that there was a distaste for manipulation and ruse.

This moral confusion about proprieties—whom it is proper to tip, and whom not—expressed itself in other strange substitutions. It was not only that she wanted to pay her lover and her friend for services rendered, sexual or literary—clearly she had little overt recognition of the *quid pro quo* uses of philanthropy. It was not only that she loved her maid Gross more than her mother, and Arthur White her "man" more than her brother—it is understood that voluntary entanglements are not really entanglements at all. But there were more conspicuous replacements. Lacking babies, she habitually fondled small dogs: there is an absurd photograph of Edith Wharton as a young woman of twenty-eight, by then five years into her marriage, with an angry-looking Pekingese on each mutton-leg shoulder; the animals, pressed against her cheeks, nearly obscure her face; the face is cautious and contemplative, as of one not wanting to jar precious things. A similar photograph shows her husband gazing straight out at us with rather empty pale eyes over a nicely trimmed mustache and a perfect bow tie—on his lap, with no special repugnance, he is holding three small dogs, two of them of that same truculent breed, and though the caption reads "Teddy Wharton with his dogs," somehow we know better whose dogs they are. His body is detached; his expression, very correct and patient, barely hides— though Lewis argues otherwise—how he is being put upon by such a pose.

Until late in life, she never knew a child. Effie, the little girl in *The Reef,* is a child observed from afar—she runs, she enters, she departs, she is sent, she is summoned, at one moment she is presented as very young, at another she is old enough to be having lessons in Latin. She is a figment of a child. But the little dogs, up to the end of Edith Wharton's life, were always understood, always thought to have souls, always in her arms and in her bed; they were, Lewis says, "among the main joys of her being." Drawing up a list of her "ruling passions" at forty-four, she put "Dogs" second after "Justice and Order." At sixty-two she wrote in her journal of "the *us*ness" in the eyes of animals, "with the underlying *not-us*ness which belies it," and meditated on their "eternal inarticulateness and slavery. Why? their eyes seem to ask us."

The fellow feeling she had for the *not-us*ness of her Pekingese she did not have for her husband, who was, from her point of view, also *"not-us."* He too was inarticulate and mired in the slavery of a lesser intellect. He was a good enough man, interested (like his wife) in being perfectly clothed, vigorous and humorous and kind and compliant (so compliant that he once actually tried to make his way through James's *The Golden Bowl*)—undistinguished in any jot, the absolute product of his class. He had no work to do, and sought none. One of Edith Wharton's friends—a phrase instantly revealing, since her friends were practically never his; the large-hearted Henry James was nearly the only one to cross this divide—observed that Teddy Wharton's "idleness was busy and innocent." His ostensible employment was the management of his wife's trust funds, but he filled his days with sports and hunting, and his glass with fine wine. Wine was the one thing he had a connoisseur's familiarity with; and, of all the elegant good things of the world, wine was the one thing his wife disliked. When he was fifty-three he began to go mad, chiefly, it would seem, because he had married the wrong wife, with no inkling that she would turn out to be the wrong wife. Edith Newbold Jones at twenty-three was exactly what Edward Wharton, a dozen years older, had a right to expect for himself: she had heritage (her ancestor, Ebenezer Stevens, was an enterprising artillery officer in the Revolutionary War), she had inheritance (the Joneses owned the Chemical Bank of New York and much of the West Side). In brief, family and money. The dominant quality— what he had married her for, with that same idle innocence that took note only of the pleasantly obvious—was what Edith Wharton was afterward to call "tribe." The Whartons and the Joneses were of the same tribe—old Protestant money—and he could hardly predict that his wife would soon replace him in the nuptial bed with a writing board. At first he was perplexed but proud: Louis Auchincloss quotes a description of Teddy Wharton from Consuelo Vanderbilt's memoirs as "more of an equerry than an equal, walking behind [his wife] and carrying whatever paraphernalia she happened to discard," and once (Lewis tells us), walking as usual behind her, Teddy exclaimed to one of her friends, "Look at that waist! No one would ever guess that she had written a line of poetry in her life." She, meanwhile, was driven to writing in her journal, "Oh, Gods of derision! And you've given me over twenty years of it!" This outcry occurred immediately after she had shown her husband, during a wearying train journey, "a particularly interesting passage" in a scientific volume called *Heredity and Variation*. His response was not animated. "I heard the key turn in my prison-lock," she recorded, in the clear metaphorical style of her fiction.

A case can be made that it was she who turned the key on him. His encroaching madness altered him—he began to act oddly, out of character; or, rather, more in character than he had ever before dared. The equerry of the paraphernalia undertook to behave as if he were master of the paraphernalia—in short, he embezzled a part of the funds it had been his duty to preserve and augment. And, having been replaced in bed by a writing board, he suddenly confessed to his wife (or perhaps feverishly bragged) that he had recently gone to live with a prostitute in a Boston apartment, filling its remaining rooms with chorus girls; the embezzled funds paid for the apartment. The story was in the main confirmed. His madness had the crucial sanity of needs that are met.

His wife, who—granted that philanthropy is not embezzlement—was herself capable of money ruse, and who had herself once rapturously fallen from merely spiritual friendship, locked him up for it. Against his protestations, and those of his sister and brother, he was sent to a sanitorium. Teddy had stolen, Teddy had fallen; he was an adulterer. She had never stolen (though there is a robust if mistaken critical tradition that insists she stole her whole literary outlook from Henry James); but she had fallen, she was an adulteress. Teddy's sexual disgrace was public; hers went undivulged until her biographer came upon it more than three decades after her death. But these sardonic parallels and opposites illumine little beyond the usual ironies of the pot and the kettle. What had all at once happened in Edith Wharton's life was that something *had* happened. Necessity intervened, her husband was irrefutably a manic-depressive. He had hours of excitement and accusation; more often he was in a state of self-castigation. He begged her for help, he begged to be taken back and to be given a second chance. ". . . when you came back last year," she told him, "I was ready to overlook everything you had done, and to receive you as if nothing had happened." This referred to the Boston apartment; she herself had been in a London hotel with Fullerton at nearly the same time. In the matter of her money she

was more unyielding. Replying to his plea to be allowed to resume
the management of her trusts and property, she took the tone of a
mistress with a servant who has been let go, and who is now discovered still unaccountably loitering in the house. "In order that no
further questions of this kind should come up, the only thing left for
me to do is to suggest that you should resign your Trusteeship.
. . . Your health unfortunately makes it impossible for you to take
any active part in the management of my affairs." Gradually, over
months, she evolved a policy: she did everything for him that seemed
sensible, as long as it was cold-hearted. He was removed, still un-
cured, from the sanitorium, and subjected to a regime of doctors,
trips, traveling companions, scoldings. In the end, when he was most
sick and most desperate, she discarded him, handing him over to the
doctors the way one hands over impeding paraphernalia to an
equerry. She discarded him well before she divorced him; divorce,
at that period and in her caste, took deliberation. She discarded him
because he impeded, he distracted, he was a nuisance, he drained her,
he wore her out. As a woman she was contemptuous of him, as a
writer she fought off his interruptions. The doctors were more polite
than Henry James, who characterized Teddy Wharton as able to
"hold or follow no counter-proposal, no plan of opposition, of his
own, for as much as a minute or two; he is immediately *off*—irrelevant and childish . . . one's pity for her is at the best scarce bearable."
    She too pitied herself, and justly, though she forgot to pity *him*.
He had lost all trust in himself, whatever he said he timidly or
ingratiatingly or furiously took back. He was flailing vainly after the
last flashes of an autonomy his wife had long ago stripped from him.
And during all that angry space, when she was bitterly engaged in
fending off the partisan ragings of his family, and coldly supervising
his medical and traveling routines, she, in the stern autonomy of her
morning bed, was writing *Ethan Frome,* finishing *The Reef,* bringing
off short stories. She could do all this because she did not look into
her husband's eyes and read there, as she had read in the eyes of her
little dogs, the helpless pathos of "Why?" It was true that she did
not and could not love him, but her virtue was always according to
principle, not passion. Presumably she also did not love the French

soldiers who were sick with tuberculosis contracted in the trenches of the First World War; nevertheless for them she organized a cure program, which she termed "the most vital thing that can be done in France now." Whatever the most vital thing for Teddy might have been—perhaps there was nothing—she relinquished it at last. The question of the tubercular soldiers was, like all the claims on her spirit that she herself initiated, volitional and opportune. She had sought out these tragedies, they were not implicated in the conditions of her own life, that peculiar bed she had made for herself— "such a great big uncompromising 4-poster," James called it. For the relief of tubercular soldiers and other good works, she earned a French medal, and was made a Chevalier of the Legion of Honor. An arena of dazzling public exertion. But in the lesser frame of private mess she did nothing to spare her husband the humiliation of his madness. It is one thing to go mad, it is another to be humiliated for it. The one time in her life drift stopped dead in its trackless spume, and a genuine claim made as if to seize her—necessity, redder in tooth and claw than any sacrifice one grandly chooses for oneself —she turned away. For her, such a claim was the Gorgon's head, to gaze on which was death.

Writer's death. This is something most writers not only fear but sweat to evade, though most do not practice excision with as clean a knife-edge as cut away "irrelevant and childish" Teddy from Edith Wharton's life. "Friend, client, child, sickness, fear, want, charity, all knock at once at thy closet door and say—'Come out unto us.' But keep thy state," Emerson advised, "come not into their confusion." And Mann's Tonio Kröger declaims that "one must die to life to be utterly a creator." This ruthless romantic idea—it cannot be lived up to by weaklings who succumb to conscience, let alone to love—is probably at bottom less romantic than pragmatic. But it is an idea very nearly the opposite of Wilson's and Kazin's more affecting view of Edith Wharton: that joylessness was her muse, that her troubles energized her for fiction—the stimulus of "some exceptional emotional strain," according to Wilson, "so many personal maladjustments," according to Kazin, which made the novelist possible. If anything made the novelist possible, it was the sloughing off of the sources of emotional strain and personal maladjustment. As for the parallel new-feminist opinion that a woman writes best when she risks "unbearable wisdoms," it does not apply: what wisdom Edith Wharton found unbearable she chose not to bear.

The rest was chatter. Having turned away from the Gorgon's head, she spent the remainder of her life—indeed, nearly the whole of it—in the mainly insipid, sometimes inspired, adventure of elevated conversation. She had her friends. There were few women—whether because she did not encounter her equals among women, or because she avoided them, her biographer yields no hint. The majority were men (one should perhaps say "gentlemen")—Lapsley, Lubbock, Berenson, Fullerton, Simmons, James, Bourget, D'Humières, Berry, Sturgis, Hugh-Smith, Maynard, Gregory, Grant, Scott . . . the list is longer still. Lewis fleshes out all these names brilliantly, particularly Berry and Fullerton; the great comic miraculous James needs no fleshing out. James was in a way afraid of her. She swooped down on him to pluck him away for conversation or sightseeing, and he matched the "commotion and exhaustion" of her arrivals against the vengeance of Bonaparte, Attila, and Tamerlane. "Her powers of devastation are ineffable," he reported, and got into the habit of calling her the Angel of Devastation. She interrupted his work with the abruptness of a natural force (she might occur at any time) and at her convenience (she had particular hours for her work, he had all hours for his). He read her novels and dispatched wondrous celebrating smokescreens of letters ("I applaud, I mean I value, I egg you on") to hide the insufficiency of his admiration. As for her "life," it was a spectacle that had from the beginning upset him: her "desolating, ravaging, burning and destroying energy." And again: "such a nightmare of perpetually renewable choice and decision, such a luxury of bloated alternatives." "*What* an incoherent life!" he summed it up. Lewis disagrees, and reproaches James for partial views and a probable fear of strong women; but it may be, on all the lavish evidence Lewis provides, that the last word will after all lie with drift, exactly as James perceived it in her rushing aimlessness aimed at him.

Before Lewis's landmark discovery of the Wharton-Fullerton liaison, Walter Van Rensselaer Berry—Wharton's distant cousin, an international lawyer and an aristocrat—was commonly regarded as the tender center and great attachment of her life. Lewis does not refute this connection, though he convincingly drains it of sexual particularity, and gives us the portrait of a conventionally self-contained dry-hearted lifelong bachelor, a man caught, if not in recognizable drift, then in another sort of inconclusiveness. But Walter Berry was Edith Wharton's first literary intellectual—a lightning bolt of revelation that, having struck early, never lost its electrical sting. Clearly, she fed on intellectuals—but in a withdrawn and secretive way: she rarely read her work aloud, though she rejoiced to hear James read his. She brooded over history and philosophy, understood everything, but was incapable in fiction or elsewhere of expressing anything but the most commonplace psychology. This was, of course, her strength: she knew how human beings behave, she could describe and predict and surprise. Beyond that, she had a fertile capacity for thinking up stories. Plots and permutations of plots teemed. She was scornful of writers who agonized after subject matter. Subjects, she said, swarmed about her "like mosquitoes," until she felt stifled by their multiplicity and variety.

The truth is she had only one subject, the nineteenth century's unique European literary subject: society. Standard American criticism, struggling to "place" Edith Wharton in a literary environment unused to her subject, has contrived for her the role of a lesser Henry James. This has served to indict her as an imitative figure. But on no significant level is the comparison with James pertinent, except to say that by and large they wrote about the same kinds of people, derived from the same class. Otherwise the difference can be seized in a breath: James was a genius, Wharton not. James invented an almost metaphysical art, Wharton's insights lay close against their molds: what she saw she judged. James became an American in the most ideal sense, Wharton remained an estranged New Yorker. James was an uncanny moralist, Wharton a canny realist. James scarcely ever failed—or, at least, his few failures when they occurred were nevertheless glorious in aspiration and seamless in execution. When Wharton failed, she fell into an embarrassing triteness of language and seeing.

It is a pity that her name is attached so unrelentingly—thanks to the American high school—to *Ethan Frome*, a desolate, even morbid, narrow, soft-at-the-center and at the last unsurprising novella not at all typical of her range. It is an outdoor book that ends mercilessly indoors; she was an indoor novelist. She achieved two permanent novels, one—*The House of Mirth*—a spoiled masterpiece, a kind of latterday reverse *Scarlet Letter*, very direct yet eerie, the other *The Age of Innocence*, a combination of ode and elegy to the New York of her childhood, affirmation and repudiation both. A good many of her short stories and some of the novellas ("The Old Maid," for instance) are marvels of shapeliness and pointedness. This applies also to stories written during her late period, when she is widely considered to have debased her gift. The common accusation—Wilson makes it—is that her prose finally came to resemble women's-magazine fiction. One can venture that she did not so much begin to sound like the women's magazines, as that they began to sound like her, a condition that obtains until this moment. No one has explored Wharton's ongoing subliminal influence on current popular fiction (see almost any issue of *Redbook*); such an investigation would probably be striking in its disclosure of the strength of her legacy. Like any hokey imitation long after the model is lost to consciousness, it is not a bad compliment, though it may be awkward to admit it. (One of the least likely tributes to the Roman Empire, after all, is the pervasiveness of nineteenth-century American civic architecture.) But *The House of Mirth* and *The Age of Innocence* are, like everything unsurpassable because deeply idiosyncratic, incapable of spawning versions of themselves; in these two novels she is in command of an inwardness commensurate with structure. In them she does not simply grab hold of society, or judge it merely; she turns society into an exulting bird of prey, with blood on its beak, steadily beating its wings just over our heads; she turns society into an untamable *idea*. The reader, apprehensive, yet lured by the bird's lyric form, covers his face.

She could do all that; she had that power. Lewis, writing to justify and defend, always her sympathetic partisan, nevertheless hedges. Having acknowledged that she had "begun to locate herself—with a certain assurance, though without vanity—in the developing course of American literature," he appends a doubt:

But in another part of her, there remained something of the conviction drilled into her in old New York that it was improper for a lady to write fiction. One could do so only if one joked about it—if one treated it, to borrow Lubbock's word, as "an amusement." She sometimes sounded as if her writing were her entertainingly guilty secret, and in her memoirs she referred to it (borrowing the title of a popular children's book of her own New York youth) as her "secret garden."

But in the winter of 1911 [she was then at work on *The Reef*], as on perhaps half a dozen other occasions, it was the believing artist that was in the ascendancy during the hard-driving morning hours.

Somehow it is easy to doubt that she had this doubt—or, if she once had it, that she held it for long. To believe in her doubt is to make the bad case of the orthodox critics who, unlike Lewis, have shrunk from taking her seriously as an artist because as an American aristocrat she was born shockingly appurtenanced, and therefore deserves to be patronized for her sorrows. To believe in her doubt is to make the bad case of the new feminists, for whom female sex is, always and everywhere, an impediment difficult to transcend—even when, for an obsessed writer of talent, there is nothing to transcend. To believe in her doubt is to reverse the terms of her life and her work. Only "half a dozen other occasions" when Wharton was a "believing artist"? Only so few? This would mean that the life outside her bed—the dressed life of conversation and travel, the matchstick life of drift—was the primary life, and the life with her writing board—the life of the believing artist—the deviation, the anomaly, the distraction.

But we know, and have always known (Freud taught us only how to reinforce this knowledge), that the secret self is the true self, that obsession is confession. For Edith Wharton that is the only acceptable evaluation, the only possible justice. She did not doubt her allegiance. The writing came first. That she kept it separate from the rest was a misrepresentation and a mistake, but it may also have been a species of holy instinct—it was the one uncontaminated zone of her being: the place unprofaned. Otherwise she can be defined only by the horrific gyrations of "a life"—by the spiraling solipsism and tragic drift that led her to small dogs instead of babies, servants instead of family, high-minded male distance instead of connubial friendship, public virtue instead of private conscience, infatuation instead of the love that sticks. Only the writing board could justify these ugly substitutions. And some would say—myself not among them—that not even the writing board justified them.

the writers wrote about painting that hangs on: it is the photographs, most of them no more official than snapshots, of the side of a house, two people playing checkers on an old kitchen chair set out in the yard, three friends and a baby poking in the sand. The snapshots are all amateur. Goblets of brightness wink on eaves, fences, trees, and wash out faces in their dazzle; eyes are lost in blackened sockets. The hem of a dress is likely to be all clarity, but the heads escape—under hat brims, behind dogs, into mottled leaf-shade. And out of the blur of those hopeless poses, cigarettes, hands on knees, hands over books, anxious little pups held up to the camera, walking sticks, long grotesque nose-shadows, lapels, outdoor chairs and tables, there rises up —no, leaks down—so much tension, so much ambition, so much fake casualness, so much heartbreaking attention to the momentariness of the moment. The people in the snapshots knew, in a way we do not, who they were. Bloomsbury was self-conscious in a way we are not. It sniffed at its own perceptions, even its own perceived posterity. Somewhere early in the course of her diaries, Virginia Woolf notes how difficult it would be for a biographer to understand her—how little biographers can know, she said—only from the evidence of her journals. Disbelieving in the probity of her own biography, she did not doubt that she would have her own biographer.

She did not doubt; she knew; they knew. Hatched from the last years of the reign of Victoria, Bloomsbury was still a world where things—if not people, then ideas—could be said to reign. Though old authority might be sneered at (or something worse even than a sneer—Virginia Woolf declared her certainty that she could not have become a writer had her father lived), though proprieties might be outrageously altered ("Semen?" asked Lytton Strachey, noticing a stain on Vanessa Bell's skirt one afternoon), though sex was accessible and often enough homoerotic, though freedom might be proclaimed on Gordon Square, though livings were earned, there was nonetheless a spine of authority to support Bloomsbury: family, descent, class and community—the sense of having-in-common. Bloomsbury, after all, was an inheritance. Both E. M. Forster's and Virginia Woolf's people were associated with the liberal and intellectual Clapham Sect of the century before. Cambridge made a kind of cousinship—the staircase at Trinity that drew together Clive Bell,

Saxon Sydney-Turner, and Virginia Woolf's brother Thoby Stephen was the real beginning of the gatherings at Gordon Square.
Bloomsbury was pacifist and busy with gossip about what it always
called "buggery," but it was not radical and it did not harbor rebels.
Rebels want to make over; the Bloomsburyites reinforced themselves
with their like. The staircase at Trinity went on and on for the rest
of their lives, and even Virginia Woolf, thinking to make over the
form of the novel, had to have each newly completed work ratified
by Morgan Forster and sometimes Maynard Keynes before she
could breathe at ease again. The authority of one's closest familiars
is the unmistakable note of Bloomsbury. It was that sure voice she
listened for. "Virginia Woolf was a Miss Stephen," Quentin Bell
begins, in the same voice; it is an opening any outsider could have
written, but not in that sharp cadence. He is not so much biographer
as a later member of the circle—Virginia Woolf's sister's son, the
child of Vanessa and Clive Bell. He knows, he does not doubt. It is
the note of self-recognition; of confidence; of inheritance. Everything is in his grip.

And yet—as she predicted—Virginia Woolf's biographer fails
her. He fails her, in fact, more mournfully than any outsider could.
It is his grip that fails her. This is not only because, sticking mainly
to those matters he has sure authority over, he has chosen to omit
a literary discussion of the body of work itself. "I have found the
work of the biographer sufficiently difficult without adventuring in
other directions," he tells us, so that to speak of Quentin Bell's "sure
authority" is not to insinuate that all his data are, perhaps, out of
childhood memory or family reminiscence, or that he has not mined
library after library, and collection after collection of unpublished
papers. He is, after all, of the next generation, and the next generation is always in some fashion an outsider to the one before. But what
is in his grip is something more precise, curiously, than merely data,
which the most impersonal research can reliably throw up: it is that
particular intimacy of perspective—of experience, really—which
characterizes not family information, but family bias. Every house
has its own special odor to the entering guest, however faint—it
sticks to the inhabitants, it is in their chairs and in their clothes. The
analogy of bias to scent is chiefly in one's unconsciousness of one's

own. Bell's Woolf is about Virginia, but it has the smell of Vanessa's
house. The Virginia Woolf that comes off these pages is a kind of
emanation of a point of view, long settled, by now, into family
feeling. Stephens, Pattles, Fishers—all the family lines—each has its
distinct and legendary scent. The Stephens are bold, the Pattles are
fair, the Fishers are self-righteous. And Virginia is mad.

She was the family's third case of insanity, all on the Stephen side.
Leslie Stephen, Virginia Woolf's celebrated father—a man of letters
whose career was marked not least by the circumstance that Henry
James cherished him—was married twice, the second time to Julia
Duckworth, a widow with children. Together they produced
Vanessa and Virginia, Thoby and Adrian. A child of Leslie Stephen's first marriage, the younger of Virginia's two half-sisters, was
born defective—it is not clear whether backward or truly insane—
and was confined to an asylum, where she died old. Virginia's first
cousin—the child of her father's brother—went mad while still a
young man, having struck his head in an accident. But one wonders,
in the retrograde and rather primitive way one contemplates families, whether there might not have been a Stephen "taint." In a
family already accustomed to rumor of aberration, Virginia Woolf,
in any case, was incontrovertibly mad. Her madness was distinguished, moreover, by a threatening periodicity: at any moment it
could strike, disabling everyone around her. Vanessa had to leave her
children and come running, nurses had to be hired, rest homes
interviewed, transport accomplished. The disaster was ten times
wider than its victim.

And just here is the defect in writing out of family authority. The
odor is personal, hence partial. Proust says somewhere that the artist
brings to the work his whole self, to his familiars only those aspects
that accommodate them. The biographer close to his subject has the
same difficulty; the aspect under which Quentin Bell chiefly views
his aunt Virginia is not of accommodation but of a still narrower
partiality: discommodity, the effect on family perspective of Virginia
Woolf's terrible and recurrent insanity. It was no mere melancholia,
or poetic mooning—as, reading Leonard Woolf's deliberately truncated edition of her diary, we used to guess. A claustrophilic though
inspired (also self-inspiring) document, it made us resent the arbi-

trary "personal" omissions: was it the madness he was leaving out? Certainly we wanted the madness too, supposing it to be the useful artistic sort: grotesque moods, quirks—epiphanies really. But it was not that; it was the usual thing people get put away for, an insanity characterized by incoherent howling and by violence. She clawed her attendants and had to be restrained; she would not touch food; she was suicidal. Ah, that cutting difference: not that she longed for death, as poets and writers sometimes do for melancholy's sake, but that she wanted, with the immediacy of a method, to be dead.

Bell's Woolf, then, is not about the Virginia Woolf of the diaries, essays, and novels—not, in the Proustian sense, about the writer's whole self. And surely this is not simply because literary criticism is evaded. Bell's Woolf is not about a writer, in fact; it is about the smell of a house. It is about a madwoman and her nurse.

The nurse was Leonard Woolf. Upon him Quentin Bell can impose no family aspects, rumors, characteristics, old experience, inherited style. He does not trail any known house-scent, like Stephens, Pattles, Fishers. Though he shared the Cambridge stairs—Thoby Stephen, Saxon Sydney-Turner, Clive Bell, Lytton Strachey, and Leonard Woolf together briefly formed the Midnight Society, a reading club that met on Saturday evenings in Clive Bell's rooms—he was not an inheritor of Cambridge. Cambridge was not natural to him, Bloomsbury was not natural to him, even England was not natural to him—not as an inheritance; he was a Jew. Quentin Bell has no "authority" over Leonard Woolf, as he has over his aunt; Leonard is nowhere in the biographer's grip.

The effect is unexpected. It is as if Virginia Woolf escapes—possessing her too selectively, the biographer lets her slip—but Leonard Woolf somehow stays to become himself. Which is to say, Bell's Virginia Woolf can be augmented by a thousand other sources —chiefly by her own work—but we learn as much about Leonard Woolf here as we are likely to know from any other source. And what we learn is a strange historical judgment, strange but unfragmented, of a convincing wholeness: that Leonard Woolf was a family sacrifice. Without him—Quentin Bell's clarity on this point is ineffaceable—Virginia Woolf might have spent her life in a mental asylum. The elder Stephens were dead, Thoby had died at twenty-six, Adrian married a woman apparently indifferent to or incompatible with the Bloomsburyites; it was Vanessa on whom the grimness fell. Leonard Woolf—all this is blatant—got Vanessa off the hook. He was, in fact, deceived: he had no inkling he was being captured for a nurse.

> Neither Vanessa nor Adrian gave him a detailed and explicit account of Virginia's illnesses or told him how deadly serious they might be. . . . Her insanity was clothed, like some other painful things in that family, in a jest. . . . Thus, in effect if not in intention, Leonard was allowed to think of Virginia's illnesses as something not desperately serious, and he was allowed to marry her without knowing how fearful a care such a union might be. In fairness to all parties it must be said that, even if Virginia's brother and sister had been as explicit and circumstantial as they ought to have been, Leonard would certainly not have been deflected from his purpose of marrying Virginia. . . . As it was, he learnt the hard way and one can only wonder, seeing how hard it was, and that he had for so long to endure the constant threat of her suicide, to exert constant vigilance, to exercise endless persuasive tact at mealtimes and to suffer the perpetual alternations of hope and disappointment, that he too did not go mad.
>
> In fact he nearly did, although he does not mention it.

"He does not mention it." There was in Leonard Woolf an extraordinary silence, a containment allied to something like concealment, and at the same time open to a methodical candor. This is no paradox; candor is often the mode of the obtuse person. It is of course perilous to think of Leonard Woolf as obtuse: he was both activist and intellectual, worldly and introspective; his intelligence, traveling widely and serenely over politics and literature, was reined in by a seriousness that makes him the most responsible and conscientious figure among all the Bloomsburyites. His seriousness was profound. It was what turned a hand press "small enough to stand on a kitchen table" into the Hogarth Press, an important and innovative publishing house. It was what turned Leonard Woolf himself from a highly able agent of colonialism—at the age of twenty-four he was an official of the British ruling apparatus in Ceylon—into a convinced anti-imperialist and a fervent socialist. And it was what turned the Jew into an Englishman.

Not that Leonard Woolf is altogether without ambivalence on this question; indeed, the word "ambivalence" is his own. Soon after his marriage to Virginia Stephen, he was taken round on a tour of Stephen relations—among them Virginia's half-brother, Sir George Duckworth, in his large house in Dalingridge Place, and "Aunt Anny," who was Lady Ritchie, Thackeray's daughter, in St. George's Square. He suffered in these encounters from an "ambivalence in my attitude to the society which I found in Dalingridge Place and St. George's Square. I disliked its respectability and assumptions while envying and fearing its assurance and manners." And: "I was an outsider to this class, because, although I and my father before me belonged to the professional middle class, we had only recently struggled up into it from the stratum of Jewish shopkeepers. We had no roots in it." This looks like candor—"we had no roots"—but it is also remarkably insensible. Aware of his not belonging, he gives no evidence anywhere that the people he moved among were also aware of it. It is true that his own group of self-consciously agnostic Cambridge intellectuals apparently never mentioned it to his face. Thoby Stephen in a letter to Leonard in Ceylon is quick enough to speak of himself, mockingly, as a nonbelieving Christian—"it's no good being dainty with Christians and chapel's obviously rot"—but no one seems ever to have teased Leonard about his being an agnostic Jew. In the atmosphere of that society, perhaps, teasing would have too dangerously resembled baiting; levity about being a Christian was clearly not interchangeable with levity about being a Jew. Fair enough: it never is. But Virginia, replying to a letter in which Leonard implores her to love him, is oddly analytical: ". . . of course, I feel angry sometimes at the strength of your desire. Possibly, your being a Jew comes in also at this point. You seem so foreign." Was he, like all those dark lubricious peoples whose origins are remote from the moderating North, too obscurely other? She corrects herself at once, with a kind of apology: "And then I am fearfully unstable. I pass from hot to cold in an instant, without any reason; except that I believe sheer physical effort and exhaustion influence me." The correction—the retraction—is weak, and fades off; what remains is the blow: "You seem so foreign."

We do not know Leonard's response to this. Possibly he made

none. It would have been in keeping had he made none. Foreignness disconcerted him—like Virginia he was at moments disturbed by it and backed away—and if his own origins were almost never mentioned to his face, his face was nevertheless *there,* and so, in those striking old photographs, were the faces of his grandparents. Leonard Woolf is bemused in his autobiography by his paternal grandfather, "a large, stern, black-haired, and black-whiskered, rabbinical Jew in a frock coat." Again he speaks of this "look of stern rabbinical orthodoxy," and rather prefers the "round, pink face of an incredibly old Dutch doll," which was the face of his Dutch-born maternal grandmother—about whom he speculates that it was "possible that she had a good deal of non-Jewish blood in her ancestry. Some of her children and grandchildren were fair-haired and facially very unlike the 'typical' Jew." Her husband, however, was a different case: "No one could have mistaken him for anything but a Jew. Although he wore coats and trousers, hats and umbrellas, just like those of all the other gentlemen in Addison Gardens, he looked to me as if he might have stepped straight out of one of those old pictures of caftaned, bearded Jews in a ghetto. . . ." Such Jews, he notes, were equipped with "a fragment of spiritual steel, a particle of passive and unconquerable resistance," but otherwise the character, and certainly the history, of the Jews do not draw him. "My father's father was a Jew," he writes, exempting himself by two generations. "I have always felt in my bones and brain and heart English and, more narrowly, a Londoner, but with a nostalgic love of the city and civilization of ancient Athens." He recognizes that his "genes and chromosomes" are something else; he is a "descendant" of "the world's official fugitives and scapegoats."

But a "descendant" is not the same as a member. A descendant shares an origin, but not necessarily a destiny. Writing in his eighties, Leonard Woolf recollects that as a schoolboy he was elected to an exclusive debating society under the thumb of G. K. Chesterton and his brother, and "in view of the subsequent violent anti-Semitism of the Chestertons" he finds this "amusing"; he reports that he was "surprised and flattered." Sixty-three years afterward he is still flattered. His description of the public school that flattered him shows it to be a detestable place, hostile to both intellect and feeling:

"I got on quite well with the boys in my form or with whom I played cricket, football, and fives, but it would have been unsafe, practically impossible, to let them know what I really thought or felt about anything which seemed to me important." *Would have been unsafe.* It was a risk he did not take—unlike Morgan Forster, who, in the same situation in a similar school, allowed himself to be recognized as an intellectual and consequently to suffer as a schoolboy pariah. Leonard Woolf did not intend to take on the role of pariah, then or later. Perhaps it was cowardice; or perhaps it was the opposite, that "fragment of spiritual steel" he had inherited from the ghetto; or perhaps it was his sense of himself as exempt from the ghetto.

Certainly he always thought of himself as wholly an Englishman. In the spring of 1935 he and Virginia drove to Rome. "I was astonished then (I am astonished still)," Quentin Bell comments, "that Leonard chose to travel by way of Germany." They were on German soil three days; near Bonn they encountered a Nazi demonstration but were unharmed, and entered Italy safely. What prompted Leonard Woolf to go into Germany in the very hour Jews were being abused there? Did he expect Nazi street hoodlums to distinguish between an English Jewish face and a German Jewish face? He carried with him—it was not needed and in the event of street hoodlumism would anyhow have been useless—a protective letter from an official of the German embassy in London. More than that, he carried—in his "bones and brain and heart"—the designation of Englishman. It was a test, not of the inherited fragment of spiritual steel, but of the strength of his exemption from that heritage. If Quentin Bell is twice astonished, it may be because he calculated the risk more closely than Leonard; or else he is not quite so persuaded of the Englishness of Leonard Woolf as is Leonard Woolf.

And, superficially at least, it is difficult to be persuaded of it. One is drawn to Leonard's face much as he was drawn to his grandfather's face, and the conclusion is the same. What Leonard's eyes saw was what the eyes of the educated English classes saw. What Leonard felt on viewing his grandfather's face must have been precisely what Clive Bell and Thoby Stephen would have felt. There is an arresting snapshot—still another of those that make up the pictorial history of Bloomsbury—of Leonard Woolf and Adrian Stephen. They are both young men in their prime; the date is 1914. They are standing side by side before the high narrow Gothic-style windows of Asham House, the Sussex villa Leonard and Virginia Woolf owned for some years. They are dressed identically (vests, coats, ties) and positioned identically—feet apart, hands in pockets, shut lips gripping pipe or cigarette holder. Their shoes are lost in the weedy grass, and the sunlight masks their faces in identical skull-shadows. Both faces are serene, holding back amusement, indulgent of the photographer. And still it is not a picture of two cultivated Englishmen, or not only that. Adrian is incredibly tall and Vikinglike, with a forehead as broad and flat as a chimney tile; he looks like some blueblood American banker not long out of Princeton; his hair grows straight up like thick pale straw. Leonard's forehead is an attenuated wafer under a tender black forelock, his nose is nervous and frail, he seems younger and more vulnerable than his years (he was then thirty-four) and as recognizably intellectual as—well, how does one put the contrast? Following Leonard, one ought to dare to put it with the clarity of a certain cultural bluntness: he looks like a student at the yeshiva. Leonard has the unmistakable face of a Jew. Like his grandfather—and, again like him, despite his costume—Leonard Woolf might have stepped out of one of those pictures of caftaned Jews in the ghetto.

The observation may be obvious and boring but it is not insignificant, if only because it is derived from Leonard himself; it is his own lesson. What can be learned from it is not merely that he was himself conscious of all that curious contrast, but that his fellows could not have been indifferent to it. In a 1968 review of the penultimate volume of Leonard Woolf's memoirs, Dan Jacobson wonders, "Did his being a Jew never affect . . . his career or social life in the several years he spent as a colonial officer in Ceylon, his only companions during that time being other colonial civil servants—not in general the most enlightened, tolerant, or tactful of British social groups? Did it not arise in the political work he carried out later in England, especially during the rise of Nazism?" On all these matters Leonard is mute; he does not mention it. Not so Virginia. "He's a penniless Jew," she wrote in a letter to a friend announcing her marriage, and we know that if she had married a poor man of her own set she would not have called him a penniless Englishman. She called Leonard a Jew not to identify or explain him, but because, quite simply, that is how she saw him; it was herself she was explaining. And if she wrote light-heartedly, making a joke of marriage without inheritance, it was also a joke in general about unaccoutered Jews—from her point of view, Leonard had neither inheritance nor heritage. He was—like the Hogarth Press later on—self-created.

Of course, in thinking about Leonard Woolf, one is plainly not interested in the question of the acculturated Jew (". . . nearly all Jews are both proud and ashamed of being Jews," Leonard writes —a model of the type); it is not on the mark. What *is* to the point is the attitude of the class Leonard aspired to join. "Virginia for her part," Quentin Bell notes—and it is unnecessary to remind oneself that he is her nephew—

> had to meet the Woolf family. It was a daunting experience. Leonard himself was sufficiently Jewish to seem to her disquietingly foreign; but in him the trait was qualified. He had become so very much a citizen of her world. . . . But Leonard's widowed mother, a matriarchal figure living with her large family in Colinette Road, Putney, seemed very alien to Virginia. No place could have been less like home than her future mother-in-law's house.
>
> And how did the Woolfs regard her? Did they perceive that she thought their furniture hideous? Did she seem to them a haughty goy thinking herself too good for the family of their brilliant son? I am afraid that they probably did.
>
> [Here follows an account of Virginia's response—aloof and truculent—upon learning the character of the dietary laws, which Mrs. Woolf observed.]
>
> Virginia was ready to allow that Mrs. Woolf had some very good qualities, but her heart must have sunk as she considered what large opportunities she would have for discovering them.
>
> "Work and love and Jews in Putney take it out of me," she wrote, and it was certainly true.

This aspect of Virginia Stephen's marriage to Leonard Woolf is usually passed over in silence. I have rehearsed it here at such length not to emphasize it for its own sake—there is nothing novel about upper-class English distaste for Jews—but to make a point about

Leonard. He is commonly depicted as, in public, a saintly socialist, and, in private, a saintly husband. He was probably both; but he also knew, like any percipient young man in love with a certain segment of society, how to seize vantage ground. As a schoolboy he was no doubt sincerely exhilarated by the playing field, but he hid his intellectual exhilarations to make it look as if the playing field were all there was to esteem; it was a way, after all, of buying esteem for himself. And though he was afterward no doubt sincerely in love with Virginia Stephen (surely a woman less intelligent would not have satisfied him), it would be a mistake to suppose that Virginia herself—even given her brilliance, her splendid head on its splendid neck, the radiance of her first appearance in Thoby's rooms in Cambridge wearing a white dress and round hat and carrying a parasol, astonishing him, Leonard says, as when "in a picture gallery you suddenly come face to face with a great Rembrandt or Velasquez" —it would be ingenuous, not to say credulous, to think that Virginia alone was all there was to adore. Whether Leonard Woolf fell in love with a young woman of beauty and intellect, or more narrowly with a Stephen of beauty and intellect, will always be a formidable, and a necessary, question.

It is a question that, it seems to me, touches acutely on Leonard Woolf in his profoundly dedicated role as nurse. He was dedicated partly because he was earnestly efficient at everything, and also because he loved his wife, and also because he was a realist who could reconcile himself to any unlooked-for disaster. He came to the situation of Virginia's health determinedly and unquestioningly, much as, years later, when the German bombings had begun, he joined up with the Local Defence Volunteers: it was what had to be done. But in the case of Virginia more than merely courage was at issue; his "background" had equipped him well to be Virginia Stephen's nurse. When things were going badly he could take on the burden of all those small code-jottings in his diary—"V.n.w.," "b.n.," "V.sl.h."—and all the crises "Virginia not well," "bad night," "Virginia slight headache" horrendously implied, for the simple reason that it was worth it to him. It was worth it because she was a genius; it was worth it because she was a Stephen.

The power and allure of the Stephen world lay not in its distance

from the Jews of Putney—Bloomsbury was anyhow hardly likely to
notice the Jews of Putney, and if Virginia did notice, and was even
brought to tea there, it was through the abnormal caprice of a freakish fate—but in its illustriousness. Virginia was an illustrious young
woman: had she had no gift of her own, the luster of her father's
situation, and of the great circle of the aristocracy of intellect into
which she was born, would have marked her life. It was additionally
marked by her double fortune of genius and insanity, and though her
primary fortune—the circle into which she was born—attracted, in
the most natural way, other members of that circle, the biting and
always original quality of her mind put the less vivid of them off. Her
madness was not public knowledge, but her intellect could not be
hidden. Her tongue had a fearful and cutting brilliance. "I was
surprised to find how friendly she made herself appear," said Walter
Lamb, another of Thoby Stephen's Cambridge friends, amazed on
one occasion to have been undevoured. He courted her for a time,
pallidly, asking frightened questions: "Do you want to have children
and love in the normal way?"—as if he expected nothing usual from
Virginia Stephen. "I wish," she wrote to Lytton Strachey, after
reporting Lamb's visits, "that earth would open her womb and let
some new creature out." The courtship was brief and ended in
boredom. Lamb's offer was one of at least four proposals of marriage
from differing sources; Strachey himself had tendered her one. Since
he preferred stableboys to women, a fact they both understood very
well, it was a strange mistake. Sydney Waterlow, still another Cambridge name, was a suitor; she regarded him as "amiable." Hilton
Young, a childhood friend—cast, says Quentin Bell, from a "smooth
and well-proportioned mould"—might have been an appropriate
match, mixing politics with poetry and gaining a peerage; he was
merely "admirable." Meanwhile, Virginia was thoughtfully flirting
with her sister's husband. At twenty-nine, despite all these atten-
tions, she was depressed at being still unmarried; she was despon-
dent, as she would be for the rest of her life, over her childlessness.
Not one of those triflings had turned to infatuation, on either side.

It was fortunate. There was lacking, in all these very intelligent
men, and indeed in their type in general, the kind of sexual seriousness that is usually disparaged as uxoriousness. It was a trait that

Leonard invincibly possessed and that Clive Bell despised as "provincial and puritanical, an enemy to all that was charming and amusing in life." Clive was occupied by a long-standing affair and lived apart from Vanessa, who, at various times, lived with Roger Fry and with Duncan Grant—who was (so closely was this group tied) Lytton Strachey's cousin, and who may have been (so Quentin Bell allows us to conjecture) the father of Quentin's sister, Angelica. Vanessa typed and distributed copies of Lytton Strachey's indecent verse; once at a party she did a topless dance; it was legendary that she had at another party fornicated with Maynard Keynes "*coram publico*"—the whole room looking on. It may have been in honor of these last two occasions that Virginia Woolf, according to Quentin Bell, pronounced human nature to have been "changed in or about December 1910."

It was not a change Leonard Woolf approved of. Four years after this crucial date in human history he published a novel critical of "unnatural cultured persons" given to "wild exaggerated talk" and frivolous behavior; it was clearly an assault on Vanessa and Clive Bell and their circle. The novel, called *The Wise Virgins*, was about *not* marrying Virginia. Instead the hero is forced to marry a Putney girl, and lives unhappily ever after—only because, having been infected with Bloomsbury's licentious notions, he has carelessly gotten her with child. The fictional Leonard loses the heroine who represents Virginia, and is doomed to the drabness of Putney; in the one act he both deplores Bloomsbury and laments his deprivation of it. The real Leonard tried to pick his way between these soul-cracking contradictions. He meant to have the high excitement of Bloomsbury—and certainly "frivolity" contributed to Bloomsbury's dash and éclat —without the frivolity itself. He meant to be master of the full brilliant breadth of all that worldliness, and at the same time of the more sober and limiting range of his native seriousness.

That he coveted the one while requiring the other was—certainly in her biographer's eyes—the salvation of Virginia. No one else in that milieu could have survived—surely not as husband—her illnesses. Roger Fry, for instance, put his own mad wife away and went to live with Vanessa. As for Lamb, Waterlow, Young—viewed in the light of what Virginia Woolf's insanity extracted from her caretaker, their possibilities wither. Of all her potential husbands, only Leonard Woolf emerged as fit. And the opposite too can be said: of Bloomsbury's potential wives, only Virginia emerged as fit for Leonard. He was fit for her because her madness, especially in combination with her innovative genius, demanded the most grave, minutely persevering and attentive service. She was fit for him not simply because she represented Bloomsbury in its most resplendent flowering of originality and luminousness; so, after all, did Vanessa, an accomplished painter active with other painters in the revolution-ary vitality of the Post-Impressionists. But just as no marriage could survive Vanessa for long, so Leonard married to Vanessa would not have survived Bloomsbury for long. What Leonard needed in Vir-ginia was not so much her genius as her madness. It made possible for him the exercise of the one thing Bloomsbury had no use for: uxoriousness. It allowed him the totality of his seriousness un-checked. It *used* his seriousness, it gave it legitimate occupation, it made it both necessary and awesome. And it made *her* serious. Without the omnipresent threat of disintegration, freed from the oppression of continuous vigil against breakdown, what might Vir-ginia's life have been? The flirtation with Clive hints at it: she might have lived, at least outwardly, like Vanessa. It was his wife's insanity, in short, that made tenable the permanent—the secure—presence in Bloomsbury of Leonard himself. Her madness fed his genius for responsibility; it became for him a corridor of access to her genius. The spirit of Bloomsbury was not Leonard's, his temperament was against it—Bloomsbury could have done without him. So could a sane Virginia.

The whole question of Virginia's sexuality now came into Leon-ard's hands. And here too he was curiously ambivalent. The honey-moon was not a success; they consulted Vanessa, Vanessa the sexual creature—when had she had her first orgasm? Vanessa could not remember. "No doubt," she reflected, "I sympathised with such things if I didn't have them from the time I was 2." "Why do you think people make such a fuss about marriage & copulation?" Vir-ginia was writing just then; ". . . certainly I find the climax im-mensely exaggerated." Vanessa and Leonard put their heads together over it. Vanessa said she believed Virginia "never had understood or sympathised with sexual passion in men"; this news, she thought, "consoled" Leonard. For further consolation the two of them rehearsed (and this was before England had become properly aware of Freud) Virginia's childhood trauma inflicted by her elder half-brother George Duckworth, who had, under cover of big-brotherly affection, repeatedly entered the nursery at night for intimate fondlings, the nature of which Virginia then hardly comprehended; she knew only that he frightened her and that she despised him. Apparently this explanation satisfied Leonard—the "consolation" worked—if rather too quickly; the ability to adjust speedily to disappointment is a good and useful trait in a colonial officer, less so in a husband. It does not contradict the uxorious temperament, however, and certainly not the nursing enterprise: a wife who is seen to be frigid as well as mad is simply taken for that much sicker. But too ready a reconcilement to bad news is also a kind of abandonment, and Leonard seems very early to have relinquished, or allowed Virginia to relinquish, the sexual gratifications of marriage. All the stranger since he repeatedly speaks of himself as "lustful." And he is not known to have had so much as a dalliance during his marriage.

On the other hand, Quentin Bell suggests—a little coyly, as if only blamelessly hinting—that Virginia Woolf's erotic direction was perhaps toward women rather than men. The "perhaps" is crucial: the index to the first volume lists "passion for Madge Vaughan," "passion for Violet Dickinson," but the corresponding textual passages are all projections from the most ordinary sort of data. Madge Vaughan was a cousin by marriage whom Virginia knew from the age of seven; at sixteen she adored her still, and once stood in the house paralyzed by rapture, thinking, "Madge is here; at this moment she is actually under this roof"—an emotion, she once said, that she never equaled afterward. Many emotions at sixteen are never equaled afterward. Of Virginia's intense letter-writing to Violet Dickinson—a friend of her dead half-sister—Quentin Bell says: ". . . it is clear to the modern reader, though it was not at all clear to Virginia, that she was in love and that her love was returned." What is even clearer is that it is possible to be too "modern," if that is what enables one to read a sensual character into every exuberant or sympathetic friendship between women. Vita Sackville-West, of course, whom Virginia Woolf knew when both writers were already celebrated, was an established sapphist, and was plainly in pursuit of Virginia. Virginia, she wrote, "dislikes the quality of masculinity," but that was the view of one with a vested interest in believing it. As for Virginia, she "felt," according to her biographer, "as a lover feels—she desponded when she fancied herself neglected, despaired when Vita was away, waited anxiously for letters, needed Vita's company and lived in that strange mixture of elation and despair which lovers—and one would have supposed only lovers—can experience." But all this is Quentin Bell. Virginia herself, reporting a three-day visit from Sackville-West, appears erotically detached: "These Sapphists *love* women; friendship is never untinged with amorosity. . . . I like her and being with her and the splendour—she shines in the grocer's shop . . . with a candle lit radiance." She acknowledged what she readily called Vita's "glamour," but the phrase "these Sapphists" is too mocking to be lover's language. And she was quick to criticize Vita (who was married to Harold Nicolson) as a mother: ". . . she is a little cold and off-hand with her boys." Virginia Woolf's biographer nevertheless supposes—he admits all this is conjecture—"some caressing, some bedding together." Still, in the heart of this love, if it was love, was the ultimate withdrawal: "In brain and insight," Virginia remarked in her diary, "she is not as highly organised as I am." Vita was splendid but "not reflective." She wrote "with a pen of brass." And: "I have no enormous opinion of her poetry." Considering all of which, Quentin Bell notes persuasively that "she could not really love without feeling that she was in the presence of a superior intellect." Sackville-West, for her part, insisted that not only did Virginia not like the quality of masculinity, but also the "possessiveness and love of domination in men."

Yet Leonard Woolf dominated Virginia Woolf overwhelmingly —nor did she resist—not so much because his braininess impressed her (his straightforwardly thumping writing style must have claimed her loyalty more than her admiration), but because he possessed her in the manner of—it must be said again—a strong-minded nurse with obsessive jurisdiction over a willful patient. The issue of Virginia Woolf's tentative or potential lesbianism becomes reduced, at this point, to the merest footnote of possibility. Sackville-West called her "inviolable"; and the fact is she was conventionally married, and had conventional expectations of marriage. She wanted children. For a wedding present Violet Dickinson sent her a cradle. "My baby shall sleep in [it]," she said at thirty. But it stood empty, and she felt, all her life, the ache of the irretrievable. "I don't like the physicalness of having children of my own," she wrote at forty-five, recording how "the little creatures"—Vanessa's children—"moved my infinitely sentimental throat." But then, with a lurch of candor: "I can dramatise myself a parent, it is true. And perhaps I have killed the feeling instinctively; or perhaps nature does." Two years after declaring the feeling killed, during a dinner party full of worldly conversation with the Webbs and assorted eminences, she found herself thinking: "L. and myself . . . the pathos, the symbolical quality of the childless couple."

The feeling was not killed; it had a remarkable durability. There is no record of her response to the original decision not to have children. That decision was Leonard's, and it was "medical." He consulted three or four people variously qualified, including Vanessa's doctor and the nurse who ran the home to which Virginia was sent when most dangerously disturbed (and to whom, according to Bell, Leonard ascribed "an unconscious but violent homosexual passion for Virginia"—which would, one imagines, make one wonder about the disinterestedness of her advice). Leonard also requested the opinion of Dr. George Savage, Virginia's regular physician, whom he disliked, and was heartily urged to have babies; soon after we find him no longer in consultation with Dr. Savage. Bell tells us that "in the end Leonard decided and persuaded Virginia to agree that, although they both wanted children, it would be too dangerous for her to have them." The "too dangerous" is left unexplained; we do not even know Leonard's ostensible reason. Did he think she could not withstand pregnancy and delivery? She was neither especially frail nor without energy, and was a zealous walker, eight miles at a time, over both London and countryside; she hefted piles of books and packed them for the Hogarth Press; she had no organic impediments. Did he believe she could not have borne the duties of rearing? But in that class there was no household without its nanny (Vanessa had two), and just as she never had to do a housekeeping chore (she never laid a fire, or made a bed, or washed a sock), she need not have been obliged to take physical care of a child. Did he, then, fear an inherited trait—diseased offspring? Or did he intend to protect the phantom child from distress by preventing its birth into a baleful household? Or did he mean, out of some curious notion of intellectual purity, not to divide the strength of Virginia's available sanity, to preserve her undistracted for her art?

Whatever the reason, and to spare her—or himself—what pains we can only guess at, she was in this second instance released from "normality." Normality is catch-as-catch-can. Leonard, in his deliberateness, in his responsibility, was more serious than that, and surrendered her to a program of omissions. She would be spared the tribulations both of the conjugal bed and of childbed. She need not learn ease in the one; she need not, no, must not, venture into the other. In forbidding Virginia maternity, Leonard abandoned her to an unparalleled and unslakable envy. Her diary again and again records the pangs she felt after visits with Vanessa's little sons— pangs, defenses, justifications: she suffered. Nor was it a social suffering—she did not feel deprived of children because she was expected to. The name "Virginia Woolf" very soon acquired the same resonance for her contemporaries ("this celebrity business is quite chronic," she wrote) as it has for us—after which she was expected to be only Virginia Woolf. She learned, after a while, to be only that (which did not, however, prevent her from being an adored and delightful aunt), and to mock at Vanessa's mothering, and to call it obsessive and excessive. She suffered the envy of the childless for the fruitful, precisely this, and nothing societally imposed; and she even learned to transmute maternal envy into a more manageable variety —literary begrudging. This was directed at Vanessa's second son, Julian Bell, killed in the Spanish Civil War, toward whose literary ambitions Virginia Woolf was always ungenerous, together with Leonard; a collection of Julian's essays, prepared after his death,

Leonard dubbed "Vanessa's necrophily." Vanessa-envy moved on
into the second generation. It was at bottom a rivalry of creatureliness, in which Virginia was always the loser. Vanessa was on the side
of "normality," the placid mother of three, enjoying all the traditional bourgeois consolations; she was often referred to as a madonna; and at the same time she was a thorough-going bohemian.
Virginia was anything but placid, yet lived a sober sensible domestic
life in a marriage stable beyond imagining, with no trace of bohemi-
anism. Vanessa the bohemian madonna had the best of both hearth-
life and free life. Virginia was barred from both.

Without the authoritative domestic role maternity would have
supplied, with no one in the household dependent on her (for years
she quarreled with her maid on equal or inferior terms), and finding
herself always—as potential patient—in submission, Virginia Woolf
was by degrees nudged into a position of severe dependency. It took
odd forms: Leonard not only prescribed milk at eleven in the morning, but also topics for conversation in the evening. Lytton Strachey's sister-in-law recalls how among friends Leonard would work
up the "backbone" of a subject "and then be happy to let [Virginia]
ornament it if she wanted to." And he gave her pocket money every
week. Her niece Angelica reports that "Leonard kept Virginia on
very short purse-strings," which she exercised through the pleasures
of buying "coloured string and sealing-wax, notebooks and pencils."
When she came to the end of writing a book, she trembled until
Leonard read it and gave his approval. William Plomer remembers
how Leonard would grow alarmed if, watching Virginia closely,
he saw her laugh a little too convulsively. And once she absent-
mindedly began to flick bits of meat off her dinner plate; Leonard
hushed the company and led her away.*

—All of which has given Leonard his reputation for saintliness.
A saint who successively secures acquiescence to frigidity, childlessness, dependency? Perhaps; probably; of course. These are, after all,
conventual vows—celibacy, barrenness, obedience. But Leonard
Woolf was a socialist, not an ascetic; he had a practical political

---

*Joan Russell Noble, ed., *Recollections of Virginia Woolf by Her Contemporaries* (William
Morrow & Company, Inc., 1972).

intelligence; he was the author of books called *Empire and Commerce in Africa* and *Socialism and Co-operation;* he ran the Hogarth Press like a good businessman; at the same time he edited a monthly periodical, *The International Review;* he was literary editor of *The Nation.* He had exactly the kind of commonsensical temperament that scorns, and is repelled by, religious excess. And of Virginia he made a shrine; of himself, a monk. On the day of her death Virginia walked out of the house down to the river Ouse and drowned herself; not for nothing was that house called Monk's House. The letter she left for Leonard was like almost every other suicide note, horribly banal, not a writer's letter at all, and rich with guilt—"I feel certain I am going mad again. I feel we can't go through another of those terrible times. . . . I can't go on spoiling your life any longer." To Vanessa she wrote, "All I want to say is that Leonard has been so astonishingly good, every day, always; I can't imagine that anyone could have done more for me than he has. . . . I feel he has so much to do that he will go on, better without me. . . ."

Saints make guilt—especially when they impose monkish values; there is nothing new in that. And it was the monk as well as her madness she was fleeing when she walked into the Ouse, though it was the saint she praised. "I don't think two people could have been happier than we have been," the note to Leonard ended. A tragic happiness—such a thing is possible: cheerful invalids are a commonplace, and occasionally one hears of happy inmates. A saintly monk, a monkish nurse? All can be taken together, and all are true together. But the drive toward monkishness was in Leonard. What was natural for himself he prescribed for Virginia, and to one end only: to prevent her ongoing nervous crises from reaching their extreme state; to keep her sane. And to keep her sane was, ultimately, to keep her writing. It is reasonable to imagine that without Leonard Woolf there would have been very little of that corpus the name Virginia Woolf calls to mind—there would have been no *Mrs. Dalloway,* no *To the Lighthouse,* no *The Waves,* no *Common Reader.* And it may be that even the word Bloomsbury—the redolence, the signal—would not have survived, since she was its center. "She would not have been the symbol" of Bloomsbury, T. S. Eliot said, "if she had not been the maintainer of it." For Bloomsbury as an intellectual "period" to have escaped oblivion, there had to be at least one major literary voice to carry it beyond datedness. That voice was hers.

The effort to keep her sane was mammoth. Why did Leonard think it was worth it? The question, put here for the second time, remains callous but inevitable. Surely it would have been relieving at last (and perhaps to both of them) to let her slide away into those rantings, delusions, hallucinations; she might or might not have returned on her own. It is even possible that the nursing was incidental, and that she recovered each time because she still had the capacity to recover. But often enough Leonard—who knew the early symptoms intimately—was able to prevent her from going under; each pulling-back from that brink of dementia gained her another few months of literary work. Again and again he pulled her back. It required cajolery, cunning, mastery, agility, suspiciousness, patience, spoon-feeding, and an overwhelming sensitiveness to every flicker of her mood. Obviously it drained him; obviously he must have been tempted now and then to let it all go and give up. Almost anyone else would have. Why did he not? Again the answer must be manifold. Because she was his wife; because she was the beloved one to whom he had written during their courtship, "You don't know what a wave of happiness comes over me when I see you smile";* because his conscience obliged him to; because she suffered; because—this before much else—it was in his nature to succor suffering. And also: because of her gift; because of her genius; for the sake of literature; because she was unique. And because she had been a Miss Stephen; because she was Thoby Stephen's sister; because she was a daughter of Leslie Stephen; because she was, like Leonard's vision of Cambridge itself, "compounded of . . . the atmosphere of long years of history and great traditions and famous names [and] a profoundly civilized life"; because she was Bloomsbury; because she was England.

For her sake, for art's sake, for his own sake. Perhaps above all for his own sake. In her he had married a kind of escutcheon; she represented the finest grain of the finest stratum in England. What

---

*From an unpublished letter in the Berg Collection. Quoted in *The New York Times,* June 14, 1973.

he shored up against disintegration was the life he had gained—a birthright he paid for by spooning porridge between Virginia Woolf's resisting lips.

Proust is right to tell us to go to a writer's books, not to his loyalties. Wherever Leonard Woolf is, there Virginia Woolf is not. The more Leonard recedes or is not present, the more Virginia appears in force. Consequently Quentin Bell's biography—the subversive strength of which is Leonard—demands an antidote. The antidote is, of course, in the form of a reminder—that Virginia Woolf was a woman of letters as well as a patient; that she did not always succumb but instead could be an original fantasist and fashioner of an unaccustomed way of seeing; that the dependency coincided with a vigorous intellectual autonomy; that together with the natural subordination of the incapacitated she possessed the secret confidence of the innovator.

Seen through Leonard's eyes, she is, in effect, always on the verge of lunacy. "I am quite sure," he tells us in his autobiography, "that Virginia's genius was closely connected with what manifested itself as mental instability and insanity. The creative imagination in her novels, her ability to 'leave the ground' in conversation, and the voluble delusions of the breakdown all came from the same place in her mind—she 'stumbled after her own voice' and followed 'the voices that fly ahead.'" At the same time her refusal to eat was associated with guilt—she talked of her "faults"—and Leonard insists that "she remained all through her illness, even when most insane, terribly sane in three-quarters of her mind. The point is that her insanity was in her premises, in her beliefs. She believed, for instance, that she was not ill. . . ."

Seen through the books, she is never "ill," never lunatic. Whether it was mental instability or a clear-sighted program of experiment in the shape of the novel that unhinged her prose from the conventional margins that had gone before is a question not worth speculating over. Leonard said that when mad she heard the birds sing in Greek. The novels are not like that: it is not the data that are altered, but the sequence of things. When Virginia Woolf assaulted the "old" fiction in her famous *Mr. Bennett and Mrs. Brown,* she thought she was recommending getting rid of the habit of data; she thought this was to be her fictive platform. But when she grappled with her own inventions, she introduced as much data as possible and strained to express it all under the pressure of a tremendous simultaneity. What she was getting rid of was consecutiveness; precisely the habit of premises. If clinging to premises was the sanity of her insanity, then the intent of her fiction was not an extension of her madness, as Leonard claimed, but its calculated opposite. The poetry of her prose may have been like the elusive poetry of her dementia, but its steadfast design was not. "The design," she wrote of *Mrs. Dalloway,* "is so queer and so masterful"; elated, she saw ahead. She was an artist; she schemed, and not through random contractions or inflations of madness, but through the usual methods of art: inspired intellection, the breaking down of expectation into luminous segments of shock.

A simpler way of saying all this is that what she achieved as a stylist cannot really be explained through linking it with madness. The diaries give glimpses of rationalized prefigurations; a letter from Vanessa suggests moths, which metamorphosed into *The Moths,* which became *The Waves.* She knew her destination months before she arrived; she was in control of her work, she did what she meant to do. If the novels are too imaginatively astonishing to be persuasive on this point, the essays will convince. They are read too little, and not one of them is conceptually stale, or worn in any other way. In them the birds do not sing in Greek either, but the Greek—the sign of a masterly nineteenth-century literary education—shows like a spine. In the essays the control of brilliant minutiae is total—historical and literary figures, the particulars of biography, society, nationality, geography. She is a courier for the past. In Volume III of the *Collected Essays,* for instance, the range is from Chaucer through Montaigne through some Elizabethans major and minor, through Swift and Sterne and Lord Chesterfield, Fanny Burney and Cowper. She was interested also in the lives of women, especially writers. She studies Sara Coleridge, the poet's daughter; Harriette Wilson, the mistress of the Earl of Craven; Dr. Johnson's Mrs. Thrale; and Dorothy Osborne, a talented letter-writer of the seventeenth century. The language and scope of the essays astound. If they are "impressionistic," they are not self-indulgent; they put history before sensibility. When they are ironic, it is the kind of irony that enlarges the discriminatory faculty and does not serve the cynical temper. They mean to interpret other lives by the annihilation of the crack of time: they are after what the novels are after, a compression of then and now into the simultaneity of a singular recognition and a single comprehension. They mean to make every generation, and every instant, contemporaneous with every other generation and instant. And yet—it does not contradict—they are, taken all together, the English Essay incarnate.

The autonomous authority of the fiction, the more public authority of the essays, are the antidotes to Bell's Woolf, to Leonard's Virginia. But there is a third antidote implicit in the whole of the work, and in the drive behind the work, and that is Virginia Woolf's feminism. It ought to be said at once that it was what can now be called "classical" feminism. The latter-day choice of Virginia Woolf, on the style of Sylvia Plath, as a current women's-movement avatar is inapposite and mistaken. Classical feminism is inimical to certain developing strands of "liberation." Where feminism repudiates the conceit of the "gentler sex," liberation has come to reaffirm it. Where feminism asserts a claim on the larger world, liberation shifts to separatism. Where feminism scoffs at the plaint of "sisters under the skin," and maintains individuality of condition and temperament, liberation reinstates sisterhood and sameness. Where feminism shuns self-preoccupation, liberation experiments with self-examination, both psychic and medical. Classical feminism as represented by Virginia Woolf meant one thing only: access to the great world of thinking, being, and doing. The notion of "male" and "female" states of intellect and feeling, hence of prose, ultimately of culture, would have been the occasion of a satiric turn for Virginia Woolf; so would the idea of a politics of sex. Clive Bell reports that she licked envelopes once or twice for the Adult Suffrage League, but that she "made merciless fun of the flag-waving fanaticism" of the activists. She was not political—or, perhaps, just political enough, as when Chekhov notes that "writers should engage themselves in politics only enough to protect themselves from politics." Though one of her themes was women in history (several of her themes, rather; she took her women one by one, not as a race, species, or nation), presumably she would have mocked at the invention of a "history of women"—what she cared for, as *A Room of One's Own* both lucidly and passionately lays out, was access to a unitary culture. Indeed, *Orlando* is the metaphorical expression of this idea. History as a record of division or exclusion was precisely what she set herself against: the Cambridge of her youth kept women out, and all her life she preserved her resentment by pronouncing herself undereducated. She studied at home, Greek with Janet Case, literature and mathematics with her father, and as a result was left to count on her fingers forever—but for people who grow up counting on their fingers, even a Cambridge education cannot do much. Nevertheless she despised what nowadays is termed "affirmative action," granting places in institutions as a kind of group reparation; she thought it offensive to her own earned prestige, and once took revenge on the notion. In 1935 Forster, a member of the Committee of the London Library, informed her that a debate was under way concerning the admission of women members. No women were admitted. Six years later Virginia Woolf was invited to serve; she said she would not be a "sop"—she ought to have been invited years earlier, on the same terms as Forster, as a writer; not in 1941, when she was already fifty-nine, as a woman.

Nor will she do as martyr. Although Cambridge was closed to her, literary journalism was not; although she complains of being chased off an Oxbridge lawn forbidden to the feet of women, no one ever chased her off a page. Almost immediately she began to write for the *Times Literary Supplement* and for *Cornhill;* she was then twenty-two. She was, of course, Leslie Stephen's daughter, and it is doubtful whether any other young writer, male or female, could have started off so auspiciously: still, we speak here not of "connections" but of experience. At about the same time she was summoned to teach at Morley, a workers' college for men and women. One of her reports survives, and Quentin Bell includes it as an appendix. "My four women," she writes, "can hear eight lectures on the French Revolution if they wish to continue their historical learning"—and these were working-class women, in 1905. By 1928, women had the vote, and full access to universities, the liberal professions, and the civil service. As for Virginia Woolf, in both instances, as writer and teacher, she was solicited—and this cannot be, after all, only because she was Leslie Stephen's daughter. She could use on the spot only her own gifts, not the rumor of her father's. Once she determined to ignore what Bell calls the "matrimonial market" of upper-class partying, into which for a time her half-brother George dragooned her, she was freed to her profession. It was not true then, it is not true now, that a sublime and serious pen can be circumscribed.

Virginia Woolf was a practitioner of her profession from an early age; she was not deprived of an education, rather of a particular college; she grew rich and distinguished; she developed her art on her own line, according to her own sensibilities, and was acclaimed for it; though insane, she was never incarcerated. She was an elitist, and must be understood as such. What she suffered from, aside from the abysses of depression which characterized her disease, was not anything like the condition of martyrdom—unless language has become so flaccid that being on occasion patronized begins to equal death for the sake of an ideal. What she suffered from really was only the minor inflammations of the literary temperament. And she was not often patronized: her fame encouraged her to patronize others. She could be unkind, she could be spiteful, she could envy—her friendship with Katherine Mansfield was always unsure, being founded on rivalry. Mansfield and her husband, the journalist John Middleton Murry, "work in my flesh," Virginia Woolf wrote, "after the manner of the jigger insect. It's annoying, indeed degrading, to have these bitternesses." She was bitter also about James Joyce; she thought him, says Bell, guilty of "atrocities." Her diary speaks of "the damned egotistical self; which ruins Joyce," and she saw *Ulysses* as "insistent, raw, striking and ultimately nauseating." But she knew Joyce to be moving in the same direction as herself; it was a race that, despite her certainty of his faults, he might win. By the time of her death she must have understood that he *had* won. Still, to be outrun in fame is no martyrdom. And her own fame was and is in no danger, though, unlike Joyce, she is not taken as a fact of nature. Virginia Woolf's reputation in the thirty and more years since her death deepens; she becomes easier to read, more complex to consider.

Diary-Keeping

Again these lyrical, allusive, and alluring names! Lytton, Carring-
ton, Clive, Roger, Vanessa, Duncan, Leonard, Maynard, Gertler,
Ka, Kot, Janet, Aldous, Bob, Arnold, Ottoline, Morgan, Logan,
Katherine, Desmond, Murry, Nick, Saxon, Alix . . . Miniaturized by
the Cyclops eye of hindsight, with the gold dust shaken out of them,
one or two have broken out of legend to survive—E. M. Forster
solidly and on his own, also the economist Keynes; the rest shakily
and in shadow, reduced to "period" names: the polemicist Toynbee
rapidly growing quaint, Aldous Huxley's novels long ago turned
problematical, Katherine Mansfield fallen even out of the antholo-
gies, Sidney and Beatrice Webb fixed in Fabian caricature. The
"men of letters"—Robert Trevelyan, John Middleton Murry, Desmond MacCarthy, Logan Pearsall Smith: how far away and small
they now seem! And the painters, Vanessa Bell, Duncan Grant,
Mark Gertler, and the art critics, Clive Bell and Roger Fry—lost
molecules in the antiquity of modernism. And Saxon Sydney-
Turner? Less than a molecule; a civil servant in the British Treasury.
Lytton Strachey? A minor psychological historian given to phrasing

The Diary of Virginia Woolf, Volume One: 1915–1919, edited by Anne Olivier Bell,
Introduction by Quentin Bell (Harcourt Brace Jovanovich, 1977).
Published in *The New York Times Book Review,* October 2, 1977.

both fustian and trite; he had his little vogue. Leonard Woolf? An ungainly writer and social reformer active in anticolonial causes, an early supporter of the League of Nations—who thinks of him as anything other than Virginia Woolf's husband?

Merited fame, when it outlives its native generation (we may call this genius if we wish), is the real Midas touch. "Bloomsbury" means Virginia Woolf and her satellites. The men and women she breathed on shine with her gold. She did not know she was their sun, they did not know they were her satellites; but it is easy now, seventy years after they all seemed to glitter together, to tell the radiance from the penumbra. Even now—she is still ascending—she is not a genius to everyone; Lionel Trilling dismissed her, probably for her purported "subjectivity," and the women's movement claims but distorts her, for the same reason. Her genius does no one any good, has no social force or perspective, and—like most literature—is not needed: it is the intolerant genius of riddle. But not the sort of riddle-of-the-absurd that is left there, amorphous and mystical on the page. She will not fail to deliver. Her riddles are all concretely and dazzlingly solved by organization into ingenious portraiture. Hers is a beaklike and unifying imagination, impatient (unlike Forster's) with muddle or puzzle; she will seize any loose flying cloth and make it over for a Jolly Roger. Identity discovered in flux is all. So the mystery of her own mother was deciphered through Mrs. Ramsay in *To the Lighthouse*; and so the stippled occasions of daily life are drawn into coherency through the device of a secret diary.

This first volume, covering the years of the Great War, tells of shortages and moonlit air raids, of strikes and huddling in cellars, of frustrations with servants and in-laws; it is also the period of the founding of the Hogarth Press, the acquisition of Monk's House, and the publication of Virginia Woolf's earliest novels, *The Voyage Out* and *Night and Day*; it is the time when many of the remarkable essays that became *The Common Reader* were beaten out under the guise of journalism written against a deadline. All these matters amaze because they are familiar; we know them from a dozen other sources; we are already in possession of Virginia Woolf, after all— and yet how shocking to peer through her window at last, how astounding to hear her confirm everything in her own voice! A diary is a time machine; it puts us not simply on the doorstep but inside the mind, and yields to curiosity its ultimate consummation.

Yet Virginia Woolf's diary is not (to stumble on that perilous word again) "subjective." There are few psychological surprises. A Freudianly-inclined reader might be interested in the juxtaposition, in a single paragraph, of a memory of a childhood fear of "being shut in"; zoo animals that "grunt and growl"; and a visit to an "invalid" just emerged from a healthy childbirth. But there is no intent to record moods. Learning that Lady Ottoline Morrell keeps a diary, Virginia notes with light contempt that it is "devoted however to her 'inner life'; which made me reflect that I haven't an inner life." By and large, this is an accurate enough description of her own diary-keeping. It eschews "feelings"; it is dense with happenings: visits, party-goings, walks, scenery and season, political meetings, concerts, conversations; the purchase of a wristwatch, a pen (the dipping kind), a glass bottle, new spectacles. It is built not on sensibility but on the *pointillisme* of chronicle.

Chronicle is the foundation, but the structure is all explicit portraiture, and each portrait is fixed, final, locked into its varnish forever. If she begins in murk, with hints and signs, she carries her inquisitiveness into graphic intelligibility.

Of Robert Trevelyan, poet and classicist:

> . . . he manages to be more malevolent than anyone I know, under a cover of extreme good nature. He reminds me of the man with the pointed stick, who picks up scraps of paper. So Bob collects every scrap of gossip within reach.

Of Beatrice Webb:

> She has no welcome for one's individuality. . . . Marriage [she said] was necessary as a waste pipe for emotion, as a security in old age . . . & as a help to work. We were entangled at the gates of the level crossing when she remarked, "Yes, I daresay an old family servant would do as well."

Of Sidney Webb:

> . . . one could even commit the impropriety of liking him personally, which one can hardly do in the case of Mrs. Webb.

Of Lytton Strachey's fame:

> How did he do it, how is he so distinct & unmistakable if he lacks
> originality & the rest? Is there any reputable escape from this impasse
> in saying that he is a great deal better than his books?

Of the painter Mark Gertler:

> He is a resolute young man; & if good pictures can be made by willing
> them to be good, he may do wonders. No base motive could have its
> way with him; & for this reason I haven't great faith in him. Its too
> moral and intellectual an affair. . . . I advised him, for arts sake, to keep
> sane; to grasp, & not exaggerate, & put sheets of glass between him
> & his matter. . . . But he can think pianola music equal to hand made,
> since it shows the form, & the touch & the expression are nothing.

Of Lytton's brother James Strachey (whom Freud later analyzed):

> He has all the right books, neatly ranged, but not interesting in the
> least—not, I mean, all lusty & queer like a writer's books.

They parade by, these portraits, by the dozens, then by the hun-
dreds; they cascade and grow orchestral; the diary, as she acknowledges, begins to comprehend its own meaning. The portraits are
extraordinary not only for the power of their penetration, but for
language as strong and as flexible and as spontaneous as that of any
of the English masters, including Dickens. And they have the gift
of seeing through the flummery of their moment: though Lytton
Strachey is a more significant friend to the style of Virginia Woolf's
imagination than Leonard Woolf (whose comings and goings to
reformers' meetings crisscross these pages), though they converse in
the bliss of perfect rapport, she judges him with the dispassion of
posterity. Nearly all the portraits have this singular contemporary
balance—contemporary, that is, with *us*.

But she is also malicious in the way of the class she was born into.
She calls the common people "animals," "a tepid mass of flesh
scarcely organized into human life." Unlike the majority of her class,
she mocked the war; but the celebrations that mark its end she
ridicules as "a servants peace." Of famine following massacre: "I
laughed to myself over the quantities of Armenians. How can one

mind whether they number 4,000 or 4,000,000? The feat is beyond me." She has no piety or patriotism, but retains the Christian bias of the one, and the Imperial bias of the other. "I do not like the Jewish voice; I do not like the Jewish laugh," she writes of Leonard's sister, and the two visiting Ceylonese with whom Leonard is forming committees on colonial oppression she refers to as "persistent darkies." In all these instances there may be the little devil's-tail flick of self-derision; still, the spite stands. Though hospitality is constant, her sister Vanessa is not much on her mind, but she misses no opportunity to disparage Leonard's family; and perhaps, one discovers, even Leonard himself. In an ominous sentence seemingly directed at a speech by the socialist theosophist Annie Besant, but more dangerously at the principled Leonard, she comments, "It seems to me more & more clear that the only honest people are the artists, & that these social reformers & philanthropists get so out of hand, & harbour so many discreditable desires under the guise of loving their kind, that in the end there's more to find fault with in them than in us." In all Leonard's plethora of meeting after meeting, there is no way that "us" can be made to include Virginia Woolf's husband.

Yet, for all that, the social distaste and the portraits—those astonishing projections into the long view—are not what the diary is about, or for. Why does she keep it, and keep it up? How explain the compulsion to write nearly every day, from New Year's Day 1915 until the onset of mental illness in February; then again from August 1917 unceasingly until December 1919? To write through bombings, flu, strikes, Leonard's malaria, changes of residence (the Woolfs voyaged continually between London and the country), house-buying, hand-printing? Above all, to write while writing? It was a discipline she admits to wanting to be only a pleasure, but clearly she needed to do it. The reasons she gives are various: to interpret the thirty-seven-year-old Virginia to the "old Virginia" of fifty; or "my belief that the habit of writing thus for my own eye only is good practice" for writing well; and sometimes one sees how it is a "therapy journal" for writer's depression, in which the terror of self-doubt is ministered to again and again by the furious craving for praise. Now and then a future reader twinkles in these private pages—why else would she meticulously speak of "my father Sir Leslie," and is it for herself she notes that "almost always the afternoon is dry in England"? On occasion the diary serves as a pouch for leakings of unwritten essays—energetic readings of Byron and Milton. And of course it is nice to know that Virginia Woolf, catered to by two servants—how easy it was for her to have crowds of friends for dinner and tea and weekends!—once lost her underpants in the street in the middle of winter. (She lets this pass without comment; the sneer comes two entries later, when women get the vote.)

But all these useful reasons, pretexts, needs—her eye sidelong on us, more directly on her own intelligence—are not to the point, and especially do not explain the explosions of portraiture. "I might in the course of time [she tells herself in a meditation on the "kind of form which a diary might attain to"] learn what it is that one can make of this loose, drifting material of life; finding another use for it than the use I put it to, so much more consciously & scrupulously, in fiction." That was April 1919. Two months earlier, she had already made that find, but failed to recognize it. On February 5, adopting the tone of a governess, she scolds, "What a disgraceful lapse! nothing added to my disquisition, & life allowed to waste like a tap left running. Eleven days unrecorded."

Life allowed to waste, and still she did not see what she meant. The following October 7, during a railway strike that "broke in to our life more than the war did," the riddle begins to unravel: "Is it [the diary] worth going on with? . . . I wonder why I do it. Partly, I think, from my old sense of the race of time 'Time's winged chariot hurrying near'—Does it stay it?"

In the end she knew what she meant, and what keeping the diary was for. It was literally a keeping—not for disclosure, but for "staying," for making life stay, for validating breath. Her diary, though it is a chronicle and a narrative, is all the same not intended solely for a "record." A record is a hound padding after life. But a diary is a shoring-up of the ephemeral, evidence that the writer takes up real space in the world. For Virginia Woolf, as these incandescent streams of language show, the life she lived and the people she knew did not become real until they were written down.

Morgan and Maurice:
A Fairy Tale

Possibly the most famous sentence in Forster's fiction is the one that comes out of the blue at the start of Chapter Five of *The Longest Journey:* "Gerald died that afternoon." The sentence is there with no preparation whatever—no novelistic "plant," no hidden tracks laid out in advance. Just before the turning of the page we have seen Gerald resplendent in his sexual prime, "with the figure of a Greek athlete and the face of an English one," a football player of no special distinction but the fact of his glorious aliveness. Then, without warning, he is "broken up."

The suddenness of Gerald's death has been commented on almost too often by Forster seminarians; it is, after all, a slap in the reader's face, and must be accounted for. Asked about it in a 1952 interview (it was then forty-five years since the book had first appeared), Forster would only say, "It had to be passed by." An insulting answer. Forster is a gentleman who never insults unintentionally; he also intends to shock, and he never shocks inadvertently. Shock is the nearest he can come to religious truths. If you are reading a Forster story about a vigorous young man and happen, in the most

E. M. Forster, *Maurice* (W. W. Norton & Co., 1971).
Book review published in *Commentary,* December 1971.

natural way, to forget for just that moment how Death lies in ambush for all of us, Forster will rub your nose in reminders. How dare you forget that Death is by, how dare you forget Significance? Like those medieval monks who kept a skull on their desks, Forster believes in the instructiveness, the salubriousness, of shock. He believes that what is really important comes to us as a shock. And like nature (or like religion bereft of consolation), he withholds, he is unpredictable, he springs, so as to facilitate the shock.

That is in the fiction. His own life seemed not like that. He endured the mildest of bachelor lives, with, seen from the outside, no cataclysms. He was happiest (as adolescents say today, he "found himself") as a Cambridge undergraduate, he touched tenuously on Bloomsbury, he saw Egypt and India (traveling always, whether he intended it or not, as an agent of Empire), and when his mother died returned to Cambridge to live out his days among the undergraduates of King's. He wrote what is called a "civilized" prose, sometimes too slyly decorous, occasionally fastidiously poetic, often enough as direct as a whip. His essays, mainly the later ones, are especially direct: truth-telling, balanced, "humanist"—kind-hearted in a detached way, like, apparently, his personal cordiality. He had charm: a combination of self-importance (in the sense of knowing himself to be the real thing) and shyness. In tidy rooms at King's (the very same College he had first come up to in 1897), Forster in his seventies and eighties received visitors and courtiers with memorable pleasantness, was generous to writers in need of a push (Lampedusa among them), and judiciously wrote himself off as a pre-1914 fossil. Half a century after his last novel the Queen bestowed on him the Order of Merit. Then one day in the summer of 1970 he went to Coventry on a visit and died quietly at ninety-one, among affectionate friends.

That was the life. That none of this was meant to be trusted, not, certainly, to be taken at face value—least of all the harmonious death —suddenly came clear last year, when the British Museum let it be known it was in possession of an unpublished Forster novel, written in 1913, between the two masterpieces *Howards End* and *A Passage to India;* and that the novel was about homosexual love. Biographically, the posthumous publication of *Maurice* is the precise equiva-

lent of "Gerald died that afternoon." (Trust the fiction, not the life.)
It was to be sprung on us in lieu of a homily, and from the grave
itself—another audacious slap in the face.

But literary shock, especially when it is designed to be didactic,
has a way of finally trivializing. The suddenness of Gerald's death
presses so hard for Significance that Significance itself begins to give
way, and wilts off into nothing more impressive than a sneer.
Forster, prodding the cosmos to do its job of showing us how puny
we are, is left holding his little stick—the cosmos has escaped him,
it will not oblige. Gerald's death may surprise, but the teaching fails:
death qua death is not enough. We must have grief to feel death, and
Forster did not give us enough Gerald to grieve over. We were never
allowed to know Gerald well, or even to like him a little; he is an
unsympathetic minor character, too minor to stand for the abyss.
Shock does not yield wisdom on short acquaintance.

Maurice is meant to convey wisdom on longer acquaintance: here
is a full-scale history of a homosexual from earliest awakening to
puzzlement to temporary joy to frustration to anguish, and at last to
sexual success. In *Maurice* it is society Forster prods, not the cosmos;
it is one of Forster's few books in which death does not reverberate
in any major way. But like the cosmos in *The Longest Journey*, society
in *Maurice* eludes Forster's stick. In *Howards End* it did not: he
impaled English mores in the house-renting habits of Mr. Wilcox,
and wrote of the money-and-property mentality in such a way as to
dishevel it permanently. *Howards End* is, along with *Middlemarch*
thirty-odd years before, the prototypical English Wisdom Novel—
wisdom in the category of the-way-things-really-are, the nest of
worms exposed below the surface of decency. *Maurice* is even more
ambitious: it appears not merely to attack and discredit society, but
to outwit it. How? By spite; by spitting in the eye of conventional
respectability; by inventing a triumphant outcome against the grain
of reality and (then) possibility. "A happy ending was imperative,"
Forster explained in a message that accompanies the novel in the
manner of a suicide note (and is, in fact, styled by him a "Terminal
Note"); like a suicide note it represents defense, forethought, revenge—the culmination of extensive fantasizing. "I shouldn't have

bothered to write otherwise. I was determined that in fiction anyway two men should fall in love and remain in it for the ever and ever that fiction allows."

The key words are: in fiction. *Maurice*, in short, is a fairy tale. I don't choose this term for the sake of an easy pun, or to take up the line of ribaldry, and certainly not to mock. I choose it because it is the most exact. *Maurice* is not merely an idyll, not merely a fantasy, not merely a parable. It is a classical (though flawed and failed) fairy tale in which the hero is stuck with an ineradicable disability. In the standard fairy tale he may be the youngest of three, or the weakest, or the poorest and most unlikely—in Maurice's instance he is the oddest, and cannot love women. In the prescribed manner he encounters sinister advice and dissembling friends and gets his profoundest wish at the end, winning—as a reward for the wish itself —the hand of his beloved. The essence of a fairy tale is that wishing *does* make it so: the wish achieves its own fulfillment through its very steadfastness of desire. That is why fairy tales, despite their dark tones and the vicissitudes they contain so abundantly, are so obviously akin to daydreams—daydreaming is a sloughing-off of society, not an analysis of it. To wish is not to explain; to wish is not to reform. In real life wishing, divorced from willing, is sterile and begets nothing. Consequently *Maurice* is a disingenuous book, an infantile book, because, while pretending to be about societal injustice, it is really about make-believe, it is about wishing; so it fails even as a tract. Fairy tales, though, are plainly literature; but *Maurice* fails as literature too. In a fairy or folk tale the hero, even when he is a trickster, is a model of purity and sincerity. What is pure and sincere in him is the force of his wish, so much so that his wish and his nature are one. But Maurice as hero has a flaw at the center of him; he is conceived impurely and insincerely.

This impurity Forster himself appears to concede. "In Maurice," the Terminal Note explains further, "I tried to create a character who was completely unlike myself or what I supposed myself to be: someone handsome, healthy, bodily attractive, mentally torpid, not a bad business man and rather a snob. Into this mixture I dropped an ingredient that puzzles him, wakes him up, torments him and finally saves him." The impurity, then, is the ingredient of homosexuality dropped into a man who is otherwise purely Mr. Wilcox, lifted temperamentally intact out of *Howards End:* a born persecutor whom fear of persecution "saves" from the practice of his trait.

But whatever Forster's hope for Maurice was, this is not the sensibility he has rendered. It is impossible to believe in Maurice as a businessman or a jock (in Cambridge vocabulary, a "blood"). He is always Ricky of *The Longest Journey* (which means he is always Morgan Forster) got up in a grotesque costume—The Sensitive Hero as Callous Philistine—and wearing a wobbly wig. Whenever Maurice is most himself, the prose gives a lurch: it is Forster remembering, with a mindful shudder, to throw in a liter of mental torpidity here, a kilo of investment shrewdness there. But all that is artifice and sham. Forster loves music; Maurice is ignorant of it; consequently Maurice's self-knowledge occurs partly through Tchaikovsky. Forster at school recoiled from games and fell in love with Hellenism; Maurice has "physical pluck" and is an indifferent scholar (his "Greek was vile"); consequently on Prize Day he delivers a Greek Oration. No matter how Forster sidesteps it, Maurice keeps coming out Forster. After a while the absurdity of the effort to coarsen Maurice—to de-Morgan him, so to speak—fatigues; Forster's pointless toil at this impossibility becomes, for the reader, an impatience and an embarrassment. It is embarrassing to watch a writer cover his tracks in the name of exploring them. Purporting to show a hard man turn soft under the pressure of alienation from the general run of society, Forster instead (and without admitting it) shows a soft man turn softer—so soft he slides off into the teleology of the fairy tale. This falsification is the real impurity of the novel. Its protagonist falls apart at the marrow, like a book left outdoors overnight in the rain. *Maurice* cannot hold because Maurice is made of paper and breaks like dough at the first moist lover's squeeze.

One suspects Forster knew this. How could he not? He had already published three nearly perfect minor novels and one extraordinary major one. He had already created the Schlegels and the Wilcoxes. Written in his own handwriting across the top of the British Museum's typescript of *Maurice,* and put there possibly as

late as 1960, were the Delphic words: "Publishable, but is it worth
it?" The ambiguity is typical. Is the reference to the homosexual
theme—or to the level of craftsmanship? That Forster was distinctly
capable of detecting a falling-off from his own standard we know
from his account of *Arctic Summer,* a work he abandoned midway
because of "fiction-technicalities." Comparing the texture of his
unfinished novel with the "density" of *A Passage to India,* he explained, "There must be something, some major object toward
which one is to approach. . . . What I had in *Arctic Summer* was
thinner, a background and color only." If he was able to sense the
thinness of one novel and then let it go, why did he preserve *Maurice,*
which he must surely have perceived as at least equally thin? In 1960,
the date of the Terminal Note, thirty-three years had already passed
since Forster's invention (in *Aspects of the Novel*) of the terms "flat"
and "round" to describe the differences between characters in novels. A flat character is always predictable; a round character is not.
Maurice is neither flat nor round, but something else—a ghost—and
Forster must have known it. How could he not? What made him
want to hang on to a protagonist so dismally flawed? The answer
may be in the "something, some major object toward which one is
to approach." In *Maurice* it is painfully easy to see what that major
object is: sex, overt and unfudged. Forster preserved the approach
but did not arrive. "There is no pornography," the Terminal Note
scrupulously reports. So much the worse for Maurice. He is there
—he was put to paper neither flat nor round—only for the sake of
the sex scenes; and the sex scenes are hardly there at all. Maurice—
neither flat nor round—is the ghost of undepicted, inexplicit coitus,
of the missing "pornography."

Except for those absent sex scenes—one feels them struggling to
be born, and Forster stamping them regretfully out at their earliest
gasp—*Maurice* has no reason to be. It is a novel, if one can say such
a thing, without a cause. Or, rather, the only genuine cause for it,
the force that got it written, was a fresh and potent interest in all
those matters that did *not* get written: the caresses in detail, the
embraces, the endearments precisely depicted. Instead we are only
handed plot. And to be handed plot is, in the case of *Maurice,* to be
handed something worn out almost to risibility. It is not that *Maurice*

has no plot; it does, and I suppose I am bound to recount a little of it; but it is a plot that Forster has dealt with at least twice before in the two novels of which *Maurice* is the shadow-novel, and, in fact, in what may have been the very first short story he ever wrote.

In all of these—"Albergo Empedocle," *The Longest Journey, A Room with a View*—a poetic but naïve hero (or heroine) falls in love with a woman (or man) who appears at first to be even more sensitive and poetic, but who betrays by turning out to be unable to love with equal tenderness or sincerity. In *The Longest Journey* Ricky, charmed by the ecloguelike scene he witnesses of the "Greek athlete" Gerald kissing Agnes in the dell, marries Agnes and finds instead that he has surrendered his spirit to coldness and cynicism. In *A Room with a View* Lucy, whose poetic nature is expressed in music, becomes engaged to Cecil; Cecil is brilliant, and therefore seems to be in love with art, Leonardo, and Italy, but is in reality "like a Gothic statue," which "implies celibacy, just as a Greek statue implies fruition." "Albergo Empedocle" describes the breakup of an engagement between Mildred, a young woman intellectually immersed in Hellenism, and Harold, who suddenly feels himself to be the reincarnation of a Greek youth. For the moment Mildred is romantically enraptured at the notion. But she ends up thinking her fiancé mad—whereupon he displays his love for another youth, ancient Greek-style. All these tender lovers, genuinely won to the Greek ideal of the body, are betrayed by a capricious and false Hellenism.

Maurice too finds his hard-earned Hellenism betrayed. In the joyfully liberating atmosphere of Cambridge he is introduced to music, Plato, and Clive Durham, a worshiper of Greece and a lapsed Christian. Like the others, they have their day in the dell and become lovers, though mainly sentimentally (Clive "abstained . . . almost from caresses"). Then Clive goes on a pilgrimage to Greece, and there—in Greece; irony!—"becomes normal." He has "turned to women," and enters the life of conventional county society, marrying coldly and growing more and more worldly and opportunistic. Maurice's outlook darkens. He too tries to "become normal." There follow relatively good, though thin, Forsterian scenes with a doctor (who can only say "Rubbish" to the idea of homosexuality) and a

hypnotist (who decides the case is hopeless). Then comes the happy
ending. Just as Lucy in *A Room with a View* flees from Cecil to marry
the Panlike figure of George Emerson, Maurice flees his family, his
work, and society altogether, going off to live tenderly ever after
with a rough-mannered but loving gamekeeper.

"There is no pornography." In short, a daydream without pictures. But what *Maurice* lacks, and what is necessary to it because
it belongs at the heart of its imagining, *is* the pictures, *is* the "pornography"—or what Forster significantly continued to think of as
pornography. What surely was not necessary was the reflex of
Forster's ineluctable plot—the same story of compulsive attraction
and callous faithlessness that he was driven to manipulate again and
again, looking for some acceptable means to tell what he *really*
wanted to tell about the importance of the body. It was pointless to
write a book like *Maurice* unless the body in its exact—not implied,
not poeticized—male lineaments could be truly shown. Forster did
not show it truly. It is clear enough that he longed to show it truly
—he lingers over those blurry passages in which he might have
shown it truly, and instead reaches desperately for the expedient of
poetry. "And their love scene drew out. . . . Something of exquisite
beauty arose in the mind of each at last, something unforgettable and
eternal, but built of the humblest scraps of speech and from the
simplest emotions." And of the flesh. But it is the flesh that Forster
omits.

The reason for this omission, it seems to me, is not that in the
England of 1913 Forster still did not dare to put it explicitly in (Gide
in France had already launched *Corydon,* but that was France), and
not even that Forster still belonged mentally to the England of 1897.
No. The reason—unlikely though it may appear at first hearing—
is that Forster thought homosexuality wrong: naturally wrong, with
the sort of naturalness that he did not expect to date. (The Terminal
Note admits that *Maurice* "certainly dates" in other respects, and
mentions its "half-sovereign tips, pianola-records, norfolk jackets.")
But if *Maurice* is a fairy tale, it is not because two men do not ever,
then or now, out of fiction as well as in, live together happily and
permanently, but because Forster himself believed that except in

fiction and daydream they ought not to. Against his deepest wish he set his still deeper belief. *They ought not to:* despite the fact that he was always openly in favor of the liberalization in England of laws concerning homosexuality, despite the fact that as early as 1928, beginning with the *Well of Loneliness* case, he went to court to testify against the suppression of a homosexual novel, the first of a succession of such books he publicly defended and praised.

Forster's own books are full of veiled* portraits of repressed or hidden or potential homosexuals, from Ansell in *The Longest Journey* to Tibby in *Howards End* (who warms the teapot "almost too deftly," is called "Auntie Tibby" for fun, and is declared not to be "a real boy"). The description of Cecil in *A Room with a View* fits not only what the young Tibby will become, but what Maurice's lover Clive already is: "He is the sort who are all right as long as they keep to things—books, pictures—but kill when they come to people." Many of Forster's clergymen are seen to be embittered ascetics who, had they not suppressed the body, would have loved men. Mr. Borenius, the rector in *Maurice,* jealously accuses the gamekeeper of being "guilty of sensuality." It is because Forster himself is always on the side of sensuality, of "fruition" as against "celibacy," that all his spokesmen-characters, with profound sadness, eventually yield up their final judgment—on moral and natural grounds, and despite Forster's renowned liberalism—against homosexuality. *Maurice,* where the wish for lasting homoerotic bliss is allowed to come true, is no exception to Forster's moral conviction.

It is precisely on this issue of sensuality that Forster's reservations rest. Forster believes, with Christianity, that the opposite of sensuality is sterility. And not sterility in any metaphorical sense—not in

---

*So successfully "veiled," in fact, that Lionel Trilling, who had published a critical volume on Forster's fiction as early as 1943, commented to me in a 1972 letter that "it wasn't until I had finished my book on Forster that I came to the explicit realization that he was homosexual. I'm not sure whether this was because of a particular obtuseness on my part or because . . . homosexuality hadn't yet formulated itself as an issue in the culture. When the realization did come, it at first didn't seem of crucial importance, but that view soon began to change." The two did not meet until after the publication of Trilling's book. In the wake of that "slight personal acquaintance," Trilling explained, his view "changed radically."

the meaning of an empty or unused life. With Christianity, Forster believes that sensuality is designed to beget progeny. The most melancholy passage in *Maurice* occurs at Maurice's most ecstatic moment—when he is at last physically in possession of Clive:

> An immense sadness—he believed himself beyond such irritants—had risen up in his soul. He and the beloved would vanish utterly—would continue neither in Heaven nor on Earth. They had won past the conventions, but Nature still faced them, saying with even voice, "Very well, you are thus; I blame none of my children. But you must go the way of all sterility." The thought that he was sterile weighed on the young man with a sudden shame. His mother or Mrs. Durham might lack mind or heart, but they had done visible work; they had handed on the torch their sons would tread out.

And it is Ansell in *The Longest Journey* who gives the homosexual's view of progeny, which is renunciation. He is strolling in the British Museum talking of "the Spirit of Life" when he is told that Ricky and Agnes are expecting a child. His response: "I forgot that it might be." Then: "He left the Parthenon to pass by the monuments of our more reticent beliefs—the temple of the Ephesian Artemis, the statue of the Cnidian Demeter. Honest, he knew that here were powers he could not cope with, nor, as yet, understand." Artemis the protectress of women, Demeter the goddess of fertility. Thus Ansell. And thus Auden. Somewhere Auden has written that homosexual men do not love their sterility; that homosexuals too would welcome parenthood; but out of decency and selflessness forgo it.

"Be fruitful and multiply." That Forster alone perhaps of all homosexual writers is willing to take seriously the Biblical injunction, and is left feeling desolated by it, is a measure of how attached he remained to Christian morals. In this attachment he was unlike any homosexual in his Cambridge generation, and possibly unlike any English-speaking homosexual in the generations afterward, Auden excepted. The Gay Liberation argument that homosexual activity is a positive good in a world afflicted by overpopulation would not have won Forster over.

* * *

Homosexuality did not begin with Lytton Strachey, but homosexual manners did. All those habits and signals that we now associate with the educated homosexual sensibility can be said to have had their start in Cambridge when Strachey was an undergraduate; and Strachey set the style for them. Sects and persuasions, like nationalities, have their forerunners and traditions: presumably Franciscans still strive to retain the mind-set of Saint Francis, Quakers recall George Fox, the white American South continues to feel itself patrician. Forster himself was influenced in liberal thinking by his ancestors in the Clapham Sect, an abolitionist group. The recollection need not be conscious; we inherit, rather than mimic, style. So with educated homosexual manners. The passion for beauty and distinction, the wit with its double bur of hilarity and malice, the aesthetic frame of mind, even the voice that edges thinly upward and is sometimes mistaken for "effeminacy"—all these are Stracheyisms. Strachey at Cambridge and afterward was so forceful in passing on Stracheyism that he founded a school, active to this day. It had, and has, two chief tenets: one was antiphilistinism expressed as élitism (one cannot imagine Strachey making a hero of a gamekeeper with no grammar, or addressing, as Forster did, a Working Men's College); the other was a recoil from Christianity. In these tenets especially Forster did not acquiesce.

Though Forster knew Strachey well at Cambridge (he even confesses that a Cambridge character in *Maurice* was modeled on Strachey), he remained peripheral to the Strachey set. This astounding group was concentrated in the Cambridge Conversazione Society, better known as the Apostles, which mingled older alumni and undergraduates, never much more than a dozen at a time, and was devoted to intellectual wrangling, high wit, snobbery toward "bloods," and, in an underground sort of way, homosexuality: its brilliant members kept falling in and out of love with one another. At one time Strachey and John Maynard Keynes were both furious rivals for the love of one Duckworth; afterward Keynes, like Clive

Durham, "became normal" and married a ballerina. Through all this Forster kept himself apart and remote, "the elusive colt of a dark horse," as Keynes called him. The Apostles churned out barristers, chief justices, governors of outlying parts of the Empire, dons, historians, economists, mathematicians, philosophers, many of them with family attachments to one another: in short, the ruling intellectual class of England more or less reproducing itself. The smaller "aesthetic" section of this privileged and brainy caste withdrew to become Bloomsbury; but from Bloomsbury too Forster held himself in reserve. One reason was his temperamental shyness, his inclination toward an almost secretive privateness. The more compelling reason was that he did not think or feel like the Apostles, or like Bloomsbury. He was more mystical than skeptical. The ideal of freedom from all restraint made him uncomfortable in practice. Unlike Strachey, he did not scoff easily or vilify happily (though it ought to be noted that there is a single radiant "Balls" in *Maurice*), and did not use the word "Christian" as a taunt. To the Apostles—self-declared "immoralists," according to Keynes—and to Bloomsbury he must have seemed a little out of date. He never shared their elation at smashing conventional ideas; though himself an enemy of convention, he saw beyond convention to its roots in nature. Stracheyan Bloomsbury assented to nothing, least of all to God or nature, but Forster knew there were "powers he could not cope with, nor, as yet, understand." Bloomsbury was alienated but not puzzled; Forster was puzzled but not alienated. His homosexuality did not divide him from society, because he saw that society in the largest sense was the agent of nature; and when he came to write *A Passage to India* he envisioned culture and nature as fusing altogether. Homosexuality led him not away from but toward society. He accepted himself as a man with rights—nature made him—but also very plainly as a deviant—nature would not gain by him. It is no accident that babies are important in his books.

The shock of the publication of *Maurice*, then, is not what it appears to be at first sight: Forster as Forerunner of Gay Lib. Quite the opposite. He used his own position as an exemplum, to show what the universe does not intend. If that implies a kind of rational martyrdom, that is what he meant; and this is what shocks. We had not thought of him as martyr. For Forster, "I do not conform" explains what does conform, it does not celebrate nonconformity. He was a sufferer rather than a champion. Now suddenly, with the appearance of *Maurice*, it is clear that Forster's famous humanism is a kind of personal withdrawal rather than a universal testimony, and reverberates with despair. Christopher Lehmann-Haupt in a recent *Times* review remarks that Maurice's homosexuality is "a symbol of human feelings." But Forster would disagree that homosexuality stands for anything beyond what it is in itself, except perhaps the laying-waste of the Cnidian Demeter. Homosexuality to Forster signified sterility; he practiced it like a blasphemer, just as he practiced his humanism like a blasphemer. There is no blasphemy where there is no belief to be betrayed; and Forster believes in the holiness of the goddess of fertility: Demeter, guardian of the social order and marriage. The most dubious social statement Forster ever made is also his most famous one: if I had to choose between betraying my country or my friend, I hope I would have the guts to betray my country. He says "I"; the note is personal, it is not an injunction to the rest of us. *Maurice* instructs us explicitly in what he understands by "friend"; in Maurice's boyhood dream the word "friend" foretells the love of a man for a man. We have encountered that charged word in Forster before. The statement about betrayal cannot be universalized, and Forster did not mean it to be. Declarations about bedmates do not commonly have general application.

Does it devalue the large humanistic statement to know that its sources are narrowly personal? Yes. And for Forster too: he does not ask society to conform to him, because he believes—he says it again and again everywhere in his books, but nowhere more poignantly than in his novel about homosexual love—he believes in the eternal stream. He died among affectionate friends, but not harmoniously; he was not content to go the way of all sterility, to vanish utterly. Books are not progeny, and nature does not read.

* * *

I append to my observations about Forster's *Maurice* a reply to a
correspondent who charged me with not loving Forster enough.

Forster as Moralist: A Reply to Mrs. A. F.

Lionel Trilling begins his book about Forster with this observation:
"E. M. Forster is for me the only living novelist who can be read
again and again and who, after each reading, gives me what few
writers can give us after our first days of novel-reading, the sensation
of having learned something." To this statement another can be
added, virtually a corollary: Forster is also one of those very few
writers (and since Forster's death, there is none now living) who
excite competitive passions—possessive rivalries, in fact—among serious readers, each of whom feels uniquely chosen to perceive the
inner life of the novels.

In recent years Forster has grown thinner for me, especially as
essayist. Not that I would now deny Forster's powers or his brilliance, or claim that the masterpieces are not masterpieces, still giving out, as Trilling said almost thirty years ago, "the sensation of
having learned something." But what we learn from the novels is not
what we learn from the essays. The novels do not preach morality
and the essays, in their way, do. Or, to put it differently, the novels
preach a novelistic morality—in the early ones, the ethics of Spon-
taneity; in *A Passage to India*, the anti-ethics of a mystical nihilism.
But the essays—preëminently "What I Believe," which Mrs. F. cites
—tell us how we are to go about living from moment to moment.
"Where do I start?" Forster asks. And answers: "With personal
relationships." Of this approach Mrs. F. says: "I like it well."

I do not, because it strikes me as incomplete and self-indulgent.
Nevertheless I recognize Mrs. F.'s tone—it was once mine, and I
think we can spot our erstwhile psychological twins—at the end of
her letter, when she concludes that I do "not love [Forster] enough
—for what he *did* do." I withdraw from the contest and agree that

Letter published in *Commentary*, May 1972.

Mrs. F. is right. She *does* love Forster's ideas and qualities, if not more than I once did, certainly more than I do now.

And the reasons I have, so to speak, fallen out of love with Forster are the very reasons she is still in thrall to him. A novelist, as she says, is both psychologist and metaphysician (and social historian). That is why we become most attached to those novels which give us an adequate account of the way the world seems to us. Novelists interpret us, and when we "choose" a novelist we are really choosing a version of ourselves. The same is true of essayists. What I no longer choose to choose among Forster's ideas is "Only Connect," which signifies, of course, "personal relationships." When I said in my remarks on *Maurice* that it devalued "the large humanistic statement to know that its sources are narrowly personal," I was not referring to Forster's novelistic imagination (of course the women in his novels are women and not disguised male homosexuals), but to his liberalism. We are now unambiguously apprised of Forster's homosexuality, and *Maurice* makes it shudderingly plain that Forster considered homosexuality to be an affliction, the ineradicable mark of a fated few. To use language grown shabby from repetition, he regarded himself as part of an oppressed minority; and, applying Only Connect, he could stand in for and champion other oppressed minorities—Indians under English colonialism, for instance, who suffered from the English public-school mentality precisely as he had suffered from it. But this, after all, is a compromised liberalism. There is nothing admirable in it; it is devalued by the presence of the vested interest. It is no trick, after all, for a Jew to be against anti-Semitism, or for a homosexual to be against censorship of homosexual novels. The passion behind the commitment may be pure, but the commitment is not so much a philosophy of liberalism as it is of self-preservation. Morality must apply some more accessible standard than personal hurt. In *Howards End* Mr. Wilcox, disapproving of Helen's affair with Leonard Bast, gets his nose rubbed in a reminder of his own affair, long ago, with Mrs. Bast: what's sauce for the goose is sauce for the gander. But suppose the gander has had no sauce? I am not a homosexual; if I had been in England in 1935, should I not have been disturbed by the law that interfered with the untrammeled publication of *Boy*, as Forster was? (See his essay

"Liberty in England.") Liberalism, to be the real thing, ought to be disinterested.

But the inadequacy of Only Connect—that it is *not* disinterested —is not the whole of my charge against "personal relationships" as the ultimate moral standard. Deciding your behavior person by person (Forster was apparently the inventor of an early form of situation ethics) seems to me a localized, partial, highly contingent, catch-as-catch-can sort of morality. "This is my friend; I love him; therefore I will not kill him" is, in my view, inferior to saying, once and for all, "Thou shalt not kill." The reason is not simply that the overall Commandment is relatively more efficient than figuring it out one person at a time as you go along, but also that it is more reliable. "This is my friend; I love him" can too easily turn into "This was my friend; now I hate him." And if that is all there is to it, if there is no larger motive than "personal relationships" to govern human behavior, one might as well kill him. It is not only that "Love and loyalty to an individual can run counter to the claims of the State" (though the single example Forster can think of to illustrate this possibility is Brutus and Cassius vis-à-vis Caesar, not exactly the sort of situation that one is likely to encounter on an everyday basis)— it is also, as Forster himself recognizes, that love and loyalty can run counter to themselves; in short, they rot. They are "a matter for the heart, which signs no documents." That is why, taking up—as Forster himself does—the question of reliability, and writing about these matters on stone some four thousand years before Forster, Moses thought that having it down on a document might not be a bad idea. "But reliability," Forster sensibly answers Moses, "is not a matter of contract—that is the main difference between the world of personal relationships and the world of business relationships." It is also one of the differences between personal relationships and universal ethics. To Forster, Moses comes out a businessman with a contract, and in the same essay (we are still in "What I Believe") he says he prefers Montaigne and Erasmus. "My temple stands," he asserts, "not upon Mount Moriah but in that Elysian Field where even the immoral are admitted." It is not a very great distance from an Elysian Field that makes no distinction between innocents and murderers (for we have a right to take the persons Forster calls "immoral" at their most extreme) to the *ou-boum* of the Marabar Caves, which swallows up both good and evil into one of the unknown black holes of the universe, similarly without distinction. The problem with Forster's "personal relationships"—or, to use Mrs. F.'s term, his personal loyalties—is that they tend to slip away at the first intrusion of something spooky or ineffably cosmic—of something, in brief, that suggests his notion of Religion, which is pagan in the sense of fearfulness, imbued with the uncanniness of *lacrimae rerum*, un-human, without relation to the world of men. When Mrs. Moore in the cave hears the *ou-boum* of nothingness, she "lost all interest, even in Aziz [who had become her good friend], and the affectionate and sincere words that she had spoken to him seemed no longer hers but the air's."

Mrs. Moore in the Marabar Caves is obviously an extreme example of the dissolution of a friendship. But Forster, as we know, is fond of extremes, so it is not too much to say that Mrs. Moore is also an extreme example of someone who—quoting Mrs. F. quoting Forster —"hate[s] the idea of causes." Her hatred of causes does not strengthen her in friendship. She betrays her friend by losing interest in him, because the universe has shown her that it is impersonal, and that friendship and betrayal and loss are all the same to it. She has no "cause"—no motivation, no ideal contract—that restricts her from betraying her friend. Forster's dedication to personal relationships without contract is doomed to work only very rarely, not only because friendship succeeds only very rarely, but because it is, in a world of friends and non-friends, not enough. "Do not lie about your friend, whom you love" is, in moral distance, a light-year from "Do not tell lies about anyone at all"—or, as it is more commonly formulated, "Do not bear false witness." A contractual, or communal, ethics, when violated, at least leaves the standard intact. A catch-as-catch-can ethics, based on your feelings for your friend, leaves everything in a shambles when it is violated.

A case can of course be made that Forster's ethics of privacy derives through Romanticism with its discovery of the Individual from Nonconformism with its emphasis on regulating personal morality through conscience. Whatever their sources, though, the moral and political positions that emerge from "What I Believe" seem to me to be disturbingly partial. They may do a certain credit to the sensibility of a hurt man who knows enough to be thoughtful about the hurts of others, but they fail of universal application. Forster never comes head-on against the problem of how to get the "bloods" to behave less callously. Or, rather, he dodges the problem by loading it: by giving Mr. Wilcox an old affair to hide, by making Maurice a homosexual. His whole men turn out not to be whole at all; Forster appears incapable of accepting the *principle* of not hurting without first making a hurt felt. His humanity goes from wound to wound. His politics, his morality, ultimately his liberalism, all signify the humanism of cripples. It is too thin. The thugs escape.

The difficulty, I think, is that Mrs. F. mixes up these specific questions raised by Forster's political and moral positions with a general analysis of the novelistic imagination. Her description of the "miracle" of the fictive imagination is superb and very nearly complete, but I am puzzled about why she has introduced it. My judgment on Forster's humanism does not lead logically to any judgment on his capacity to imagine. If I believe, as I do, that Forster's sense of himself as a kind of martyr taints the candor of his liberalism with a hidden self-interest, how does this relate to Mrs. F.'s notion that I somehow also believe the novels to be homosexual disguises? They are obviously not homosexual disguises. Nothing in what I wrote suggested they might be. That there are in Forster's fiction men with homosexual tendencies has always been clear and is now clearer. A pair of obvious examples: Ricky and Ansell, Aziz and Fielding. Revisited in the aftermath of *Maurice* (I have, for instance, been rereading *A Passage to India*), they have new resonances; so does the passionate "friend" in the essay called "Notes on the English Character" (1920), who is an adumbration of Aziz as Forster himself in that essay is an adumbration of Fielding. As for Forster's use of the word "friend": until some industrious clod of a graduate student gives us the definitive concordance for that word in Forster's *oeuvre*, we shall not know how often he intended it wistfully and how often straightforwardly. But until we get the concordance, we will have to rely on impressions—and my impression is that it is a word

Forster most often uses wistfully. I feel certain—it is an impression
—that the friend for whom Forster would betray his country is
thought of wistfully. When you betray your country, that is treason,
a capital offense. Betraying your country for your friend, you die.
I quote Mrs. F. quoting Maurice in a passage she herself calls "the
epitome of the homosexual 'friend' ": "He could die for such a friend
. . . they would make any sacrifice for each other, and count the
world nothing." Maurice would betray his country for such a friend;
Forster is largely indistinguishable from Maurice; and yet Mrs. F.
writes, "I don't believe you can imagine him to mean by 'friend'
anything different from what you or I or anyone would mean by it."
My impression is otherwise.

But all this is about friendship between men. Against the rest—
Mrs. F.'s catalogue of "love, courtship, marriage, sisterhood, father-
hood, sonhood"—nothing can be insinuated. Forster believed, as I
have said, in Demeter, the most domestic of all the goddesses.

So two cheers for Forster's Friendship. "Two cheers are quite
enough," Forster remarked of Democracy, saving his third for
"Love the Beloved Republic." If, as Mrs. F. asserts, I do not love
Forster enough for what he has done, it is not because I fail to
celebrate his novelistic imagination, but rather because I would dislike living in his Republic, where personal relationships govern (one
might dare to say seethe) and there are no communal contracts. I
save half my third cheer for the Covenant; and the other half, following Forster in all his novels but the last, for Demeter.

Truman Capote Reconsidered

Time at length becomes justice. A useful if obscure-sounding literary aphorism, just this moment invented. What it signifies is merely this: if a writer lives long enough, he may himself eventually put behind him the work that brought him early fame, and which the world ought to have put aside in the first place.

I remember reading somewhere not long ago a comment by Truman Capote on his first novel: it was written, he said, by somebody else.

Cruel time fleshes out this interesting, only seemingly banal, remark: who is this tiny-fingered flaccid man, with molasses eyes and eunuch's voice, looking like an old caricature of Aeolus, the puff-cheeked little god of wind? We see him now and then on television talk shows, wearing a hayseed hat, curling his fine feet, his tongue on his lip like a soft fly, genially telling dog stories. Or we read about the vast celebrity parties he is master of, to which whole populations of the famous come, in majestic array of might and mind. Or we hear of him in New Orleans some months ago, in the company of Princess Radziwill, observing the Rolling Stones and their congrega-

---

Essay published in *The New Republic*, January 27, 1973.

tions, with what secret thoughts print will soon make plain. Or we catch him out as a cabal-sniffing inquisitor in *Playboy,* confiding in an interview how "other backgrounds" are not being "given a chance" because of the "predominance of the Jewish Mafia" in American letters. Or, back on television again, we learn from him about the psychology of criminals—which inadvertently lets us in a little on the psychology of people who are attracted to the psychology of criminals. Or we discuss, for months, his puzzling coinage "nonfiction novel," as if some new theory of literature had broken on the world—what he means, it turns out on publication, is the spawn of garden-variety interview journalism, only with this out: he is not to be held morally accountable for it.

(He is not even to be held accountable for his first non-nonfiction novel: it was written by Somebody Else.)

Were all these non-qualities implicit in that long-ago Somebody Else—that boy whose portrait on the back cover of *Other Voices, Other Rooms* became even more celebrated than the prose inside? Who can forget that boy?—languid but sovereign, lolling in the turn of a curved sofa in bow tie and tattersall vest, with tender mouth and such strange elf-cold eyes. Like everyone else whose youth we have memorized and who has had the bad luck to turn up on television afterward, he was bound to fatten up going toward fifty; and like everyone else who has made some money and gained some ease in the world, he was bound to lose that princely look of the furious dreamer.

On the face of it he was bound to become Somebody Else, in short: not only distant physically from the Dorian Gray of the memorable photograph, and not simply psychologically distant according to the chasm between twenty-three and forty-eight, and not merely (though this chiefly) distant from the sort of redolent prose craft that carried *Other Voices, Other Rooms* to its swift reputation. An even more radical distancing appears to intervene.

It's not only ourselves growing old that makes us into Somebody Else: it's the smell of the times too, the invisible but palpable force called *Zeitgeist,* which is something different from growth, and more capricious. Books change because we change, but no internal rea-

sons, however inexorable, are enough to account for a book's turning
to dust twenty-four years afterward. *Other Voices, Other Rooms* is
now only dust—glass dust, a heap of glitter, but dust all the same.

Robert Gottlieb, editor-in-chief of Knopf, some time ago in *Publishers Weekly* took shrewd notice of how the life expectancy of
books is affected: Solzhenitsyn, he said, can write as he does, and
succeed at it, because in Russia they do not yet know that the
nineteenth century is dead.

A century, even a quarter of a century, dies around a book; and
then the book lies there, a shaming thing because it shows us how
much worse we once were to have liked it; and something else too:
it demonstrates exactly how the world seems to shake off what it does
not need, old books, old notions of aesthetics, old mind-forms, our
own included. The world to the eager eye is a tree constantly prun-
ing itself, and writers are the first to be lopped off. All this means
something different from saying merely that a book has dated. All
sorts of masterpieces are dated, in every imaginable detail, and yet
survive with all their powers. *Other Voices, Other Rooms* is of course
dated, and in crucial ways: it would be enough to mention that its
Southern family has two black retainers, an old man and his granddaughter, and that when he dies the old man is buried under a tree
on the family property, the way one would bury a well-loved dog,
and that the granddaughter, having gone north for a new life, is
gang-raped on the way, and comes back to the white family's kitchen
for love and safety. . . . In Harlem now, and in Washington, Watts,
Detroit, Newark, and New Rochelle, they are dancing on the grave
of this poetry. It was intolerable poetry then too, poetry of the
proud, noble, but defective primitive, but went not so much unnoticed as disbelieved; and disbelief is no failing in an aesthetic confec-
tion. Even then no one thought Jesus Fever, the old man, and Zoo,
the kitchen servant, any more real than the figures on a wedding
cake; such figures are, however vulgar, useful to signify outright the
fundamental nature of the enterprise. Dated matter in a novel (these
signals of locale and wont) disposes of itself—gets eaten up, like the
little sugar pair, who are not meant to outlive the afternoon. Dated
matter in a novel is not meant to outlive the *Zeitgeist*, which can last

a long time, often much longer than its actual components, digesting everything at hand.

But *Other Voices, Other Rooms* is not a dead and empty book because Zoo is, in today's understanding, the progenitrix of black militancy, or because the times that appeared to welcome its particular sensibility are now lost. Indeed, the reason "dated matter" has so little effect on *Other Voices, Other Rooms* is that it is a timeless book, as every autonomous act of craft is intended to be. A jug, after all, is a jug, whether bought last week at the five-and-dime or unearthed at Knossos: its meaning is self-contained—it has a shape, handles, a lip to pour. And *Other Voices, Other Rooms* has a meaning that is similarly self-contained: Subjectivity, images aflash on a single mind, a moment fashioned with no reference to society, a thing aside from judgment. One can judge it as well made or not well made; but one cannot judge it as one judges a deed.

And this is why it is not really possible to turn to the *Zeitgeist* to account for *Other Voices, Other Rooms'* present emptiness. In fiction in the last several years there have been two clearly recognizable drives: to shake off the final vestiges of narration as a mechanism to be viewed seriatim, and to achieve an autonomous art—"where characters," William Gass explains in a remark derived from Gnosticism in general and from MacLeish in particular, "unlike ourselves, freed from existence, can shine like essence, and purely Be." The atmosphere of our most recent moments—Gass's sentence is their credo —ought both to repulse and retrieve *Other Voices, Other Rooms:* it begins deep in narrative like Dickens (a boy setting out on his own to find the father he has never seen), but ends in Being, and shines like "essence," which I take to be, like Tao or satori, recognizable when you have it but otherwise undefinable—and not, surely, accessible, like a deed, to judgment.

The literary *Zeitgeist* is, to use the famous phrase, Against Interpretation; and it is into such a philosophy, freed from existence, and above all freed from the notion of the morally accountable Deed, that *Other Voices, Other Rooms* ought almost flawlessly to glide. For just as its outmoded Negroes do not matter—essence transcends history —so also does the impediment of its rusty narrative works vanish in the dazzle of its prose-poem Being. *Other Voices, Other Rooms* is, as we always boringly say, a vision: a vision apart from its components, which include a paralyzed father who signals by dropping red tennis balls, a Panlike twin, a midget, a transvestite cousin, the aforementioned sad-happy darkies, not one but two decaying manses (one of which is called the Cloud Hotel), and the whole apparatus of a boy's *rite de passage* into probable homosexuality. But the vision is not the sum of any combination of its parts, no more than some or all of the churches of the world add up to the idea of a planet redeemed. Joel Knox, the boy who comes to Skully's Landing in search of his father, is nevertheless after a redemption that has nothing to do with the stuff of the story he passes through; and at the close of the novel he *is* redeemed, because the novel itself is his redemption, the novel is a sacrament for both protagonist and novelist.

A less fancy way of saying all this is that *Other Voices, Other Rooms* is the novel of someone who wanted, with a fixed and single-minded and burning will, to write a novel. The vision of *Other Voices, Other Rooms* is the vision of capital-A Art—essence freed from existence. And what is meant by the cant phrase "the novel ought to be about itself" is this: the will to write a novel expresses the novel itself; the will to make art expresses art itself—"expresses" not in the sense that one is equivalent to the other, but that the fulfillment of desire is itself a thing of value, or enough for literature. This is so much taking the imagining to signify the thing itself (which is, after all, *literature*) that quotidian life—acts followed by their consequences—is left behind at the Cloud Hotel. To quote the theoretician Gass again: "Life is not the subject of fiction."* One would be willing to broaden this comment to strike a more percipient grain: life is not the subject of the sort of fiction that is at home in the American *Zeitgeist* at this moment—despite some beginning strands of dissent. The novel that is said to be "about itself," or "about its own language," belongs not to the hard thing we mean when we say "life," but rather to tran-

---

*It ought to be noted, though, that much of Gass's fiction brilliantly contradicts his theory of fiction. Yet as the prevailing embodiment of this type of aesthetic formulation, Gass's credo is significant currency, representative enough to warrant its appearance elsewhere in this volume. See "Toward a New Yiddish," p. 151.

scendence, incantation, beatification, grotesquerie, epiphany, rhap-
sody and rapture—all those tongues that lick the self: a self conceived
of as sanctified (whether by muses or devils or gods) and superhu-
man. When life—the furious web of society, manners, institutions,
ideas, tribal histories, and the thicket of history-of-ideas itself—when
life is not the subject of fiction, then magic is. Not fable, invention,
metaphor, the varied stuff of literature—but *magic.* And magic is a
narcissistic exercise, whether the magic is deemed to be contained
within language or within psychology: in either case the nub is
autonomous inwardness.

The *Zeitgeist* is just now open to all this. Yet *Other Voices, Other
Rooms*—a slim, easy, lyrical book—can no longer be read. Dead and
empty. And what of 1948, the year of its publication? What was that
time like, the time that sped Capote and his novel to a nearly legendary celebrity that has not since diminished?

In 1948, cruising the lunchbag-odorous Commons of Washington
Square College, I used to keep an eye out for *Other Voices, Other
Rooms.* That place and that time were turbulent with mainly dumb,
mainly truculent veterans in their thirties arrived under the open
enrollment of the GI Bill, and the handful of young aesthetes, still
dewy with high-school Virgil *(O infelix Dido!),* whose doom it was
to wander through that poverty-muttering postwar mob in hapless
search of Beauty, found one another through Truman Capote. Other
voices, other rooms—ah, how we felt it, the tug of somewhere else,
inchoate, luminous, the enameled radiance of our eternal and gifted
youth. Instead, here were these veterans, responsible clods, jerks, and
dopes, with their preposterous eye-wrinkles, their snapshots of preposterous wives and preposterous little children, the idiotic places
they lived in, dopey Quonset huts on some dopey North Brother
Island, slow-witted all, unable to conjugate, full of angry pragmatic
questions, classroom slumberers grinding their joyless days through
English and history and language, coming alive only for Marketing
and Accounting, sniggering at Sheats and Kelley, hating Thomas
Wolfe, with every mean money-grubbing diaper-stinking aging
bone hating Poetry and Beauty and Transfiguration. . . .

Capote was the banner against this blight. To walk with Capote in your grasp was as distinctive, and as dissenting from the world's values, as a monk's habit. Capote: that is what the pseudonym signified: a concealing cloak, to be worn by enraptured adepts.

If *Other Voices, Other Rooms* was written by Somebody Else, it was, even more so, read by Somebody Else. Who made Capote famous? I, said the fly, with my covetous eye—I and all those others who clung to him and made him our cult, I and my fellow cabalists for whom he embodied Art Incarnate (among them the late Alfred Chester, who, priestlike, claimed to have Capote's unlisted telephone number). He was not much older than we were, and had already attained what we longed for: the eucharist of the jacket biography. So we seized the book, the incongruous moment, the resplendent and ecstasy-stung words:

> . . . the run of reindeer hooves came crisply tinkling down the street, and Mr. Mystery, elegantly villainous in his black cape, appeared in their wake riding a most beautiful boatlike sleigh: it was made of scented wood, a carved red swan graced its front, and silver bells were strung like beads to make a sail: swinging, billowing-out, what shivering melodies it sang as the sleigh, with Joel aboard and warm in the folds of Mr. Mystery's cape, cut over snowdeep fields and down unlikely hills.
>
> . . .
>
> Whereupon the room commenced to vibrate slightly, then more so, chairs overturned, the curio cabinet spilled its contents, a mirror cracked, the pianola, composing its own doomed jazz, held a haywire jamboree: down went the house, down into the earth, down, down, past Indian tombs, past the deepest root, the coldest stream, down, down, into the furry arms of horned children whose bumblebee eyes withstand forests of flame.

Who could withstand these forests of flaming prose? In the generation of his own youth Capote was the shining maggot in the fiction of the young.

The *Zeitgeist* then had nothing to do with it. The *Zeitgeist* now ought to have everything to do with it, but masses of the young do not now read the early Capote; the new cults form around antistylists like Vonnegut and Brautigan.

Something needs to be explained. It is not that the novel was written, and read, by Somebody Else; after twenty years all novels are. It is not that the mood of the era is now against Poetry and Transfiguration; the opposite is true. Above all, it is not that *Other Voices, Other Rooms* is dead and empty only now; it always was.

What needs to be explained is the whole notion of the relation of *Zeitgeist* to fiction. In fact there is none, yet there is no fallacy more universally swallowed. For what must be understood about an era's moods is this: often they are sham or nostalgia or mimicry, and they do not always tell the truth about the human condition; more often than not the *Zeitgeist* is a lie, even about its own data. If, as Gottlieb persuades us, Solzhenitsyn comes to us with all the mechanism of the Tolstoyan novel intact, and yet comes to us as a living literary force, it is not because the nineteenth century is not yet dead in the Russian mind, although that may be perfectly true. It is because, whatever its mechanics, the idea of the novel is attached to life, to the life of deeds, which are susceptible of both judgment and interpretation; and the novel of Deed is itself a deed to be judged and interpreted. But the novel that is fragrant with narcissism, that claims essence sans existence, that either will not get its shoes drekky or else elevates drek to cultishness—the novel, in short, of the aesthetic will—*that* novel cannot survive its cult.

Further: one would dare to say that the survival of the novel as a form depends on this distinction between the narcissistic novel and the novel of Deed.

On the surface it would seem that Capote's progress, over a distance of seventeen years, from *Other Voices, Other Rooms* to *In Cold Blood*—from the prose-poetry of transfiguration to the more direct and plain, though still extremely artful, prose of his narrative journalism—is a movement from the narcissistic novel to the novel of Deed; Capote himself never once appears in the pages of his crime story. But there is no forward movement, it is all only a seeming; both the novel and the "nonfiction novel" are purely aesthetic shapes. In *Other Voices, Other Rooms* it is the ecstasy of language that drives the book; in *In Cold Blood* it is something journalists call "objectivity," but it is more immaculate than that. "My files would almost fill a whole small room up to the ceiling," Capote told an interviewer; for years he had intertwined his mind and his days with

a pair of murderers—to get, he said, their point of view. He had
intertwined his life; he was himself a character who impinged, in
visit after visit, on the criminals; and yet, with aesthetic immaculate-
ness, he left himself out. Essence without existence; to achieve the
alp of truth without the risk of the footing. But finally and at bottom
he must be taken at his word that *In Cold Blood* has the blood of a
novel. He cannot have that *and* the journalist's excuse for leaving
himself out of it—in the end the "nonfiction novel" must be called
to account like any novel. And no novel has ever appeared, on its
face, to be more the novel of Deed than this narrative of two killers
—despite which it remains judgment-free, because it exempts itself
from its own terms. Chekhov in "Ward No. 6," one of the most
intelligent short novels ever written, understood how the man who
deals with the fate of the imprisoned begins to partake of the nature
of the imprisoned; this is the great moral hint, the profound unholy
question, that lurks in *In Cold Blood.* But it is evaded, in the name
of objectivity, of journalistic distance, all those things that the novel
has no use for. In the end *In Cold Blood* is, like *Other Voices, Other
Rooms,* only another design, the pattern of a hot desire to make a
form; one more aesthetic manipulation. It cannot go out of itself—
one part of it leads only to another part. Like *Other Voices, Other
Rooms,* it is well made, but it has excised its chief predicament, the
relation of the mind of the observer to the mind of the observed, and
therefore it cannot be judged, it escapes interpretation because it flees
its own essential deed. Such "objectivity" is as narcissistic as the
grossest "subjectivity": it will not expose itself to an accounting.

Despite every appearance, every modification of style, Capote is
at the root *not* Somebody Else. The beautiful reclining boy on the
jacket of *Other Voices, Other Rooms* and the middle-aged television
celebrity who tells dog stories are one, more so than either would
imagine; nothing in Capote as writer has changed. If the world has
changed, it has not touched Capote's single and persistent tone.
Joel Knox in the last sentence of *Other Voices, Other Rooms* looks
back "at the boy he had left behind." False prophecy. Nothing has
been left behind—only, perhaps, the younger writer's habit of the
decorated phrase. What continues in Capote, and continues in

force, is the idea that life is style, and that shape and mood are what matter in and out of fiction. That is the famous lie on which aesthetics feeds the centuries. Life is not style, but what we do: Deed. And so is literature. Otherwise Attic jugs would be our only mentors.

Literary Blacks and Jews

In 1958, in his celebrated collection *The Magic Barrel*, Malamud published a short story about a Negro and a Jew. It was called "Angel Levine," and it contrived for Manischevitz, a Joblike figure who has "suffered many reverses and indignities," the promise of redemption through a magical black man. Manischevitz has already lost his cleaning establishment through fire, his only son through war, his only daughter through a runaway marriage with a "lout." "Thereafter Manischevitz was victimized by excruciating backaches and found himself unable to work. . . . His Fanny, a good wife and mother, who had taken in washing and sewing, began before his eyes to waste away . . . there was little hope."

A black man appears. His idiom is elaborate in Father Divine style: "If I may, insofar as one is able to, identify myself, I bear the name of Alexander Levine." Manischevitz at first doubts that this derby-hatted figure is a Jew, but the Negro says the blessing for bread in "sonorous Hebrew" and declares himself to be a "bona fide angel of God," on probation. Of this Manischevitz is not persuaded. "So if God sends to me an angel, why a black?"

Essay published in *Midstream*, June/July 1972.

The angel departs, rebuffed by Manischevitz's distrust. Then "Fanny lay at death's door," and Manischevitz, desperate, goes "without belief" in search of the black angel. In a Harlem synagogue he witnesses a small knot of Negro worshipers in skullcaps bending over the Scroll of the Law, conducting something very like a Baptist theology session: "On de face of de water moved de speerit. . . . From de speerit ariz de man." Passing through a lowlife cabaret, Manischevitz is jeered at: "Exit, Yankel, Semitic trash." When at last he finds the black Levine, he is broken enough to burst out with belief: "I think you are an angel from God." Instantly Fanny recovers, and as a reward Levine is admitted to heaven. "In the flat Fanny wielded a dust mop under the bed. . . . 'A wonderful thing, Fanny,' Manischevitz said. 'Believe me, there are Jews everywhere.' "

A distinction must be made. Is it the arrival of a divine messenger we are to marvel at, or is it the notion of a black Jew? If this is a story with a miracle in it, then the only miracle it proposes is that a Jew can be found among the redemptive angels. And if we are meant to be "morally" surprised, it is that—for once—belief in the supernatural is rewarded by a supernatural act of mercy. But the narrative is altogether offhand about the question of the angel's identity: Levine is perfectly matter-of-fact about it, there is nothing at all miraculous in the idea that a black man can also be a Jew. In a tale about the supernatural, this is what emerges as the "natural" element—as natural-feeling as Manischevitz's misfortunes and his poverty. Black misfortune and poverty have a different resonance—Manischevitz's wanderings through Harlem explain the differences—but, like the Jews' lot, the blacks' has an everyday closeness, for Manischevitz the smell of a familiar fate. To him—and to Malamud at the end of the fifties—that black and Jew are one is no miracle.

A little more than a decade later, with the publication of *The Tenants,** the proposition seems hollow. Again Malamud offers a parable of black and Jew culminating in fantasy, but now the fantasy has Jew slashing with ax, black with saber, destroying each other in a passionate bloodletting. The novel's last paragraph is eerily liturgi-

*Farrar, Straus and Giroux, 1971.

cal—the word "mercy" repeated one hundred and fifteen times, and once in Hebrew. Nevertheless *The Tenants* is a merciless book. Here are the two lines which are its last spoken exchange:

"Bloodsuckin Jew Niggerhater."
"Anti-Semitic Ape."

It took the narrowest blink of time for Malamud, who more than any other American writer seeks to make a noble literature founded on personal compassion, to come from "Believe me, there are Jews everywhere" to this. How was the transmutation from magical brotherhood to ax-murder wrought? Is it merely that society has changed so much since the late 1950s, or is it that the author of "Angel Levine" was, even then, obtuse? If the difference in Malamud's imaginative perception lies only in our own commonplace perception that the social atmosphere has since altered in the extreme —from Selma to Forest Hills—then "Angel Levine," far from being a mythically representative tale about suffering brothers, is now no more than a dated magazine story. One test of the durability of fiction is whether it still tells even a partial truth ten years after publication. The conclusion of *The Tenants* seems "true" now—i.e., it fits the current moment outside fiction. But a change in social atmosphere is not enough to account for the evanescence or lastingness of a piece of fiction. There are other kinds of truth than sociological truth. There is the truth that matches real events in the world —in *The Tenants*, it is the black man and the Jew turning on each other—and there is the truth that accurately describes what can only be called aspiration. Even in the world of aspiration, it is a question whether "Angel Levine" remains true. And on the last page of *The Tenants*, when Jew and black cut sex and brains from each other, Malamud writes: "Each, thought the writer, feels the anguish of the other." This is the truth of invisible faith, and it is a question whether this too can survive.

"The anguish of the other" is a Malamudic assumption, endemic in his fiction. The interior of many of Malamud's fables resounds with the injunction that for the sake of moral aspiration one must *undergo*. Yakov Blok of *The Fixer* is an ordinary man with ordinary failings, born a Jew but not yet an accountable Jew until he has undergone, in his own flesh, the terror of Jewish fate. In *The Assistant* Morris Bober's helper, the Italian Frank Alpine, formerly a hold-up man, becomes a Jew through gradually taking on the obligations of a Jew, ultimately even undergoing painful but "inspiring" circumcision. The idea of the *usefulness* of submitting to a destiny of anguish is not a particularly Jewish notion; suffering as purification is far closer to the Christian ethos. Jewish martyrs are seen to be only martyrs, not messiahs or even saints. Malamud's world often proposes a kind of hard-won, eked-out saintliness: suffering and spiritual goodness are somehow linked. The real world of humanity —which means also the real world of the Jews—is not like this. "Bad" Jews went up in smoke at Auschwitz too—surely embezzlers as well as babies, not only *tsadikim* but misers too, poets as well as kleptomaniacs. Not one single Jew ever deserved his martyrdom, but not every martyr is a holy man. For Malamud all good men are Job.

Nevertheless there remains a thin strand of connection between Malamud's visionary "Angel Levine" and a commonplace of Jewish temperament, between the messianic insistence on the anguish of the other and the common sense of ordinary, "bad," Jews. The sociological—the "real"—counterpart of Malamud's holy fables is almost always taken for granted by Jews: it is, simply put, that Jews have always known hard times, and are therefore naturally sympathetic to others who are having, or once had, hard times. The "naturally" is what is important. It is a feeling so normal as to be unrelated to spiritual striving, self-purification, moral accountability, prophecy, anything at all theoretical or lofty. This plain observation about particularized suffering requires no special sensitiveness; *naturally* there are Jews everywhere, and some of them are black.

But what has surprised some Jews, perhaps many, is that this Jewish assumption—this quiet tenet, to use a firmer word, that wounds recognize wounds—is not only *not* taken for granted by everyone else, especially by blacks, but is given no credibility whatever. Worse, to articulate the assumption is to earn the accusation of impudence. Nowadays the accusers would include numbers of Jews who point out how thoroughly racism has infiltrated the life of Jewish neighborhoods and institutions; Jews, they say, are as racist as anyone—maybe more so, in view of (the litany begins) those

Jewish shopkeepers who have traditionally been the face-to-face exploiters of the black ghetto. For all these accusers, "Angel Levine" must seem not just dated, obsolete, a sentimental excrescence of that remote era when Jews were as concerned with CORE as they were with UJA—but *wrong*. And many young blacks writing today would regard its premise not only as not a moral hope, but as a hurtful lie. Or else would see Manischevitz's salvation as simply another instance of Jewish exploitation, this time of black benevolence.

Black distrust of this heritage of Jewish sympathy is obviously a social predicament, but it is, curiously, a literary one as well. If the distrust has caused a blight on the sympathy, it turns out also that the distrust antedates the withering of that sympathy. The historical weight of "Angel Levine" was this: Negroes are not *goyim*, not in the full oppressive meaning of that word. How could they be? Anti-Semitism is not properly a Negro appurtenance—it is not histori-cally black, any more than plantation-slave guilt is properly a Jewish burden. Thirteen years later *The Tenants* appears to reply: but no, the black man is a *goy* after all; and perhaps always was. Between these contradictory and irreducible formulations, Jewish astonish-ment came to fruition. It was as improbable for the Jew to imagine himself in the role of persecutor—or even indifferent bystander—as it was for him to imagine the black man in that same role. Yet by the late sixties Jews and blacks were recognizable, for and by one another, in no other guise. In a 1966 symposium in *Midstream* on the relations between blacks and Jews, the sociologist C. Eric Lincoln wrote: "One could argue the expectation that if the Jews are not especially moved by faith, then they ought to be moved by experi-ence. Perhaps so. But the best way to forget an unpleasant experience is not by becoming implicated in someone else's troubles." If this sounded like a sensible generality, it was nevertheless shocking to Jews because it was so thoroughly contrary to the way Jews had been experiencing their own reality, their own normality.

But 1966 counts as almost recent; it is, anyway, midway in time between the redemptiveness of "Angel Levine" and the murderous conclusion of *The Tenants*—the corrosion of relations had already begun. It began perhaps not so much because of the emergence of black political violence and Jewish fear of that violence, and not even because anti-Semitism had again become the socialism of the militant masses, but more fundamentally out of the responsiveness of America itself: the Jews have been lucky in America, the blacks not. Manischevitz's daughter—we can imagine it—moves out of the foul old neighborhood to Long Island; the black Levine, according to Malamud, has no place green to go but heaven.

Jews are nowadays reminded that this difference—America felt simultaneously as Jewish Eden and black inferno—has always been exactly the thing that called into question the authenticity of Jewish sympathy; that this disparity from the beginning made the Jews suspect to resentful blacks, that Jewish commitment to black advancement, much less black assertion, *had* to be undermined by the Jews' pleasure in an America open and sweet to them. The statement "The blacks have not been lucky in America" is used now as a reproof to these luckier Jews for the impudence of their empathy, and to show it up as a lie—an ineluctable time-bomb sort of lie: if Jewish identification with black causes was after all not intended to be traitorous, then it was destined by Jewish success to become so. That most American Jews are themselves less than eighty years distant from their own miseries in the Russian Pale is said to be wiped out by their American good luck, and all at once; Jews who lay claim to historical memory are ridiculed as pretentious or bullying—present security is taken for a mandatory form of amnesia.

But this very formulation—the hell of being black in America—that is today raised against Jews to chide them for the vanity and presumptuousness of assuming historical parallels, is nevertheless not tolerated when Jews themselves proffer it. Either it is taken as still another meaningless white *mea culpa,* or else as a sign of greenhorn uppityness: the Jew putting on airs in the pretense of a *mea culpa* he hasn't been around long enough to earn. Lack of sympathy is an obvious offense; sympathy turns out to be more offensive yet. The point is surprising but unsubtle. If the current wound-licking withdrawal of Jews is now seen as an outrage or an expected betrayal, what of that earlier, poignantly spontaneous Jewish concern? In the very hour of its freest, most impassioned expression, it was judged as a means to take the Negro's humanity away from him—

even then. To illustrate this astounding statement one must turn from the social side to the literary.

Sociologists—I hope I am permitted this fractionally unfair jibe—arrive at their preconceptions cautiously and soberly, but it is the smoothness of their preconceptions they are all the while aiming for. Literary minds work rawly and unashamedly through their beliefs, and have the skeptical grace to arrive at no man's land. Both Jew and black in *The Tenants* are literary men. Their war is a war of manhood and of art. The book has no conclusion and stops in the middle of an incoherency. Eight years before the publication of *The Tenants*, five years after the appearance of "Angel Levine," at the absolute height of "Jewish concern" for the condition of being black in America, a Jew and a black, both literary men, acted out an adumbration of the tragic discord (this phrase is not too grandiose) of *The Tenants*. Their war was a war of manhood (what does it mean to be human) and of art (what are a writer's most urgent sources). Their clash led to no tangible conclusion and stopped in the middle of a double questioning: "how it seems to Ellison I cannot really say," Irving Howe wrote at the last, "though I should like very much to know." "You should not feel unhappy about this or think that I regard you either as dishonorable or an enemy. I hope," Ralph Ellison had already written, "you will come to view this exchange as an act of, shall we say, 'antagonistic cooperation'?"

("Each, thought the writer, feels the anguish of the other.")

The exchange is seminal and ought to be republished all in one place for its superb documentary value—a collision rich in felt honesty and therefore somehow strange, hurtful and agonizing, eluding decent summarization. Ellison's side in particular is a remarkably useful notation in the history not so much of black as of Jewish self-understanding. That there is space here only to give the argument with the sort of crude speed one would ordinarily eschew is probably, for purposes of illuminating a single point, all to the good—that single point being the response of one profoundly gifted black writer to "Jewish concern."

It ought to be made instantly clear that nothing in Howe's "Black Boys and Native Sons"—the essay that triggered the debate with

Ellison, first published in *Dissent* (Autumn 1963)—was overtly written from the viewpoint of a Jew. The essay was, first of all, a consideration of Baldwin and Wright, and finally of Ellison himself. Baldwin, Howe observed, had at the start of his career backed off from Wright's "nightmare of remembrance," hoping to " 'prevent myself from becoming *merely* a Negro; or even, merely a Negro writer.' " And Ellison, Howe noted, was the "Negro writer who has come closest to satisfying Baldwin's program." Appraising Ellison's novel *Invisible Man,* Howe marveled at "the apparent freedom it displays from the ideological and emotional penalties suffered by Negroes in this country," but at the same time admitted he was troubled by "the sudden, unprepared, and implausible assertion of unconditioned freedom with which the novel ends." "To write simply about 'Negro experience' with the esthetic distance urged by the critics of the fifties, is a moral and psychological impossibility," Howe charged, "for plight and protest are inseparable from that experience." And while acknowledging that "the posture of militancy, no matter how great the need for it, exacts a heavy price from the writer," Howe set his final sympathies down on the side of Wright's "clenched militancy" and Baldwin's ultimately developed "rage."

As against Ellison's affirmation of America as a place of "rich diversity and . . . almost magical fluidity and freedom," Howe wrote:

> What, then, was the experience of a man with a black skin, what *could* it be in this country? How could a Negro put pen to paper, how could he so much as think or breathe, without some impulsion to protest, be it harsh or mild, political or private, released or buried? The "sociology" of his existence formed a constant pressure on his literary work, and not merely in the way this might be true for any writer, but with a pain and a ferocity that nothing could remove.

Afterward Ellison was to characterize these phrases as "Howe, appearing suddenly in blackface." The reply to Howe, an essay of great flexibility and authority, came in the pages of *The New Leader* the following winter, and what Ellison made plain was that he was first of all a writer and a man, and took his emotional priorities from that: "Evidently Howe feels that unrelieved suffering is the only 'real' Negro experience, and that the true Negro writer must be ferocious. . . . One unfamiliar with what Howe stands for would get the impression that when he looks at a Negro he sees not a human being but an abstract embodiment of living hell."

In coming out for the autonomy of art, Ellison seemed to leave Howe stuck with all the disabilities, crudenesses, and ingenuousness of the militant Protest Novel. Yet in almost the next breath here is Ellison defending his own militancy as unassailable: "I assure you that no Negroes are beating down my door, putting pressure on me to join the Negro Freedom Movement, for the simple reason that they realize that I am enlisted for the duration. . . . Their demands, like that of many whites, are that I publish more novels. . . . But then, Irving, they recognize what you have not allowed yourself to see: namely that my reply to your essay is itself a small though necessary action in the Negro struggle for freedom." Here Ellison suddenly seems to be giving Howe a victory. Even in *not* writing the Protest Novel he is protesting; *by virtue of being black* his heart is instantly recognizable—by fellow blacks—as being in the right place, "enlisted." —And had not Howe argued, "But even Ellison cannot help being caught up with the *idea* of the Negro"?

This part of the argument—complex and blazing, essentially the classic quarrel between critic and imaginative artist, and between the artist's own two selves, the "esthetic" and the "engaged"—is also an uncanny fore-echo of one of Malamud's preoccupations in *The Tenants*. There, however, it is the Jew who assumes Ellison's overall position of the free artist committed first of all to the clean fall of his language, and the black man who expresses Howe's implacability. What this reversal portends we shall see in a moment, but first it is necessary to look at Ellison's consideration of Howe as Jew. It comes very suddenly—and I think justly—in his reply, and points to the absence anywhere in Howe's remarks of the admission that he is a Jew. Whether or not Howe himself thought this relevant is not the issue; what is important is that Ellison thought it relevant, and scornfully rounded on Howe for having called himself a "white intellectual."

. . . in situations such as this [Ellison wrote] many Negroes, like myself, make a positive distinction between "whites" and "Jews." Not to do so could be either offensive, embarrassing, unjust or even dangerous. If I would know who I am and preserve who I am, then I must see others distinctly whether they see me so or no. Thus I feel uncomfortable whenever I discover Jewish intellectuals writing as though *they* were guilty of enslaving my grandparents, or as though the *Jews* were responsible for the system of segregation. Not only do they have enough troubles of their own, as the saying goes, but Negroes know this only too well.

The real guilt of such Jewish intellectuals lies in their facile, per- haps unconscious, but certainly unrealistic, identification with what is called the "power structure." Negroes call that "passing for white." . . . I consider the United States freer politically and richer culturally because there are Jewish Americans to bring it the benefit of their special forms of dissent, their humor and their gift for ideas which are based upon the uniqueness of their experience.

The statement reads admirably. But if Ellison wants to "see others distinctly," including Howe's distinctiveness as a Jewish rather than a "white" intellectual, he must not object to Howe's seeing *him* distinctly, as a man participating in a certain social predicament— i.e., getting born black in America. Defining an individual's social predicament does not automatically lead to stripping him of his personal tastes and talents, as Ellison assumes earlier in his essay, when he speaks of "prefabricated Negroes . . . sketched on sheets of paper and superimposed upon the Negro community." Jews also have their predicament, or call it their destiny, as Jews; but destiny is something profoundly different from a stereotype.

The second part of Ellison's remarks, ringing though they are, is where the real difficulty lies. If Ellison thought Howe obtuse because he visualized the black as a man in perpetual pain, if Ellison thought Howe was distorting his own more open perception of the effect on blacks of their civil inequities ("matters," Ellison wrote, "about which I could do nothing except walk, read, hunt, dance, sculpt, cultivate ideas")—what could a Jew think of Ellison's Jewish projec- tions? What could be "special" about forms of Jewish dissent that do

not include dissent on behalf of others?* What else, in the eye of
history, could "special forms of dissent" *mean* if not the propensity
to be enlisted in social causes not intimately one's own? What could
be the purpose of ideas based upon the uniqueness of Jewish experience if that uniqueness did not signify at least in part a perennial
victimization, and if that experience did not expend itself beyond
compassion into identification? How then does it happen that Ellison, in attributing so many useful and distinctive things to Jews, has
it all add up to nothing less ugly than "passing for white"?

The trouble, I think, is a simple one. At bottom it is Ellison, not
Howe, who fails to nail down the drift of distinctive experience, who
imagines the Jew as naturally identifying with the white "power
structure." Ellison has some of the psychology right, to be sure—it
was a case of "perhaps unconscious" identification, but in a way
Ellison was curiously unable to conceive of, except for the instant
it took for him to ridicule the idea: "Howe, appearing suddenly in
blackface." But Howe's call for the "impulsion to protest" was not
a matter of burnt cork—he was not coming on as a make-believe
Negro (and certainly not as a make-believe member of the "power
structure"), but rather as a Jew responding implicitly and naturally
—i.e., vicariously—to an urgent moment in history, applying to that
moment the "benefit of [his] special form of dissent." That the
"identification" was authentic, the vicariousness pragmatic, the dissent genuinely felt, untouched by manipulativeness or cynicism, the
next several years in America rapidly made clear, the proof being the
rise of black programs of "ferocity," both political and literary—
which, interestingly enough, a Jewish critic was able to foretell
through the exercise of his own familial sensibility.

In this interpretive retelling, I have perhaps made Howe out to be
too much the prototypical Jew. This may be unfair to him. I do not
know his personal views or whether he would welcome this characterization. But the exchange with Ellison, at this distance and after

*Howe has written elsewhere that he became a socialist through realization of what
poverty was. And it was the poverty of the rural South that brought it home to him,
though at the very moment he was reading about it he was himself an impoverished youth
living wretchedly in a Bronx tenement in the middle of the Depression. (That the
connection was made through *reading* is perhaps also to the point.)

so many reversals in the putative black-Jewish alliance (how long ago that now seems, how unreal the very phrase), has taken on the power, and some of the dread, of a tragic parable. Ellison's inability to credit the Jew with a plausible commitment was, as it turned out, representative not only of what was to come, but of what had long been. From the Ellisonian point of view, "Angel Levine" never *was* true: impossible for black man and Jew to share the same skin and the same pair of eyes out of which to assess reality. Ellison's side of the argument, it seems to me, utterly undermines the "sociological" premises of "Angel Levine"—black and Jew are not, will never be seen to be, mutually salvational. But it is not only the nonfictive referents of the tale that are undermined. Little by little even the moral truthfulness begins to seep out of the vision itself—what was radiant, if illusioned, hope at the time "Angel Levine" was conceived has disintegrated into a kind of surrealism, an arbitrary act of art, set apart from any sources of life. Literature (even in the form of fantasy) cannot survive on illusion.

This is perhaps why Malamud went forward from the failed dream of "Angel Levine" to the warlike actualities of *The Tenants*. Ellison, meanwhile, is revealed by the passage of time to be not simply representative but prophetic. Society becomes for the black, if not yet magically fluid, then not nearly so much of a shut box as it is for Malamud's Jew in the claustrophobic world of *The Tenants*, or for the Jew in an America now seen to be inhabited by black as well as white *goyim*, with few temperamental allies. Black political fluidity has increased immeasurably since Ellison wrote, expressing itself in a kind of overall ascendancy of purpose, while Jewish political self-consciousness is static, confined to a handful of Congressional constituencies. But even then, while acknowledging the chasm between himself and the power structure, Ellison made it plain that he was at home in America in the most comfortable sense of country-culture. In the very same essay addressed to Howe there is an account of quail hunting in snowy Ohio fields, and a note of gratitude to Hemingway for having written so well on wing shooting "that I could keep myself and my brother alive during the 1937 Recession by following his descriptions." Few Jews, even of the third or fourth generation, will recognize in themselves this sort of at-homeness with the land, whereas even urban Poles and Italians have land-memory to draw upon. What emerges from the encounter with Howe is that Ellison has a Gentile ease in America—an easier scorn, even, for its blemishes—that Howe and Malamud, with their bookish moral passion, have not. "I could do nothing except walk, read, hunt, dance, sculpt, cultivate ideas." It is almost as if the Jew can do nothing but cultivate ideas.

What happened between Ellison and Howe (behind the back, as it were, of literature) was bound to be seized on by the larger metaphor of the novel. In my own case I have not found it possible to think about *The Tenants* without first turning Howe-Ellison round and round; together they make a bemusing artifact in a reverse archaeology. Dig them up and discover, in genteel form, the savage future.

I came to rehearse their exchange because, in my first reading of *The Tenants,* I was, like many readers, rabidly discontent with Malamud's conception of his black character, Willie Spearmint, later called Spear. Willie Spear is a black writer who has the flavor of an Eldridge Cleaver rather than an Ellison; and this seemed to matter. Malamud, it appeared, had deliberately chosen—for novelistic bite and drama—an unruly spear-carrier, when he might have chosen a poised aristocrat of prose. And up against Spear he set the Jewish writer Harry Lesser, a man almost too fastidious in his craft. The balance was unequal, the antagonists unfairly matched, the Jew too hesitant and disciplined, the black too spontaneous and unschooled.

That the antagonists *have* to be a match for each other at first strikes one as important, because *The Tenants* is partly, despite its directness of language and gesture, a theater piece designed as stately discourse. Though I admit the comparison is inflated, nevertheless one is put in mind of the eye-to-eye feud of Elizabeth and Mary, Queen of Scots, in Schiller's *Maria Stuart;* or of Shaw's Joan at her trial, another example of an elevated contest of societal interpretation. *The Tenants* is obviously barer and coarser than these—airless and arid, a flat plain pitting philosopher-king against philosopher-king. Except for these two figures—the Jew and the black—the book is, by and large, unpeopled. The two writers meet in an almost empty tenement about to be torn down. Lesser still lives in his old apartment, refusing to move out until his novel is finished. Already ten years of his life have gone into trying to finish it. Willie is a squatter—hauls in a typewriter, rustles up an old table and chair, and begins.

The friendship that springs up between them is not really a writers' friendship. In a literary sense it is the relation of higher and lower. Lesser is always the pro, the polisher, authority, patron of opinion; he has published before, one book is moderately famous. Willie, out of the ghetto, is the rough-hewn disciple. Lesser is the cultivated representative of Society-at-Large, and when he speaks as writer he speaks not as a Jew but as a clear-cut descendant of the American literary tradition from Hawthorne to James—that very James, in fact, who, visiting the Lower East Side in 1904, worried about the effect of Yiddish-influenced impurities on his clean ancestral English. Lesser too feels himself superior: a natural inheritor, like James, of the language, while Willie is only a crude aspirant, likely to damage his material by clumsiness. Lesser observes:

> He has not yet mastered his craft. . . . What can I say to a man who's suffered so much personal pain, so much injustice, who clearly finds in his writing his hope and salvation, who defines himself through it? He comes in the end, as in the old slave narratives, to freedom, through his sense of writing as power—it flies up and carries him with it—but mainly in his belief that he can, in writing, help his people overthrow racism and economic inequality. That his freedom will help earn theirs. The Life he writes, whatever he calls it, moves, pains, inspires, even though it's been written before, and better, by Richard Wright, Claude Brown, Malcolm X, and in his way, Eldridge Cleaver. Their self discoveries have helped Willie's. Many black men live the same appalling American adventure, but it takes a unique writer to tell it uniquely, as literature. To make black more than color or culture, and outrage larger than protest or ideology. . . . Lesser sees irrelevancy, repetition, underdeveloped material; there are mistakes of arrangement and proportion, ultimately of focus.

Reading this, it is easy to think: Ah, but this is unjustly conceived. Willie is a straw man. Why not a black writer who is not only fully literate, but *accomplished?* Suppose Malamud had given us Ellison instead of Willie—then what? Lesser, like Ellison, believes first of all in the primacy, the loveliness, of the sentence; for him literature is the personal courage by which the language is seized. Beyond that lies propaganda. Granted that two-literary-intellectuals-talking-to-each-other does not make a novel (Mann and the Russians excepted), or, at least, would not make *this* novel, Malamud seems to be asking for the sort of resentment that would soon come to surround his formulation: Jewish Intellectual versus Tough Black Militant. Unequal warfare in the Republic of Letters. Could it not—for fairness —somehow have been contrived as Jewish Intellectual versus Black Intellectual?

There were, of course, good novelistic reasons why it could not. For instance, the conflict that eventually interposes itself between Lesser and Willie is not intellectual but rawly sexual. Willie has a Jewish girl friend, Irene, whom Lesser covets and ultimately wins. Irene is unfortunately a fiction-device and lives only intermittently. Her narrative task is to convert the two writers into enemies through sexual jealousy. Lesser's importuning landlord, Levenspiel, is also a fiction-device—he is there to give us the novel's pivotal "problem," to put time pressure on a stubborn Lesser—but Levenspiel, by contrast, manages to live vividly: "Have a little mercy, Lesser, move out so I can break up this rotten house that weighs like a hunch on my back. . . . Hab rachmones, Lesser, I have my own ambition to realize." All this is beside the point. Levenspiel and Irene and Willie's black friends who slide in and out from the wings are all interruptions in the dialogue between Lesser and Willie; they are pretexts for necessary "action," for novelistic progress. They are not what the book fundamentally intends.

If *The Tenants* progresses, it is not through plot but through revelation. The revelation is one-sided: it happens inside Lesser. We do not really know what happens inside Willie. And what happens inside Lesser is this: the clear realization that the black writer who shares his quarters and also his literary hopes is, more than he is writer, more than he is lover, more even than he is fleshly human being, a ferocious, a mythic, anti-Semite.

It is a revelation to Lesser because, at the start of their closeness, it did not "show." When Willie is angry at Lesser he says "white," he says "ofay," he does not yet see distinctly into his rage at the Jew.

Lesser, himself a failing writer, views Willie as a possibly ascending one. All that is in Willie's way is technique. He tells Willie, "Not that you don't work hard but there has to be more emphasis on technique, form. . . ." They discuss form:

> Lesser asks Willie to grant him good will. "I know how you feel, I put myself in your place."
>
> In cold and haughty anger the black replies. "No ofay mother-fucker can put himself in *my* place. This is a *black* book we talkin about that you don't understand at all. White fiction ain't the same as *black*. It *can't* be."
>
> "You can't turn black experience into literature just by writing it down."
>
> "Black ain't white and never can be. It is once and for only black. It ain't universal if that's what you are hintin up to. What I feel you feel different. You can't write about black because you don't have the least idea what we are or how we feel. Our feelin chemistry is different than yours. Dig that? It *has* to be so. I'm writin the soul writin of black people cryin out we are still slaves in this fuckn country and we ain't gonna stay slaves any longer. How can you understand it, Lesser, if your brain is white?"
>
> "So is your brain white. But if the experience is about being human and moves me then you've made it my experience. You created it for me. You can deny universality, Willie, but you can't abolish it."
>
> "Bein human is shit. It don't give you any privileges, it never gave us any."
>
> "If we're talking about art, form demands its rights, or there's no order and maybe no meaning. What else there isn't I think you know."
>
> "Art can kiss my juicy ass. You want to know what's really art? *I* am art. Willie Spearmint, *black man*. My form is *myself*."

Up to the moment of Willie's conclusion—"*I* am art"—this exchange is only another chapter of Howe-Ellison, with Willie as Howe, speaking in behalf of "being caught up with the *idea* of the Negro," and Lesser as Ellison, speaking in behalf of the universal values of art and humanity. But the two positions, Ellison's and Willie's, intermingle somewhat. Willie, like Ellison, does not trust his antagonist to "know how you feel, . . . [to] put myself in your place." Addressing Howe, Ellison simultaneously denies and affirms universality: as a black man he considers himself first of all a man, one who despite external disabilities is pleased to walk, read, hunt, etc., like all men; but again as a black he denies that anyone not black can creditably take into himself the day-to-dayness of the black predicament. Willie accepts only the denial: only a black can know what it is to be black, no one else. As for "being human," not only does Willie reject the term "universal," but he sees himself as almost physiologically different ("Our feelin chemistry is different than yours"), and he goes further yet—he freezes himself into the image of a totem, a *"black man."* The statement "My form is *myself"* is beyond humanity, beyond even art. It stands for something more abstract than either: a political position taken at its most absolute. For a totem *is* an absolute politics: an object, an artifact, a *form* representing an entire people, together with its interests, its cult, its power, its history and fate. The totem has no fluidity, its being is its meaning. Willie has turned the politics of a group into an object—himself, *black man.* In Willie Art is Politics, Politics is Art.

This is why it would not have served Malamud's deepest intention if he had chosen not Willie, but a more "realistic," pragmatic, literate, humane, relatively apolitical, less symbolic black for the novel. In *not* choosing an Ellison, of course, Malamud took on himself both a risk and a certainty. The certainty was the charge of "stereotype" and "blacklash," to which *The Tenants* has already been preëminently subject. The risk—a "stereotype" having indeed been chosen —was the failure of the novel as art. To a degree this *has* happened —to the very degree that Willie's stereotyped expectations lead to banalities masking as passions. Something was necessary to stimulate Willie's active vengeance, so we are given a plot-fulcrum, Willie's girl Irene. In return for Lesser's stealing his girl, Willie destroys Lesser's work of ten years; the war is on. Irene exists to accommodate neither Willie nor Lesser, but the exigencies of a made fiction. All this is too obviously and distractingly schematic—even the lineaments of "parable" cannot contain it—and if I seem to be bringing it up again now, it is only to contrast it with the novel's authentic passions. These are in the mimicry of Willie's writing. I will come to them in a moment.

Suppose, though, Malamud *had* chosen an Ellisonlike character to confront his Lesser. The first advantage would have been safety in the world external to the novel: with equal contenders, fewer readers might have cried bigot. And internally, also, there would have been an advantage: the contenders might have met and if necessary separated on the *cultural* issues, as Howe and Ellison did, not on the extraneous ones of purloined women and violated manuscripts. ("But," Malamud might counter, "purloined women and violated literature are the stuff of Willie's culture.") It might even be argued that, if novelistic conflict was what was wanted, if dramatic misunderstanding and distrust were what was wanted, a fictionalized Howe-Ellison clash could have provided them as surely as Lesser-Willie, and with the black man's "humanity" intact, all stereotypes avoided and averted. Inside the air of Malamud's novel, Ellison—or, rather, "Ellison"—would still have found Jewish literary empathy suspect, as the actual Ellison did in the more open world of nonfictional debate; and there would not have occurred, between two civilized beings, the perilous contrast between the "civilized" Jew Lesser and the "savage" Willie. (As the book now stands, though, there is nothing to choose at the end between Willie's and Lesser's savagery.) And not only this: with "Ellison" instead of Willie to do battle with Lesser, the novel would have been intellectually richer, thicker, clearer, the parable more perfect, the fright more frightening because in seemingly safer hands.

With so much to lose from Willie, with so much to gain from "Ellison," why did Malamud opt for what is so plainly a grossness, a caricature, above all a stereotype?

Here is Willie at his grossest:

". . . You tryin to kill off my natural writin by pretendin you are interested in the fuckn form of it though the truth of it is you afraid of what I am goin to write in my book, which is that the blacks have to murder you white MF's for cripplin our lives." He then cried out, "Oh, what a hypocrite shitass I am to ask a Jew ofay for advice how to express *my* soul work. Just in readin it you spoil what it says. I ought to be hung on a hook till some kind brother cuts off my white balls."

Ellison had complained to Howe (implying Howe was guilty of it too) that nonblack writers tend to create "prefabricated Negroes . . . sketched on sheets of paper and superimposed upon the Negro community." Surely this quotation from Willie fits Ellison's imputations; Willie is unabashedly "prefabricated."

But the real question is: who cast this die, who prefabricated Willie? Not Malamud. The source of a stereotype is everything. When, in the late 1890s, William Dean Howells praised the black poet Paul Dunbar's dialect verse for having "the charming accents of the Negro's own version of our [*sic*] English," chiefly because it exploited "the limited range of the race," which was "the range between appetite and emotion," the stereotype imposed on Dunbar by a white critic killed the poet and the man; he died in bitterness at thirty-four, wretched over the neglect of what he regarded as his real work—"But ah, the world, it turned to praise / A jingle in a broken tongue." In the sixty or so years since Dunbar's death, the "jingle in a broken tongue" has entered the precincts of "soul," and the notion of "our English," when espoused by blacks, receives serious pedagogical and linguistic consideration as a legitimate alternative, a separate language with a distinctive grammar. The stereotype, emerging from Howells, was an insult and a misappropriation; emerging from black pride, it begins to gather the honors of honest coinage.

Malamud did not make Willie. He borrowed him—he mimicked him—from the literature and the politics of the black movement. Willie is the black dream that is current in our world. Blacks made him. Few blacks disavow him. The black middle class, which is ambivalent about Willie, nevertheless does not disavow him—not simply out of loyalty to the underclass (the loyalty is what is in doubt), but out of covert gratitude.* Almost no black writer has

---

*Orde Coombs wrote some years back in *Harper's* (January 1972), "The thirty-to-forty-year-old black who holds down a good job in the North must know that his present success is a direct result of past tumult. All his talent, all his effort would not have otherwise given him a toehold in television, in consulting firms, in brokerage firms, in advertising, and in publishing. . . . Many of these black men know they owe their livelihoods to their poorer, more militant brethren. . . . *In fact, only one group has really benefited from the turbulence; and that is the middle class.*" (Coombs's emphasis.)

disavowed Willie. Ellison is the exception: ". . . what an easy con-game for ambitious, publicity-hungry Negroes this stance of 'mili-tancy' has become!" he exclaimed to Howe, but that was eight years ago, and since then, though Willie has grown louder and published amply (he is famous as LeRoi Jones, for instance), Ellison has had nothing to say about him. Surely Baldwin does not disavow Willie; he has become him.

In short, Willie is what he intends himself to be (which is also what he is intended to be by those blacks who do not deny him): a totem, emblem of a community unified in and through Willie's spirit, what he calls his "form"—not man, as Ellison would have it, but *black man*.

What is the meaning of Willie in his self-declared "form"? Willie's form takes up not freedom and fluidity, but unmovable hatred and slavish vengeance. His vengeance is "literary" in two ways: the burning of Lesser's book, and the creation of his own—but "his own" ends as a travesty and spoliation of all humane literary values. Only through the destruction of Jewish culture, says Willie's form, can black culture arise. Lesser finds Willie's notes: "I have got to write better. Better and better. Black but better. Nothing but black. Now or never." And whereas earlier—before the pivotal jealousy episode—writing "black" for Willie had for the most part meant telling the poignant and honest story of his ruined, scarred, and panicked childhood in the ghetto,* now, writing black for ven-geance, Willie dreams pogroms. For him literature serves politics—not as propaganda consciously does, as an "arm" or partner or exten-sion or tool of politics—but intrinsically, below the level of rational motivation. Willie's only politics is coextensive with nearly the whole of his literary imagination; it is the politics and the imagina-tion of anti-Semitism.

Lesser finds another of Willie's notes:

> It isn't that I hate the Jews. But if I do any, it's not because I invented it myself but I was born in the good old U. S. of A. and there's a lot

---

*Malamud has mastered the idiom typical of this fiction. For anyone doubtful about Malamud's ear—or, rather, literary eye—an anthology called *What We Must Be: Young Black Storytellers* (Dodd, Mead, 1971) is instructive.

of that going on that gets under your skin. And it's also from knowing the Jews, which I do. The way to black freedom is against them.

Now that Willie has stopped seeing Lesser as a more experienced writer and can think of him only as a Jew, Lesser too alters. He is rewriting his lost manuscript in fear and anguish, but the vision slips from him, he is in terror of Willie. "I treated you like any other man," he tells Willie. Willie replies, "No Jew can treat me like a man," and Lesser, afraid for his life, turns as savage as Willie, with this difference: ". . . it sickened him deeply"; he remains self-conscious. Nevertheless he gets an ax and chops up Willie's typewriter. On that typewriter Willie had written pages of anti-Semitic (some of it "anti-Zionist") poetry and prose, fantasying the murder of Jews. The work of the two writers is contrasted. Lesser's destroyed book is about a writer's struggle to love. The writer is named Lazar Cohen; he is much like Malamud's Fidelman, an artist with a Jewish name who conceives of himself only as artist, almost never as Jew. Willie's stories are about blacks torturing Jews. In one of them, "a Jew slumlord in a fur-collar coat, come to collect his blood-money rents," is stabbed and killed by three blacks, who strip his corpse naked and propose to eat it, but change their minds. "He tastes Jewtaste, that don't taste like nothin good." The story, as Lesser finds it in Willie's notes, ends:

> Then they [the murderers] go to a synagogue late at night, put on yarmulkas and make Yid noises, praying.
> In an alternate ending the synagogue is taken over and turned into a mosque. The blacks dance hasidically.

With the apparition once again of a black synagogue, with the word "hasidically," Malamud suddenly and astonishingly blows in a whiff of "Angel Levine"—are his blacks becoming Jews again? Lesser has a fantasy: in a mythical Africa there is a double tribal wedding. A rabbi presides. The chief's son, who turns out to be Willie, is marrying a Jewish girl, who is Irene. Lesser is marrying a black woman. The rabbi exhorts the couples, "Someday God will bring together Ishmael and Israel to live as one people. It won't be the first miracle." Inside his dream Lesser says critically of it, "It's something I imagined, like an act of love, the end of my book, if I dared."

But Malamud himself does not dare. "Angel Levine" is not merely out of date, it is illusion; at the close of *The Tenants* Malamud explicitly acknowledges that it is illusion. Lesser's ax—it is the final vision of the novel—sinks into Willie "as the groaning black's razor-sharp saber, in a single boiling stabbing slash, cut[s] the white's balls from the rest of him." It is curious, horrible, and terrifying to take in what Malamud in *The Tenants* openly posits: that the Jew in America, beginning as Howe did with a cry of identification with black suffering, is self-astonished to find himself responding now in the almost forgotten mood of *zelbshuts*—the *shtetl*'s term for weaponry stored against the fear of pogroms. Lesser, a hesitant intellectual, is driven to hauling an ax. But *The Tenants* insists on more than this. Like much of Malamud's work, and specifically like *The Assistant* and *The Fixer*, it offers the metaphoric incarnation of a Malamudic text: whoever wants to kill the Jew has already killed the human being in himself.

It is not only no failing, it is the best achievement of the novel that Willie, its black militant, is a stereotype devoid of any easy humanity. The clichés appropriate for a political strategy are unsuitable for describing the soul of a living person. Given the extraliterary truth that black militancy, in and out of print, has now come to define itself if not largely then centrally through classical anti-Semitism, to bestow on a fictional Willie a life beyond his bloody fantasies would have been a savagery akin to Willie's own. To put it another way: to have ascribed to Willie the full and continuing aspects of a decent breathing human being *but for his hatred of Jews* would have been to subvert the meaning of human.

The Tenants is a claustrophobic fable: its theme is pogrom. It remarks the minutiae of a single-handed pogrom so closely that the outer world is shut out. There is almost no city beyond Lesser's tenement, and there are no white Gentiles in the novel, no faint indication of that identification with the Gentile power structure Ellison claimed Jewish intellectuals were seeking. In *The Tenants* the Jew has no allies. Jew and black fight alone in an indifferent world.

There is no means, at this juncture, of determining whether its current worldly truths will one day seep out of *The Tenants*, as the moral radiance of "Angel Levine" had ultimately, through subversion by history, to ebb into falsehood. But—for the moment—Malamud has abandoned the hopefulness of "Angel Levine" and drawn a parable of political anxiety. "Each, thought the writer, feels the anguish of the other" is the last flicker of that hopefulness but does not convince. Willie is Lesser's doom—Lesser, dreaming of love, rigorously apolitical, isolated in his aesthetics, becomes the inescapable victim of an artist whose art is inseparable from butchery.

Yevtushenko, declaiming at the Felt Forum that bombs and balalaikas are in essence always separate,* nevertheless speaks not for Lesser but for Willie. Yevtushenko's poem condemning the bombing of Hurok's office, and the death of a secretary there, moved everyone, who could disagree? But the poem is a cheat. To be horrified at the bombing is not automatically to assent to the purity of art. Mozart was played at Auschwitz, and it is a ruse to pretend that any natural "separation" of art keeps it unblemished by political use. Malamud, in plucking Willie out of the black writing that made him, has not invented the politicization of fiction. And in inventing *The Tenants*, Malamud ironically follows Willie—he has written a tragic fiction soaked in the still mainly unshed blood of the urban body politic.

*Yevgeny Yevtushenko, the Soviet poet, gave a reading in New York City the day after a New York group had bombed the offices of Sol Hurok, the agent responsible for booking Soviet cultural events in the United States. A young Jewish woman, a secretary in Hurok's office, was killed. Yevtushenko overnight wrote a poem of commemoration; it compared the girl's death to the gassing of Jews in Auschwitz, and declared that art and politics must be kept separate. The poem noticeably subverted its own thesis.

Cultural Impersonation

NOTE

Mark Harris's *The Goy* and John Updike's *Bech: A Book* appear to arrange themselves under a common yoke: each touches on cultural impersonation, on "ethnicity," while neglecting, in a setting where it would surely be pertinent, the sacral imagination.

In *The Goy*, Harris invents a secretly brutal and oppressive midwestern American anti-Semite who impersonates a liberal philo-Semitic intellectual. In *Bech: A Book*, Updike's hero emerges as the type of fully secularized Jewish writer who is himself an impersonator of a fully secularized (if one could credit this) John Updike. Just below the skin of the best Gentiles, Harris's narrative implies, lies a heart cold to Jews. And Updike, next to Frederick Buechner our most theological writer, portrays Bech, his Jew, as theologically hollow.

Both novels rest on sociology as raw source. In spite of which, both, it seems to me, make their curious contribution (if only through the provocation of contradiction) to the liturgical language I have described elsewhere in this volume: New Yiddish.

1. Bech, Passing

I love John Updike.* When some time ago in *Commentary* Alfred Chester (my old classmate, who vanished into Algiers and then died in Jerusalem) flicked Updike off as a magician of surfaces, I wrote in my head the imaginary counter-review: Updike as Late Church Father. For years I sniffed after an opportunity to think in print about the sacral Updike, and now that the chance is palpably here, it turns out to be not *Pigeon Feathers,* or *Rabbit, Run,* or *The Centaur,* or *Of the Farm,* not even *Couples:* those fictions of salvationism and eucharistic radiance. Instead, *oif tsulokhes* (the phrase of regret Bech's Williamsburg uncles would use and toward which Bech is amnesiac), here is Henry Bech, Jew, rising, like Shylock and Bloom, out of a Christian brain.

Updike, whose small-town stories in particular have suggested him as our most "American" writer, is considerably less American, it seems to me, than, say, George P. Elliott or R. V. Cassill, secularists in a post-Christian neuterland. It is not especially American to be possessed by theology, and Updike is above all the Origen of the novel. The epigraph for *The Poorhouse Fair* is from Luke, *Couples* is

agape, not *eros.

Essay published in *Commentary,* November 1970.

emblazoned with Tillich, *Rabbit, Run* quotes Pascal concerning "the motions of Grace." In *Couples,* as in Saint Theresa, love's arrows and Christ's thorns fuse: "He thinks we've made a church of each other," someone says of one of the couples at the start, and in the last chapter fellatio becomes the Sacrament of the Eucharist: ". . . when the mouth condescends, mind and body marry. To eat another is sacred." Further rich proofs and allusions will contribute nothing: it is already well-known that John Updike is a crypto-Christian, a reverse Marrano celebrating the Body of Jesus while hidden inside a bathing suit. (Vide "Lifeguard," *Pigeon Feathers.*) Even Bech, a character, as they say, "pre-processed"—even Bech, who doesn't know much, knows *that.* In a letter that constitutes the Foreword to *Bech: A Book* (this letter, by the way, wants me to call it "sly," but I am too sly for that), Bech tells Updike: "Withal, something Waspish, theological, scared, and insulatingly ironical . . . derives, my wild surmise is, from you." The original Marranos, in Spain, were probably the first group in history to attempt large-scale passing. As everyone knows (except possibly Bech), they ended at the stake. So much for Jews posing. What, then, of Christian posing as Jew? What would he have to take on, much less shuck off?

In the case of Updike's habitation of Bech, nothing. Bech-as-Jew has no existence, is not *there,* because he has not been imagined. Bech-as-Jew is a switch on a library computer. What passes for Bech-as-Jew is an Appropriate Reference Machine, cranked on whenever Updike reminds himself that he is obligated to produce a sociological symptom: *crank, gnash,* and out flies an inverted sentence. Not from Bech's impeccably acculturated lips, of course, but out of the vulgar mouth ("Mother, don't be vulgar," Bech says in boyhood) of a tough Jewish mother lifted, still in her original wrap, straight out of *A Mother's Kisses.* The Foreword—which, like all Forewords, is afterthought and alibi—tries to account for this failure of invention by a theory of the Comic: it is, you see, all a parody: ironically humorous novelist Bech addresses ironically humorous novelist Updike and coolly kids him about putting Bech together out of Mailer, Bellow, Singer, Malamud, Fuchs, Salinger, the two Roths. The Appropriate Reference Machine is thereby acknowledged as the very center of the joke; the laugh is at the expense of the citation.

In search of a Jewish sociology, Updike has very properly gone to
the, as Bech would say, soi-distant Jewish novel. And found:

Category: *Vocabulary*
   1. Adjective: *zoftig*
   2. Nouns
      a. *shikse*
      b. *putz*
   3. Ejaculation: *ai*

Category: *Family*
   1. Beloved uncles in Williamsburg
      a. back rooms
      b. potatoes boiling, "swaddled body heat"
   2. Father (mentioned twice in passing)
      a. uxorious, a laugher
      b. no occupation given
   3. Mother
      a. buys Bech English children's books at Fifth Avenue Scribner's
      b. takes young Bech to awards meeting of facsimile of Academy
         of Arts and Letters

Category: *Historical References*
   1. "the peasant Jews of stagnant Slavic Europe"
   2. Russian "quality of life" "reminiscent of his neglected Jewish
      past"
   3. "Hanukkah"

Category: *Nose*
   Bech's: Jewish big
   (Forgive this. An in-joke. Updike's, *goyish* big, earns him the right.)

Category: *Hair*
   Bech's: Jewish dark curly

Category: *Sex*
   1. Sleeps willingly with Gentile women; like Mailer (though a
      bachelor) tries out whole spectrum of possible *shikse* types
   2. But invited to sleep with *zoftig* Ruth Eisenbraun, is less willing;
      unclear if he does or doesn't

All right. No quarrel with most of these attributes. If the only
Yiddish Bech knows is *shikse, putz,* and *zoftig,* he is about even with

most indifferent disaffected de-Judaized Jewish novelists of his generation. And I suppose there are Jewish novelists who, despite the variety in the gene pool, have *both* big noses *and* kinky hair: one (affectionate) stereotype doesn't make an anti-Dreyfusard. And if, on a State Department–sponsored visit, Bech associates the more comfortable tones of Russia—"impoverished yet ceremonial, shabby yet ornate, sentimental, embattled, and avuncular"—with his "neglected Jewish past," his is, like that of other indifferent disaffected de-Judaized Jewish novelists, a case not so much of neglect as of autolobotomy. Emancipated Jewish writers like Bech (I know one myself) *have* gone through Russia without once suspecting the landscape of old pogroms, without once smoking out another Jew. But because Bech has no Jewish memory, he emerges with less than a fourth-grade grasp of where he is. His phrase "peasant Jews" among the Slavs is an imbecilic contradiction—peasants work the land, Jews were kept from working it; but again Bech, a man who is witty in French, who in youth gave himself over to Eliot, Valéry, Joyce, who has invented a comic theory of the intelligence of groups, who thinks of himself as an Aristotelian rather than a Platonist—this same Bech is a historical cretin. If there had been "peasant Jews" there might have been no Zionism, no State of Israel, no worrisome Russians in the Middle East . . . ah Bech! In your uncles' back rooms in Williamsburg you learned zero: despite your Jewish nose and hair, you are —as Jew—an imbecile to the core. Pardon: I see, thanks to the power of Yuletide, you've heard of Hanukkah.

So much for the American Jewish novelist as sociological source. As a subject for social parody, it is fairly on a par with a comic novel about how slavery cretinized the black man. All those illiterate darkies! Bech as cretin is even funnier: they didn't bring him in chains, he did it to himself under the illusion of getting civilized.

Nevertheless a few strokes seem not to be derivative and may be Updike's alone: one, the whimsical notion that a woman who speaks sentences like "Mister Touch-Me-Not, so ashamed of his mother he wants all his blue-eyed *shikses* to think he came out from under a rock" would venture past Gimbels to any Fifth Avenue store, much less to Scribner's for English (*English!*) children's books. Having adequately researched P.S. 87, Updike might have inquired at the neighborhood branch library for Bech's sweaty-fingered, much-stamped ancient card ("Do Not Turn Down the Leaves"). Updike's second wholly original misapprehension is a descent into inane imagination. Comedy springs from the ludicrous; but the ludicrous is stuck in the muck of reality, resolutely hostile to what is impossible. That this same woman would by some means, some "pull," gain entry to a ceremony in a hall of WASP Depression *Hochkultur* is less mad than the supposition that she would ever have gotten wind of such doings. What rotogravure section carried them? Bech's mother's culture drive stops at the public-library door; Bech goes in without her, and if he ends up reading Hawthorne in Bulgaria, the credit belongs to P.S. 87. Bech's grandfather's mind came equally unfurnished: what produces a Bech is a grandfather just like him, with no conscious freight of history, no scholarliness, and the sort of ignorant piety of rote that just sustains against poverty. Remove the poverty, slip in P.S. 87, and you have Bech.

What Updike leaves out (and what Roth puts in) is the contempt of the new Bech for the old Bechs: the contempt of just appreciation. Updike writes, ". . . all the furniture they had brought with them from Europe, the footstools and phylacteries, the copies of Tolstoy and Heine, the ambitiousness and defensiveness and love, belonged to this stuffy back room." (For love's duration in close family quarters, see Roth, supra.) Footstools in steerage? From out of the cemeteries on Staten Island, ten thousand guffaws fly up. The beds left in Minsk still harbored the next wave to come. The phylacteries they threw away at the first sight of a paycheck for pants-pressing. And those who read Tolstoy or Heine alighted not in New York but in Berlin. Or stayed behind to make the Revolution. A Jew who came to New York with some Gemara in his brain was absolved from spawning Bech. Bech is a stupid Jewish intellectual. I know him well.

I am not asking Updike to be critical of Bech—it is not his responsibility: it is mine and Bech's. Besides, Updike loves Bech too much, especially where (and this is the greater part of the book) he is thoroughly de-Beched. Updike can be as funny as Dickens and as celestial as bits of *Anna Karenina*, and in *Bech: A Book* he is, now and then, in glimpses, both. This happens when he is forgetting to re-member about Bech-as-Jew; luckily, the crunch of the Appropriate Reference Machine is sometimes silenced. Updike loves Bech best when Bech is most openly, most shrewdly, most strategically, most lyrically Updike. Bech's failure—he is a celebrated writer suffering from Block—is rumor and theory, but the exact flavor of Bech's success is the stuff of Updike's virtu. Who else but Updike could take fame so for granted as to endow it with exhaustion? The exhaustion is examined with Updike's accustomed theological finesse: Bech's Block is to be taken somewhat like the modern definition of the Christian hell—no fire and brimstone in a fixed nether location; instead a sense of irreparable loss, a feeling of eternal separation from God, a stony absence of Grace. In the presence of his Block, Bech becomes christologized. In the wilderness of his London hotel lobby he is even subjected to satanic wiles: the devil is a young journalist named Tuttle into whose notebook Bech spills his spiritual seed:

> . . . Bech talked of fiction as an equivalent of reality, and described how the point of it, the justification, seemed to lie in those moments when a set of successive images locked and then one more image arrived and, as it were, superlocked, creating a tightness perhaps equivalent to the terribly tight knit of reality, e.g., the lightning ladder of chemical changes in the body cell that translates fear into action or, say, the implosion of mathematics consuming the heart of a star.

Imagine the Body of Christ describing its transubstantiation from bread. What could the devil do but flee that holiness? But then, coming ever closer, there approaches the ghostly clank of the A. R. Machine, and the eucharistic Bech folds flat and begins to flap like the leaf of an ethnic survey-analysis study:

> He said, then, that he was sustained, insofar as he was sustained, by the memory of laughter, the specifically Jewish, embattled, religious, sufficiently desperate, not quite belly laughter of his father and his father's brothers, his beloved Brooklyn uncles; that the American Jews had kept the secret of this laughter a generation longer than the Gentiles, hence their present domination of the literary world; that unless the Negroes learned to write there was nowhere else it could

come from; and that in the world today only the Russians still had it, the Peruvians possibly, and Mao Tse-tung but not any of the rest of the Chinese. In his, Bech's, considered judgment.

Here Updike, annoyed at the Machine's perpetual intrusions, allows it to grind itself into giggling berserkdom. The Machine is amusing itself; it is providing its own ethnic jokes. (The inopportune demands of Bech's Jewishness on his author should serve as sufficient warning to other novelists begging to be absorbed uninterruptedly by epiphanies: beware of any character requiring more sociology than imagination.) Bech, confronted at last by the journalist's printed report of their encounter, guesses the devil's spiritual triumph over matter: "He [Bech] had become a character by Henry Bech." Which is to say, a folk character out of Jewish vaudeville, not quite Groucho Marx, not yet Gimpel the Fool. Nevertheless unsaved. But while none of Updike's people has ever attained salvation, salvation is the grail they moon over. Bech's grail is cut in half, like his name, which is half a kiddush cup: *becher*. Over the broken brim the Jew in Bech spills out: Updike, an uncircumcised Bashevis Singer (as Mark Twain was the Gentile Sholem Aleichem), is heard in the wings, laughing imp-laughter.

The center of *Bech: A Book* is a sustained sniff of this Christian hell: it is so to speak an inverted epiphany, a negative ecstasy. Bech lectures at a Southern girls' college and experiences a Panic: "He felt dizzy, stunned. The essence of matter, he saw, is dread. Death hung behind everything. . . ." He sees "the shifting sands of absurdity, nullity, death. His death gnawed inside him like a foul parasite. . . ." "All things have the same existence, share the same atoms, reshuffled: grass into manure, flesh into worms." ". . . the grandeur of the theatre in which Nature stages its imbecile cycle struck him afresh and enlarged the sore accretion of fear he carried inside him as unlodgeably as an elastic young wife carries within her womb her first fruit." The abyss swells and contracts, until finally it shrinks from Immense Void to empty *becher* and again becomes recognizable merely as Bech's Block: "He tried to analyze himself. He reasoned that since the id cannot entertain the concept of death, which by being not-being is nothing to be afraid of, his fear must be of something narrower, more pointed and printed. He was afraid that his critics were right. That his works were indeed flimsy, unfelt, flashy, and centrifugal. That the proper penance for his artistic sins was silence and reduction . . ." It is typical of Updike that he even theologizes writing problems, though here he parodies his standard eschatology with an overlay of Freudian theodicy. The fact is Updike theologizes everything (in *Rabbit, Run* he theologized an ex-high-school basketball player); this is his saving power, this is precisely what saves him from being flashy and centrifugal. The stunning choice Updike has made—to be not simply an American but a Christian writer—distinguishes him: in this he is like a Jew (though not like Bech): America as neuter is not enough.

But he does not theologize the Jew in Bech. In seven chapters (really separate stories) he takes the mostly de-Beched Bech everywhere: from Russia to Rumania and Bulgaria, through scenes sweated with wistful wit and ironic love; from a worshipful pot-smoking ex-student through a shift of mistresses; from Virginia to stinging London to a sophomoric "Heaven" where the "Medal for Modern Fiction was being awarded to Kingsgrant Forbes" while the "sardonic hubbub waxed louder." (This last section, by the way, need not be compared for satiric force with Jonathan Swift: I suspect because both the Jewish Appropriate Reference Machine *and* the Literary Politics A. R. Machine, in tandem, were working away like *Mad.*) Wherever Updike is at home in his own mind, the book runs true, with lyric ease: the jokes work, small calculations pay off, anticlimaxes are shot through with a kind of brainy radiance. Without Bech, *Bech* might have been small but sharp, a picaresque travel-diary wryly inventing its own compunctions. But wherever the Jew obtrudes, there is clatter, clutter, a silliness sans comedy. Bech makes empty data. It is not that Updike has fallen into any large-scale gaucherie or perilous failures-of-tone. It is not that Updike's American Jew is false. It is that he is not false enough.

By which I mean made up, imagined, mythically brought up into truthfulness.

In the case of Bech—and *only* in the case of Bech—Updike does not find it worthwhile to be theological. In no other novel does he resist the itch of theology; everywhere he invests ordinary Gentile characters with mythic Christian or proto-Christian roles, adding to local American anthropology a kind of sacral sense. And when the sacral is missing, sulphur drifts up from the Void. Updike is our chief Dante: America is his heaven and hell. He has no such sense of Bech. It is as if he cannot *imagine* what a sacral Jew might be.* You might want to say he is not altogether to blame, after all: what would any accurate sociological eye see on the American landscape but Bech? Nevertheless Bech is deviation, perhaps transient deviation, from the historical Jew. Being historical cretin, Bech does not know this about himself: unable to inherit his past, he has no future to confer. He is very plausibly without progeny: though his writing Block is an Updikean Christian salvational crisis, his Jewish Block consists in being no longer able to make history. As Jew he is all sociology, which is to say all manners (acquired exilic manners); as Jew he is pathetically truncated, like his name. So Updike finds Bech and so he leaves him. Updike comes and goes as anthropologist, transmuting nothing.

It is very queer—it is something to wonder at—that Updike, who is always so inquisitive about how divinity works through Gentiles, has no curiosity at all about how it might express itself, whether vestigially or even by its absence or even through its negation, in a Jew. Being a Jew (like being a Christian) is something more than

---

*Twelve years after *Bech: A Book,* he is beginning to try. In a review of Bernard Malamud's *God's Grace* (*The New Yorker,* November 8, 1982), Updike ponders what "Jewishness" might be. It seems, he reflects, "in part a religious condition but . . . not negated by irreligion, as, say, a disavowal of faith removed a person from the lists of Christianity or Islam. A Jew, like Jehovah, simply is, in some realm beyond argument." Since the entire rabbinic tradition *is* argument (as opposed to credo), and since, consequently, nearly all varieties of Jewish intellectuality, including the Bechian secular-modern, are heirs to a mode of discourse wherein nothing is "beyond argument," it is hard to guess what Updike is imagining here. Having brilliantly assimilated the major texts of contemporary Protestant theology, he strangely does not assume (after millennia of Jewish texts) equal or greater (because more weightily cumulative) nuance and complexity in Jewish self-definition; what emerges for him is the naive, faintly mistrustful, vaguely poetic, puzzlement implicit in the phrase "A Jew, like Jehovah, simply is." This formulation, even if it does just manage to escape meaninglessness, slides nevertheless into the exotically intergalactic. "Jehovah" is a foreign word to the Jewish ear; so is "faith" in its Protestant sense. All the same, on the evidence of these two sentences, Updike appears to be getting interested in, or at least self-conscious about, the notion of the Jewish sacral; he may even be on his way to insight into the historicity of the idea of Jewish Peoplehood.

what is. Being a Jew is something more than being an alienated marginal sensibility with kinky hair. Simply: to be a Jew is to be covenanted; or, if not committed so far, to be at least aware of the possibility of becoming covenanted; or, at the very minimum, to be aware of the Covenant itself. It is no trick, it is nothing at all, to do a genial novel about an uncovenanted barely nostalgic secular/neuter Bech: Bech himself, in all his multiple avatars (shall I give you their names? no), writes novels about Bech every day. It is beside the point for Updike and Bech together to proclaim Bech's sociological there-ness. Of course Bech is, in that sense, there. But what is there is nothing. In a work of imagination Bech-as-he-is is critically unjustifiable. It is not Bech-as-he-is that interests us (if you want only that, look around you), but Bech-as-he-might-become. If to be a Jew is to become covenanted, then to write of Jews without taking this into account is to miss the deepest point of all. Obviously this is not Updike's flaw exclusively; it is, essentially, the flaw of the Jewish writers he is sporting with. It is no use objecting that Updike and others do not *aim* for the deepest point: concerning Jews, the deepest point is always most implicated when it is most omitted.

Descending, for the sake of the Jew alone, from the level of theological mythmaking to the level of social data, is Updike patronizing his Jew? One thinks, by contrast, of a Jew writing about a Gentile: I mean *Henderson the Rain King.* Meditating on the quintessential *goy,* Bellow makes up a holy culture to demonstrate him. The demonstration is not through *what is,* but through opposites: the *goy* is most revealed as not-Jew. It seems to me that a Christian writing of a Jew would profit from a similar route in showing the quintessential Jew as not-Gentile. Whereas Bech has no inner nature of his own, and only passes. Or I think of a short story, not altogether seamless but divinely driven, by George P. Elliott, in his collection *An Hour of Last Things:* a Jewish woman fevered by the beauty of a cathedral is made to waver between revulsion for Christian history and the lustful leap into the idolatry of Art. Here a secularized post-Christian WASP writer explores the most awesome, most dangerous, most metaphorical depths of Commandment.

Two questions, then, remain to puzzle. Why, for Bech, does Updike withhold his imagination from the creation of Bech *as Jew?*

And second: what motive, what need, what organic novelistic gains, emerge from the turn to Bech? As some say Mailer taunted Updike into the sexual adventurism of *Couples,* so now, it is declared, a similar competitiveness with Jewish "domination of the literary world" (Bech's self-sneering Gaullist phrase) compels him to a Jewish character. I reject the competitive motive: it seems plain that Updike experiments for himself, not for other writers, and pits himself against values, not persons. But while *Couples* turned out to be a Christian novel, *Bech* is a neuter. It may be that Updike's experiment this time lies precisely in this: to attempt a novel about no-values, about a neuter man. To find the archetypical neuter man, man separated from culture, Updike as theologian reverts to Origen and Ambrose, to centuries of Christian doctrine, and in such ancient terms defines his Jew. If the only kind of Jew Updike can *see,* among all these cities and hearts, is Bech, that is not solely because Bech is in the majority, or most typical; it is because for him Bech—the Jew as neuter man; the Jew as theological negative and historical cipher—is most real.

But seen from the perspective of the Jewish vision, or call it Jewish immanence (and what other perspective shall we apply to a Jew?), the Jewish Bech has no reality at all, especially not to himself: he is a false Jew, a poured-out *becher,* one who has departed from Jewish presence. For Updike to falsify the false—i.e., to lend the Jew in America the Grace of his imagination—would have been to get beyond data to something like historical presence, and a living Bech. But that, I suppose, would have required him to do what Vatican II fought against doing: forgive the Jew for having been real to himself all those centuries, and even now. And for that he would have had to renounce the darker part of the Christian imagination and confound his own theology.

POSTSCRIPT

Bech: A Book is followed, a dozen years later, by *Bech Is Back.* The tone of the sequel is greatly refined; for one thing, Updike has junked the Appropriate Reference Machine. Bech, left to himself,

ethnic banners banned, sociology damned, vestigial Yiddish reduced to two unspoken grunts (alas, they are the words for
"whore" and "unclean"), elegantly comic mind almost everywhere
beautifully conflated with Updike's own—Bech lives. In *Bech Is
Back*, Bech is, by and large, no more a Jewish character than I am
a WASP. This satisfies him; if his newest success—a bestseller
called *Thinking Big*—allows him the time, I hope he will write
Updike a thank-you letter, especially since, as it turns out, there is
only one bad patch for the ethnic Bech to get through: a visit to
what the chapter-title, in wall-map Sunday-school language, terms
"The Holy Land." This pilgrimage is undertaken in the company
of Bea, Bech's Episcopalian wife, all pure responsive essence,
whose name (even if accidentally) is metaphysically interesting in
context. In Israel, only Bea can rapturously, serenely, supremely,
Be; Bech cannot. He moves in this consecrated landscape as a skep-
tic and an antagonist; and here, to be sure, Updike has precisely
nailed the post-Enlightenment intellectual Jewish scoffer epito-
mized by surly Bech—for whom, after the Nazi depredations, after
the Arab wars, "events in Palestine had passed as one more mop-up
scuffle, though involving a team with whom he identified as effort-
lessly as with the Yankees." Only the last part of this judgment
rings false; Bech is non-, perhaps anti-, Zionist, and always was.

The "Holy Land" section opens in Jerusalem not, as one would
expect, with a trip to the lost Temple's Western Wall, sighed after
for two thousand years of teary Exile, but with a walk, led by a Jesuit
guide, along the Via Dolorosa. Still, Bech must not be credited with
making a beeline for the very spot that stands, in every Passion Play,
and annually at Eastertide, for the historic revilement of "perfidious"
Jews; it is Updike's walking tour he is taking, not his own. The
controversial lands west of the Jordan River are designated, tenden-
tiously, as "occupied territory" (whether in Bech's or Updike's head,
or both, it is difficult to tell), a characterization by no means linguisti-
cally immaculate or politically neutral. (Perhaps Bech, when he gets
back home, will write an attack on the Begin government's settle-
ment policy for *The New York Times Magazine*.) The Western Wall
itself appears as the Wailing Wall, an antiquated christological insult.
Bech and Bea are put up at a lavish government guest house for

distinguished visitors, "echoing," thinks Bech, "like the plaster-board corridors of a Cecil B. DeMille temple," where he is tempted to cavort like Bojangles on the wide stairs. The "tragic, eroded hills of Jerusalem" just beyond those corridors, and the brilliant Valley of Gehenna a breath's space below, do not draw Bech's eyes or his hardened heart. The holiness of the Holy Land leaves Bech cold; only his Gentile wife catches its heat. In deference to Bea's touching ardor—the ardor both of the romantic tourist and of the industrious Christian pilgrim—Bech visits the City of David dig, the two shining mosques atop the Temple Mount, and, among squabbling sectarians, the arena of Bea's generous surrender to spirit, the Church of the Holy Sepulcher. Bech's raised anti-Israel consciousness is not disappointed at a dinner with Israeli writers "in a restaurant staffed by Arabs. Arabs, Bech perceived, are the blacks of Israel." Finally, when Bea, honoring Bech's Jewishness, proposes moving to Israel to live, Bech retorts: "Jesus, no. It's depressing. To me, it's just a ghetto with farms. I *know* these people. I've spent my whole life trying to get away from them, trying to think bigger." Later he will visit the land of Bea's forebears, and find "happiness in Scotland." He will defend the Highlanders against their historic oppressors. He will be amazed and amused, edified and electrified, in Ghana, Korea, Venezuela, Kenya, Canada, Australia. Only in Israel is he depressed.

Thus, slippery, satirized, satirical Bech. Does Updike mean Bech to mean what Bech says? Does Bech say what Updike means? In his second coming, returned briefly to Jewish scenes, Bech is, as Jew, not really Redux. As Jew he merely momentarily recurs, as reduced —as reductive—as before. Nothing can transform him; he will not be elevated, even by the holy heights of Jerusalem. His secular skepticism will not be contradicted by any whiff of the transcendental; he is the only major character in Updike's fiction wholly untouched by the transcendental. He remains man sans spirit, no different from that medieval Jew whom Christendom deemed hollow, unable to be hallowed: theological negative in Jerusalem, historic cipher in Zion, carper in the precincts of Ariel. As scoffer and Jewish neuter, Bech is, yes, "real," "actual," "lifelike," abundantly "there." Updike's curled irony has not ironed him out; I recognize him. "I *know* these people," as Bech would say. As a symptom of a segment of Jewish reality, Bech is well and truly made.

Charles Dickens sold his house—it was called Tavistock House, and you will see how I am not changing the subject—to a certain Mr. J. P. Davis, a Jew. According to Edgar Johnson, Dickens's biographer, Davis's wife Eliza

> wrote Dickens a letter telling him that Jews regarded his portrayal of Fagin in *Oliver Twist* as "a great wrong" to their people. If Jews thought him unjust to them, he replied, they were "a far less sensible, a far less just, and a far less good-tempered people than I have always thought them to be." Fagin, he pointed out, was the only Jew in the story (he had forgotten the insignificant figure of Barney) and "all the rest of the wicked *dramatis personae* are Christians." Fagin had been described as a Jew, he explained, "because it unfortunately was true of the time to which that story refers, that that class of criminal almost invariably was a Jew. . . . I have no feeling towards the Jews but a friendly one," Dickens concluded his letter.

I believe Dickens; he is the best and most honorable of geniuses. I certainly believe that he believes he is telling the truth. There *is* a curious point, though, in the choice of Fagin's name. When the boy Dickens lay, so to speak, in the miserable pit of his childhood, crushed and seemingly snuffed forever by his forced employment in a warehouse, beaten up by the other boys for his "airs"—the early signs, no doubt, of the miracle he became—only one fellow-worker took pity on him, cared for him, and was consistently and deliberately tender to him. That boy's name was Bob Fagin. We know with what unkind immortality the warehouse of Dickens's unconscious repaid that first Fagin.

A quarter of a century after the completion of *Oliver Twist*, Dickens obliged Eliza Davis with an act of literary compensation: he invented Mr. Riah of *Our Mutual Friend*. Mrs. Davis wrote to thank him. Some time afterward she presented him with a Hebrew Bible.

Dickens again commented, "I would not wilfully have given an offence or done an injustice for any worldly consideration." He had already let Riah speak for him: "Men say, 'This is a bad Greek, but there are good Greeks. This is a bad Turk, but there are good Turks.' Not so with the Jews. Men find the bad among us easily enough— among what peoples are the bad not easily found?—but they take the worst of us as samples of the best; they take the lowest of us as presentations of the highest; and they say 'All Jews are alike.' "

Bech, it seems to me, is, as Jew, not the best or the highest. Since he is caricature, it will not do to have him best or highest: comedy is ill-served by loftiness. Nor is Bech, funny and fond and woeful and brave, a literary (preposterous thought) Fagin. Still, what if Updike followed Dickens in turning his Jew upside down—or, rather, in allowing him to rise? As Fagin is extravagantly lurid, so is Riah extravagantly gentle. There is a comedy in that, though unwitting: the innocent purposefulness of undoing one caricature in order to make another. Compensation snickers; restitution is risible.

It is ten years from now. The third book in the delightful series (and for the occasion the binding is not "perfect" but sewn) is called *Bech, Bound.* * Whither is Bech bound? What is his destination? And what, above all, is binding Bech? The memory of Moriah, Isaac's binding. The thongs of the phylacteries. The yoke of the Torah. The rapture of Return. The dictionary meaning of "ethnic."† By now Bech has read his Bible. He has been taking Hebrew lessons; he is learning Rashi, the eleventh-century commentator whose pellucid explications even little children can understand. Bech, as Jew, is like a little child, though pushing sixty. Akiva too began to study late. Starting with the six-volume Graetz, bound in Jewish Publication Society (Philadelphia) crimson, Bech has mooned his way in and out of a dozen histories. He is working now on the prayer book, the

*In Hebrew: *Bech, Baal-T'shuvah* (Tel Aviv: Sifriat Hapoalim, 1992).
†In Bech's beat-up old *American College Dictionary*, from college, this surprise: "pertaining to nations not Jewish or Christian; heathen or pagan; as, *ancient ethnic revels.*"

essays of Achad Ha-Am, and the simpler verses of Bialik. He seeks out the Chancellor of the Seminary for long talks. He is reading Gershom Scholem.

Bech stands on a street in Jerusalem. The holy hills encircle him —they are lush with light, they seize his irradiated gaze. He is, for the first time, Thinking Big.

What will Updike, honorable and resplendent mind, do with such a big Bech?

2. Esau as Jacob

When a book by a writer with a large following drops into the void, one wonders why. There may have been one or two other reviews of Mark Harris's *The Goy*—his first novel in ten years—but I recall only that the reviewer for *The New York Times Book Review* called it "gratuitously venomous" and took note of the circumstance that Harris was born Finkelstein. Otherwise the book has been allowed to sink out of sight almost as if it were a first novel. Yet *The Goy* is an enterprise that not only makes large claims for itself, but also, it seems to me, lays large claims on our attention and our inquiries.

One of these inquiries ought to go to the metamorphosis of the novelist himself: how does it come about that the author of baseball novels, a writer whose fiction has up to now engaged in what must be called WASP impersonation, suddenly bursts out with a book about the nature of the Jewish mind? Is it that something has happened inside Mark Harris, or inside America? That a hitherto frolicsome entertainer-novelist of Jewish origins all at once begins to write seriously about being Jewish is not very remarkable in itself—we have seen it once before, in Ludwig Lewisohn, who turned from the

---

Mark Harris, *The Goy* (The Dial Press, 1970).
Book review published in *Commentary*, June 1971.

kind of fiction that made him a popular novelist *(The Case of Mr. Crump)* to the passionate tracts (the novel *The Island Within,* the lyrical prose essay called *Israel*) that returned him to obscurity. But Harris with *The Goy* is not simply abandoning popular subject matter; and besides, in a literary community that celebrates both S. Levin and Mr. Sammler, the problem is not that *The Goy* represents a conversion, so to speak, from baseball back to being Finkelstein. The problem is that *The Goy* is purposefully designed, for whatever curious reason, to be a pariah book: its fate is its theme. It is, especially, designed to poison those abundantly philo-Semitic reviewers who mean to bring good will to the fiction of Jewish marginality.

What makes *The Goy* untouchable, particularly for critics, is that it is an attack on that very Gentile culture—the literature of "humanism"—which produces literary critics. Worse yet, it is an attack on the complex of historical and social attitudes that make up the Gentile mind itself—or call it, more definitively, the Christian mentality. It is this mentality, in its most secularized and liberalized forms, at its apparent pinnacle of clarity and effectiveness, that *The Goy* is out to get. The *Times* reviewer mistakenly called Harris's book "a repudiation of Mr. Agnew's America." In fact it is a repudiation of the America of coexistence, accommodation, moderation—of the America, in short, of most American Jews; of the "Judeo-Christian tradition"; even of the good will of the Gentile reviewer himself. It is as if Mark Harris one day in sunny Indiana had fallen upon a cave laden with all the volumes of Graetz's *History of the Jews,* Malcolm Hay's *The Foot of Pride,* James Parkes's *The Conflict of the Church and the Synagogue*—as if he had suddenly fallen from Saint Augustine and the sublimeness of Chartres into the other side of Christian history, into a vast heap of pre-Holocaust chronicling, and had come up stunned and bloodied. How the author of baseball novels comes to dream the-Jew-of-Europe is itself a dark dream: something has broken, something has imploded at the core, America has turned—for Harris—into the Europe of Graetz.

Harris begins, then, craftily: he posits Westrum. Westrum is a Christian American, a man of the West in the larger sense, of the midwest in the local sense. His father is a ferocious anti-Semite. His mother is a decent Christian woman—what is usually meant by that phrase: namely, an onlooker. Long ago she looked on while his father drove a Jewish family from town. The town itself is a bad and backward place: in it children learn that "the poor we will always have, the Indians were savages, the Jews are greedy, the blacks are lazy, the railroad is here to stay." Out of this backwash of the Reformation Westrum somehow springs fully into otherness; he appears to have grown into the world with the kind of secularized social conscience Jews are notorious for. Harris does not answer the mystery of Westrum's conscience or his otherness; or, rather, he answers it only as to its bits and scraps—Westrum, a bookish boy isolated by his bookishness in childhood, is therefore drawn to the unself-conscious bookishness of Jews. There is in Westrum that which needs Jews. What planted the need? Out of what pressure does it issue? No answer. When Jews want to be like Gentiles, we know why. We do not know why Westrum needs to be like Jews. In a *goy* it is perverse; it is abnormal. Heine's conversion, Disraeli's baptism—these make pragmatic sense. Those Jewish philosophers—Bergson, Simone Weil—who distort Judaism in order to repudiate it, these make even more sense: they help wash away the idiosyncratic configurations of the minority mythos, they clarify and affirm the claims of the West. But Westrum represents a reversal of everything we have ever known: he is a man acculturating to Jews.

The external signs of this reversal are clear enough: he learns to say *shikse;* he marries a Jew. His sons—Westrum has three—are half-Jews. Unlike the Jewish philosophers of Christianity, he can repudiate his inheritance without distortion: seeing it clearly, particularly its historical attitude toward Jews, is the point of the repudiation. But all of this is inadequate. It is not enough to have Jewish friends, a Jewish wife, Jewish children; biology is not Jewish. How then shall Westrum become like a Jew? What is the Jewish "secret"? Westrum hits it precisely: what makes a Jew is the conscious implication in millennia. To be a Jew is to be every moment in history, to keep history for breath and daily bread. How clever of Harris to make Westrum clever enough to clothe himself in history! Thus clothed, Westrum puts on the gabardine. In Philip Roth's "Eli, the Fanatic," there is a similar removal from the center to the edge: a man of the majority puts on the mien of a man of the minority; but

both are Jews. The Jew in the business suit is transformed into the
refugee in gabardine. But Harris is even more innovative. In *The Goy*
it is a *goy* who infiltrates the Jews. Westrum, having perceived the
mainstream to be bestial in its ancestral usages, is attracted to prey;
in theory it is nobler to be prey than beast.

Under the influence of this attraction he writes a vast book: *A
History of the Past World,* and perversely (for why should it?) it
makes him famous, leisured, rich. Through it he learns the quality
of Jewish priorities:

> ... Jews ... had made him think his work made sense. They believed
> in the perilous world and therefore in every effort, whether history
> or introspection, to find it out, explain it, clarify it, and maybe even
> partly solve it. They feared the outside danger. They thought that
> books, art, history, science, inquiry mattered. . . .

After several editions the title is changed to *The History of the Past
World,* and Westrum, in the shift from the generalized *A* to the
particularized *The,* at last becomes situated in the locus of peculiarity:
becomes Judaized. He works on a Presidential committee for social
justice. He is renowned for liberal views. His brother-in-law Tikvah,
having begun a history called *Potentialities for Fascism in America,*
can't finish it. "My coming on the scene," Westrum explains,
"stopped [it] forever. Its thesis is that every goy is a Jew-hater somewhere just below the surface, but as long as I appeared to be the
exception to his theory he couldn't go on, he had no theory, his
theory went bust." Entering Jewish history, Westrum causes it to
halt; when the *goy* ceases to be a *goy,* Jewish history has no subject
matter.

This, then, is Harris's seeming premise: that on occasion history
can reverse itself, that on occasion the majority will be zealous after
the minority, that now and then Esau will wish to live in Jacob's tent.

The usual proposition—Jacob putting on goatskins to imperson-
ate Esau—has often and often flowered in history; frequently
enough in the mask of fiction. Cultural impersonation is an ancient
artistic risk, and remains interesting. Outside of literature, Jews—
a minority treated to resemble the majority—can sometimes be
absorbed into the dominant biology, like those mimetic surgical

stitches which need never be ripped out; the host tissue swallows them without a trace. Acculturation—absorption—of the minority into the majority is, after all, almost a definition of civilization; of a civilization's root energy-source. When Matthew Arnold said that he would not like to have been born a Jew or a Socinian (the Socinians were sixteenth-century Unitarians), he did not mean that he disliked anyone who denied the divinity of Jesus, or even that he disapproved of the denial itself. His objection was pragmatically related to an idea about civilization. He pitied the unassimilable; he thought it "better" to be in the "mainstream"; he wanted to be civilized, by which he meant belonging to the locally prevailing mythos—to the West as Christendom.

In inventing Westrum, Harris postulates the obverse force of Arnold, a darkened counterpart—one implicated, like Arnold, with the drift of his civilization, owned by it and its owner, but with this difference: he chooses against the Arnoldian thesis. Himself the best of the majority in imaginative power and prowess, Westrum chooses to acculturate to the minority; through a voluntary act either of renunciation or taking-on, or both, he chooses to habituate his life to pariah modes. The thesis in reverse—assimilation into marginality*—is a dazzlingly innovative but grotesque meditation: grotesque because it goes against the grain of what really happens, it distorts normal historical expectation. If Harris—or anyone—could have brought this off, he would have written the novel of the century. But no one can bring it off. In literature it is perilous to be too original in one's premise—one ends not with a novel but with a fairy tale. And Harris, eschewing fantasy, does not mean to bring it off. Having startled us with his reverse proposition, Harris gradually leads us to discover that he does not intend to make it work; he accepts Arnold's law of civilization. He is not interested in staging a miracle play.

And so he peels the Judaized clothing off Westrum to reveal the spots beneath:

---

*I know of only two other works of fiction hung on this premise. One is Norma Rosen's *Touching Evil* (1969), wherein a young woman follows the Eichmann trial on television and becomes Judaized. The other is, of course, Malamud's *The Assistant*. Both of these books harbor miracle plays in that the premise is allowed to stand.

Westrum is a good father. But once, in a rage, he broke his young son's back; no one remembers whether, in that rage, he called the boy a Jew. He is a good husband, though not faithful. He is not faithful to his Jewish mistress either, and thinks about taking another, also Jewish. He woos her with a Jewish-sounding slogan: Football is Fascist. Once a football player himself, he is still a fanatic athlete, devoted to the upkeep of his body for its own sake. He clocks his daily run—a life's habit. Invited to join a prestigious think-tank, he broods on Benstock, Weinberg, Silvers, his colleagues: "All Jews here but me"—this silent phrase another life's habit. He says he does not smoke or drink, but he does both, by stealth; he says he sleeps with no one but his wife, whom he deceives by stealth. Though a humanitarian, he concludes that his typist is an unaware automaton —"he had dismissed her uniqueness," but she learns from him to deceive him by stealth.

Now he is writing not a general history, but something private, not social but self-directed, in his own mind grander than history or society: a Journal, the confessions of Westrum's soul; it is Christian to suppose that the individual soul equals the world. He "lives his life twice"—once in the staged happening, once in the shrewd sly malice of writing it truthfully down. It is a work of stealth. Disciplined and introspective as Loyolan exercises, kept up every day for years in an invented secret shorthand, this Journal, already distinguished though undisclosed, has a compulsive criminal honesty. It tells how Westrum lies without point, in small unnecessary things; how Westrum is like his father: he is attracted to prey; how Westrum is not like his father: he hates the Jews by stealth. His son, a half-Jew, Westrum has now made a Jew altogether: with his mended spine the boy can't run, can't play football, just like some bookish urban Jew. But the boy is not bookish; his grammar is bad. He is a skilled filmmaker, though, and photographs his father with a corrective intuition: he longs to mollify and flatter his powerful father, so Westrum in his Jewish son's movie comes out the ideal movie star, a handsome, clean-living, filial, patriotic, churchy, dog-loving, country-humorous WASP. When this son was circumcised Westrum joked about the bill: "Jesus, it costs me money to be a Jew"— his only Jewish joke, because he is serious about prey. He is an infiltrator, an underminer, a corrupter—he has made his wife not like having a Jewish face. He hates the meticulous conscience of her brother Tikvah. All the same, she believes in him and takes him at his (public) word—thereby changing from his wife into his public, and betrayed both ways.

> Nobody else really and truly understood [thinks Westrum's wife] that Westrum's mistrust of himself was greater than anyone else's mistrust of him, and with less reason; that he tormented himself beyond necessity; that he suffered a moral concern too exquisite. . . . He feared that he carried within himself that seed of moral indifference which had permitted his father and his father's fathers down the line to take pleasure in war, hatred, and the violent advance of their own interests, all in the name of American duty and service.
>
> If he had done her ill at all it was by giving her so good an opinion of the country. He was not the country.

The burden of *The Goy* is that Westrum *is* the country; that like Westrum the country is a lie and a deception, that moral indifference is endemic, and cannot be introspected away; is in fact increased by intellectual application. Ultimately this is a novel (or, rather, it is Tikvah's treatise completed) about its own apparent premise— which is to say, the premise tested, contradicted, traduced: the *goy* doesn't change his spots, even in America. It is a rough, supple, and ingeniously scouted book, as cruel and precise as its title: if *"goy"* has become a Yiddishism signifying roughneck and persecutor, it is also the Hebrew word that designates a nation, any nation, including the Jews. At bottom *The Goy* is not an exploration of the character of "the *goyim*," or even of the character of America; it is a novel about the imperatives of Jewish character, defined not by what is "Jewish," but by what is incontrovertibly not. That there is a cleavage between the noblest social ideals of Western civilization and its attitude toward Jews is not something we are just finding out, after all; it is not something Matthew Arnold (who dispassionately saw Jews as outside civilization), or even his less disinterested descendant T. S. Eliot (whose *Idea of a Christian Society* simply and axiomatically excludes Jews), or any other theoretician of culture had to tell us. What makes *The Goy* provocative in its despair is Harris's willingness to extend the case beyond Europe to the good *goyim* of America—to those Puritan consciences, emancipated intellectuals, liberal academicians, liberated allies, friends, wives, husbands, and half-Jewish children of Jews. Harris accuses them all.

And what makes *The Goy* such a societally pressing book is that it reflects with static precision a mentality we had thought the freedom of America—and certainly the advent of Israel—should by now have wiped out: what the *shtetl* used to call "fear of the *goy.*" Harris retains that fear; though a child of America, he has not lost the tremor of suspicion that characterizes an immigrant five minutes out of steerage. It is a nervousness that is probably not untypical of many Jewish Americans; and it is hard to decide whether it is Jews or Gentiles who should be more shamed by its persistence.

The Fourth Sparrow:
The Magisterial Reach
of Gershom Scholem

Gershom Scholem is a historian who has remade the world. He has remade it the way Freud is said to have remade it—by breaking open the shell of the rational to uncover the spiraling demons inside. But Freud, in fencing himself off from tradition, was hobbled by the need to invent everything on his own, through case history, trial and error, drug research, venturesome ingenuity, hunch and speculation above all. The little gods he collected, and the vocabulary he borrowed, took him partially and intuitively to Greek and primitive sources. All the same, in purposefully excluding himself from Hebrew origins—in turning Moses into an Egyptian, for instance—Freud inevitably struck loose from an encompassing history of ideas, ending in sensation and in a thesis of individuality suitable to the ardent physician he was; his new formulations stuck close to biology and family drama.

If Freud is regarded as an engine of thought and a sorcerer of fresh comprehension—as one of the century's originals, in short—there are nevertheless those who, without necessarily reducing Freud's stature, think the oceanic work of Gershom Scholem envelops

Conflated from *The New York Times Book Review*, September 21, 1980, and February 24, 1974.

Freud's discoveries as the sea includes even its most heroic white-caps. Or, to alter the image: Freud is a peephole into a dark chamber —a camera obscura; but Scholem is a radiotelescope monitoring the universe, with its myriads of dark chambers. This is because Scholem's voyage brought him past those boundaries Freud willfully imposed on himself. Freud dared only a little way past the margins of psychology; whereas Scholem, whose medium was history, touched on the very ground of human imagination. Freud claimed Hannibal as his hero, but Scholem delved beyond the Greek and Roman roots of the classical European education common to them both. Scholem went in pursuit of the cosmos—and that took him straight to the perplexities of Genesis and the Hebrew language. Freud shrugged off religion as "illusion," and ended his grasp of it with that word. Where Freud thought it fit to end, Scholem begins.

In his restrained little memoir, *From Berlin to Jerusalem: Memories of My Youth,* Scholem recounts how even in boyhood he was drawn by mysterious magnets to the remote heritage his parents had deliberately denied him. The elder Scholem was a Jew who, like many Jews in the Germany of his generation and afterward, longed for a kind of social invisibility. The proprietor of a print shop, he thought of himself as a properly bourgeois German; he intended his four sons to distinguish themselves by growing up indistinguishable—he required them to be turned out as educated Germans with no recognizable Jewish quirks of intellect or passion. The two older boys obliged him; the two younger, Werner and Gerhard, were infected by a powerfully Jewish desire to repair a morally flawed world. Werner became a Communist, and, to his father's outrage and shame, was court-martialed for treason, having taken part in an anti–World War I demonstration while wearing a German military uniform. Gerhard Hebraized his identity fully, called himself Gershom, sought out the Yiddish-speaking East European Jewish intellectuals he was expected to scorn, and became a Zionist. In the father's eyes the activities of both sons were "anti-German." The Marxist was unreachable in jail. The Zionist the father threw out of the house. The Marxist died in Buchenwald. The Zionist chose Jerusalem, and emerged as the monumental scholar of Jewish mysticism whose huge researches and daring insights have infiltrated and significantly enlarged the religious imagination of our age.

Scholar, yes—but also rediscoverer. When Scholem began his investigations, the antirational elements in Judaism had long been deliberately suppressed, both by tradition itself and by the historians. Though there are mystical moods in the vastnesses of Talmud, they are almost by-the-by: what dominates is the rabbis' ethical and juridical genius, in the intellectual and rationalist sense. Scholem set out to rescue from distaste and neglect, indeed from ill-repute and shame, those wellsprings of metaphoric vitality that lay in Kabbalah, a proliferating system of symbolic descriptions of creation and revelation deemed capable of seizing the quality of holiness itself. These ancient ideas, some of them bordering on a kind of Jewish Gnosticism, were hidden away in numbers of texts, some forgotten, some misunderstood, some condemned, some—like the Zohar—ringed round with traditional strictures. Scholem cut through disdain and rejection to begin, single-handedly, his life's task of reconstructing the story of Jewish mysticism.

Kabbalah—grounded in a belief in divine disclosure and the irrepressible hope of redemption—was historically both an inward movement and an outward one. When joined to messianic currents, it exploded the confines of esoteric reflection and burst into real event. The most startling event occurred in the seventeenth century, just after the massive Chmielnitzki persecutions of Polish Jews, when a popularly acclaimed redeemer, Sabbatai Ṣevi, and his prophet and theologian, Nathan of Gaza, set their generation on fire with the promise of an imminent return to Zion and an instantaneous end to exile and its oppressions. Scholem's inexhaustible masterwork on this subject, *Sabbatai Ṣevi: The Mystical Messiah*, divulges with philological, historical, and psychological force the amazing tale of that Sabbatian adventure: how it broke out spectacularly among the Jewish masses, and how it launched reverberations that penetrated into the next two centuries. The would-be deliverer, broken by threats of execution by the Turks—who held the Holy

Land—saved his life and abandoned his followers by converting to Islam, bringing a furiously spreading cataclysm of redemptive fever to a tragic and bewildering anticlimax.

Sabbatai Ṣevi is a titanic investigation into the substance and effect of illusion. It explores the rise, in the years 1665 and 1666, of a messianic movement among a profoundly subjugated people, only just recovering from the Inquisition and the Iberian expulsion, thrown into yet another devastation—the catastrophic massacres of the Jews of Poland that began in 1648 and continued until 1655. But the Sabbatian movement was not merely the response of hope to cataclysm. Sabbatai Ṣevi, born in Smyrna, Turkey, did not declare himself the true messiah of the Jews only to abolish their dispersion and restore to them their historic territory; the idea he represented was a cosmic redemption, the cleansing and renewal of all things, the retrieval of the sparks of holiness from the husks of evil which, according to Kabbalistic thought, bind them fast.

In the wake of Sabbatai Ṣevi's annunciation came an incalculable penitential wave. The messiah's work could not be completed until the world was cleared of sin, and everywhere—over the whole face of Europe, in Turkey, Morocco, Palestine, Egypt, wherever Jews lived—sanctification made vivid claims in the form of an astonishing spiritual roiling characterized by penitential exercises and charitable works. While the Gentiles around them gaped, Jews stopped in their daily tracks, gave up their livings, sold their possessions—the city of Leghorn, which had a large Jewish merchant class, nearly came to a halt—and prepared to journey to Jerusalem. Though there were doubters, no community of Jews went untouched by the messianic fervor. Legendary reports of the redeemer spread from land to land —a pandemic of ecstatic expectation.

The personality of the messiah himself is remarkably well-documented. He was plump, young, attractive. He had a beautiful singing voice, which he liked to show off in the synagogue, chanting psalms. An undistinguished writer, he was poetic in act rather than

word. He was not intellectually notable, although the study of Kabbalah, which formed his character, demands unusual conceptual
gifts: Kabbalah is a kind of Einsteinian mysticism—the brilliance of
its inventions is precisely the brilliance of an original physics. It is
no easy, amoral occultism, rather the vision of a universal moral
restitution willed so acutely that only an alteration in the perception
of the cosmos can account for it. Without the Kabbalah, Scholem
explains, there could have been no Sabbatai Ṣevi to inaugurate the
messianic dream, and no messianic dream to inaugurate the career
of Sabbatai Ṣevi.

But he was, above all, a man of afflictions, subject to periods of
"darkness," which then gave way to phases of "illumination." In
short, a classic manic-depressive; and, worn and perplexed by his
suffering during the cycle of bleakness, he traveled from Jerusalem,
where he was tolerated as peculiar though harmless, to Gaza, to
receive a healing penance from a twenty-year-old Kabbalist named
Nathan. Nathan was a young man of genius—a natural theologian,
given to bending Kabbalah with the craft of a chess master plying
new openings. Sabbatai Ṣevi confessed that now and then, in moments of exaltation, he conceived himself to be the messiah—and
Nathan, all at once irradiated, confirmed him as exactly that, con-
ferred on him his mission, and theologized his madness.

The madness expressed itself in what was termed "strange acts."
When the mania came on him, the messiah's face grew rosy and
glowing, and, lifted up by glory, he would compel his followers to
engage in unprecedented and bizarre performances. He made
changes in the liturgy, pronounced the unutterable Tetragramma-
ton, called women to the Ark, married himself to the Scrolls of the
Law, turned fasts into feasts; once he crammed three holidays into
a single week; another time he declared that Monday was the real
Sabbath. The glad tidings of the messianic age began to supersede
the Law by eroding its strict practice—prayerbooks were amended
to include the new messiah—and meanwhile the awakening to redemption burgeoned among all classes of Jews. One widespread
group was especially receptive—those refugees called Marranos,
who had survived the Inquisition in the guise of professing Chris-

tians, all the while secretly maintaining themselves as Jews. Their Catholic inheritance had inclined them toward worship of a Redeemer, and their public apostasy prepared them for the strangest of Sabbatai's strange acts: his conversion to Islam.

The political meaning of the ingathering of the exiles into Turkish-held Palestine was not lost on the sultan and his viziers, who smelled, in so much penitence and prayer, a nuance of insurrection. Sabbatai Ṣevi was arrested in Smyrna, where he had come home under the triumphant name of King Messiah, Savior and Redeemer. He was offered one or the other: execution or apostasy. He chose to save his life, and with that one signal tossed thousands of his shocked and disillusioned followers back into the ordinary fact of exile, to be swallowed up once again by unmediated, unmiraculous history. But masses of others, the "believers," continued to nurture their faith: for them the messiah's act was a sacred mystery shielding an arcane purpose. An underground literature and liturgy sprang up; Nathan promulgated a new theology of paradox to account for the apostasy, wherein the inward reality of belief was held to be more forceful than the outer reality of happening. The "true" truth is always the concealed truth. The holiness-at-the-core is the real revelation even when it is clothed in seeming evil. The sacred and the profane change places. The Sabbatians came at length to an astounding prayer: "Blessed art Thou, Lord of the Universe, who permittest that which is forbidden."

The crisis of theology brought on by the messiah's apostasy led the believers to abandonment of traditional rabbinic Judaism, and from there with astonishing directness to Reform Judaism, anarchism, Enlightenment, revolutionary utopianism, nihilism, antinomianism, orgiastic excess—all the stupendously complex, often contradictory, strands of ideology that are implicit in the imagination released from the yoke of Commandment. All this was the effect of illusion. We are not finished with Sabbatianism yet, nor with the bafflements it suggests about the mentality of its heirs (Justice Brandeis was descended from a Sabbatian family), or the antiquity of the impulse nowadays called Zionism, or the psychological atmosphere surrounding the development of Christianity in its earliest years, or the whole history of Christianity over the centuries. The career of Sabbatai Ṣevi hints that every messiah contains in himself, hence is responsible for, all the fruits of his being: so that, for instance, one may wonder whether the seeds of the Inquisition somehow lie even in the Sermon on the Mount.

Scholem's interpretations of these extraordinary matters were in themselves shockwaves for those who depended on the conventional histories. Instead of being merely a false messiah and mystagogue who inflamed a desperate people with his maniacal delusions, Sabbatai Ṣevi was now seen as a forerunner of the impassioned idealist Zionism of the nineteenth century; and Nathan of Gaza's formulations, instead of being mere popular nonsense, were revealed as the heir to a deep poetical tradition, dense with luxuriant imaginings and an inspired fecundity of moral feeling: the Kabbalists' yearning was to release the encapsulated divine sparks that would cleanse the world of evil. And beyond all that, Scholem maintained that the disintegration of orthodoxy through the development of Sabbatian mysticism led indirectly to circumstances that favored eighteenth-century Enlightenment and nineteenth-century Reform Judaism. This last—rational stirrings growing out of the heart of an intensely nonrational movement—is only one of Scholem's innumerable contributions to fresh seeing. Scholem's magisterial historical intuition, his capacity to enter and overwhelm several philosophical traditions at once, above all his reclamation of Kabbalah, empowered intellectual-rationalist Judaism to reharness the steeds of myth and mysticism, and to refresh the religious imagination at many wells and springs along the way.

These immense ideas, spilling over from Scholem's histories into literature and even into literary criticism, have made Scholem into one of the great modern masters: a knower who, through the scrupulous use of knowledge, refashions and dominates the way we look at ourselves and our notions of the world.

*　*　*

But even these perplexities are not all. The major wonder is about mysticism itself, about human imagination itself, and how it runs free in religion. Scholem and Deuteronomy do not agree; for Scholem, mysticism is endemic in the sacral orchestration of the human mind, and should not be set aside. But Deuteronomy's agnostic wisdom (29:28) concerning the effort to penetrate the nature and purposes of God is antithetical: "The secret things belong to the Lord"—which is to say, they are not for us.

About the paradoxical personality of Gershom Scholem himself, I once speculated in a story:

> The draw of the irrational has its own deep question: how much is research, how much is search? Is the scientist, the intelligent physician, the skeptical philosopher who is attracted to the irrational himself a rational being? How explain the attraction? I think of that majestic scholar of Jerusalem sitting in his university study composing, with bookish distance and objectivity, volume after volume on the history of Jewish mysticism—is there an objective "scientific interest" or is all interest a snare? Is the hidden cauldron not an enticement and a seduction to its investigator? —Or, to say it even more terribly: it may be that the quarry is all the time in the pursuer.

Accordingly, when I set out to see Scholem,* I went with his memoir under my arm, impatient to put a single question—that notorious conundrum all readers who are fascinated by his explorations surrender to: Does the scholar of Kabbalah possess a hidden self (as Kabbalah speaks of a hidden "true" God)? Is there some secret sharer within, an unrevealed soul? Is there, in brief, a shadow-Scholem?

Scholem is quick to answer: "The scholar is never the whole man." Then he does a thing that seems ordinary at the moment, but will turn out to be as tantalizingly wily as a reply from the Delphic oracle—he crosses to his wide scholar's table and hands me a piece of paper, a newspaper review. It concerns Scholem's relations with his great friend, Walter Benjamin. Who Benjamin was, and what he was to Scholem, can be surmised from the dedication prefixed to Scholem's seminal volume, *Major Trends in Jewish Mysticism:* "To

---

*Gershom Scholem died in 1982.

the memory of the friend of a lifetime whose genius united the insight of the Metaphysician, the interpretive power of the Critic and the erudition of the Scholar." Benjamin, a breathtaking essayist, a literary thinker drawn to Marxism, unable to share Scholem's Zionist convictions all the way, remained in Europe until it was too late. To avoid being murdered as a Jew he took his own life in 1940, at the age of forty-eight. (Scholem, a Zionist since his teens, arrived in then Palestine in the 1920s.) The two brilliant polymaths pursued their mutually enriching exchanges for years; when they were separated, the talk went on copiously, in stunning essaylike letters. The German edition of their correspondence was reviewed in the London *Times Literary Supplement* by George Steiner. "Perhaps you will find the shadow-Scholem *here,*" Scholem says; it is Steiner's review he has put in my hands. Among other stringently mournful speculations, I am astonished to read: "Scholem cannot forgive." I am astonished to read it because it has been delivered over to me as a kind of confession. Or perhaps not. The allusion, in any case, is to the Jews of Germany who deceived themselves into believing Germany would accept and absorb them. Presumably Benjamin was among them.

And it is these Jews—this pitiable phenomenon of a passionately loyal citizenry longing only to be good and peaceable Germans—who comprise the furious hidden text of *From Berlin to Jerusalem*. Writing of the bloodthirsty days of Nazi-dominated Munich, Scholem comments: "I had long since made my decision to leave Germany. But it was frightening to encounter the blindness of the Jews who refused to see and acknowledge all that. This greatly encumbered my relations with Munich Jews, for they became extremely jumpy and angry when someone broached that subject." In Frankfurt, Scholem broke off his friendship with Franz Rosenzweig, the remarkable author of *The Star of Redemption*, a vigorously original meditation on Judaism; in spite of his "intense Jewish orientation," Rosenzweig still hoped for "a Jewish community that considered itself German." "Thus I had," Scholem concludes, "one of the stormiest and most irreparable arguments of my youth." And again: "In view of the task of radical renewal of Judaism and Jewish society, Germany was a vacuum in which we would choke."

It is more than an irony, it is an ongoing wound, that *From Berlin to Jerusalem,* incontestably a Zionist book, continues the fraternal drama in its dedication to the Marxist brother who chose Communist "Humanity" over Jewish fate. But if Werner is not yet absolved, neither is Benjamin. "He paid dearly for his flirtation with Marxism," Scholem tells me. Not far from where we sit in the dining room, a long row of books commands an endless shelf: they are all by Walter Benjamin.

We are having this conversation over lunch in Scholem's house in Jerusalem, on green and flowering Abarbanel Street. The books climb and spread over all the walls of every room. Scholem is famous for loving chocolates, so I have brought some, but warily: he is famous also for knowing which chocolates will do and which won't. "Why am I being bribed?" cries Scholem—a very lofty elf with bold elfin ears and an antic elfin glee advertising tricks and enigmas—and I am relieved that my offering has passed muster. The pilgrimages to this house have been many. The critic Leslie Fiedler has been here. The historian Lucy Dawidowicz has been here. The scholar Yosef Yerushalmi has been here. The novelists Mark Mirsky and Norma Rosen have been here. Jorge Luis Borges has been here, in homage, but Scholem disclaims it: "Borges wrote all his work beforehand, before he read me." Patrick White, the Australian Nobel Prize winner, acknowledges Scholem's influence, particularly in the novel *The Riders of the Chariot.* Yale professor Harold Bloom's startling schematic borrowings, in *Kabbalah and Criticism* and elsewhere, prompt Scholem to quip: "It's a free country."

He seems pleased by these varied manifestations of his authority. What he does object to is the questionable uses his prestige is sometimes put to. "I was naïve," he explains. "I believed that if scholarship came, it would drive out charlatanism. Instead, the charlatans go on as before—only now they use me as a footnote." (The charlatans are presumably occult faddists who have appropriated Kabbalah.) He tells how his work is now frequently subject to a kind of veiled plagiarism: "One man wrote a book on Kabbalah and referred to

Scholem in a few footnotes. But all the rest of the book was also Scholem!"

Lunch is cold spinach soup, ambrosial in the perpetually patient sunheat of a Jerusalem afternoon; roast veal in a pastry crust; and, for dessert, Mrs. Scholem's homemade pink ices, concocted of fresh strawberries. The meal is elegant, in an atmosphere new to me—is it the way the light laps over these Biblical hills like some heavy celestial ray, is it a redolence of 1912 Berlin? Mrs. Scholem has been thinking about my question—the question about the shadow-Scholem. She shakes her head; she looks grave, but in a riddling way. "I know what the shadow is. And I found out only three years ago. I know it only three years." It has nothing to do with Benjamin; it has nothing to do with any of that. Will she tell? "No, I won't tell." It is a joke and it is not a joke. Later, when I plead with her to tell after all: "Maybe when I am one hundred years old. Until then I won't tell." Scholem, elfin, enjoying this: "What is 'information'? Nothing at all. Use your judgment. Use your imagination." It is as if he does not mind being invented. We begin to speak of the "theater of the self." "I call myself a metaphysical clown," Scholem says; "a clown hides himself in theater." I ask whether Walter Benjamin ever hid himself that way. "Benjamin never played theater." How much of Professor Scholem is theater? Scholem: "Ask Mrs. Scholem." Mrs. Scholem: "One hundred percent."

We turn over the pages of Scholem's memoir and study the photographs. There is one of Scholem and his three brothers, all of them under the age of fourteen. "His mother called them the four sparrows," Mrs. Scholem supplies. In the picture Gerhard, the smallest, is only six. I am suddenly emboldened to speculate—though not out loud—about the flight of the last sparrow; it seems to me I know by now what the shadow-Scholem must be. It is the shadow cast by the sparrow's wings on the way from Gerhard to Gershom. It is the capacity to make one's life a surprise, even to oneself—to create the content of one's own mind, to turn out to be something entirely unexpected. Nothing in the narrow Berlin of Gershom Scholem's youth prepared him for where he stands now. When, I inquire, did he begin to sense what his destiny would be? He reflects; he resists. And then: "About the age of twenty. You get the feeling of going in a straight line." And how would he account for this realization of a special intellectual calling? The rejoinder is so plain, and yet so obscure, that it shocks, like the throwing of three ordinary stones. "I wanted to learn about Judaism. I wanted to learn Hebrew. I wanted to learn as much as I could." Mrs. Scholem: "He went to the bottom of the question. Curiosity." Scholem: "Yes, curiosity."

But that cannot satisfy. And, in fact, the particulars of Gershom Scholem's journey, as he describes them in *From Berlin to Jerusalem*, do not quite satisfy either, although they are meant to yield the story of "going in a straight line"—they leave out the mystery of self-surprise. Everything strange remains strange. The eccentricity of an education against all likelihood, begun in parental contempt, seized in contradiction of everything influential—society, the times, the drift and pulse of contemporary scholarship, Germany itself—is not unraveled. The secret of how that miraculous rupture and awakening came about, leading to Scholem's rise as one of the whirlwind masters, teachers, wideners and imaginers of our age, is not revealed. The closest Scholem comes to it is in a single sentence. Alluding to his attraction to Kabbalah, he remarks, "Perhaps I was endowed with an affinity for this area from the 'root of my soul,' as the kabbalists would have put it, or maybe my desire to understand the enigma of Jewish history was also involved—and the existence of the Jews over the millennia *is* an enigma, no matter what the numerous 'explanations' may say."

Yet Scholem will go no further in self-disclosure, or even self-conjecture, than he has already gone; perhaps he cannot. "There will be no second volume of memoirs," he warns. This book, another on Walter Benjamin that follows it, and the volume of correspondence with Benjamin—a trinity of biography, autobiography, and portraiture—are all we are to have in the way of personal history.

What the memoir delivers—and it is, after all, a shining little book—is a pageant of characterizations, rife and roiling, in spots diaphanous, elsewhere speedy, skeletal, and spare. It is all a slender chain of shimmering beads on a string: quicksilver sketches of a hundred brilliant encounters—Rubashov, who became Shazar, Israel's third President, living next door to Scholem in a boarding house packed with brainy but impoverished young Russian Jews; the philosophers

Martin Buber and Hermann Cohen; Agnon, the Nobel-winning genius whose stories Scholem was the first to translate and to teach; Simmel, the prototypical self-estranged Jewish intellectual (to whom Buber "sometimes pointed out . . . that a man like himself ought to be interested in seeing to it that men of his type did not disappear"); Franz Rosenzweig; numbers of intellectual young women, German, Jewish, and half-Jewish; and glimpses of Benjamin himself. There is plenty of comedy, some of it melancholy, such as Hermann Cohen's comment to Franz Rosenzweig, reproaching the Zionists, "Those fellows want to be happy!"—"the most profound statement," Scholem writes, "that an opponent of Zionism ever made."

Still, everything flashes by with the quirky velocity of picture cards—people (Scholem is sensitive to looks), ideas, influential books (Kafka especially), Talmud study ("the dialogue of the generations"), extraordinary observations. Though crowded with radiant susceptibilities—for learning, for ideals, for intellectual friendships —yet these anecdotal portraits all run by too quickly. What we want from a memoir, I suppose, is something like the sensation of watching Hans Castorp's thoughts open into new depths before our eyes; or the actual texture of a mind in struggle that John Stuart Mill's *Autobiography* chillingly renders. One aches for a Thomas Mann to make a fat *Bildungsroman* of Scholem's early life—to unfold, for instance, the falling-away of mathematical ambition in the young scholar (who began as a powerful mathematician). What a marvel it would be for those paternal and fraternal crises to play themselves out in dramatic scenes; for the late nights of boarding-house cake-nibbling and philosophy to shout themselves across the page; for the playful and gifted mother who took such twinkling pleasure in writing Scholem's school compositions to draw nearer to us—for every unforeseeable and perplexing wave in Scholem's life to break into novelistic plenitude! But no, the enigma with its aura of conjecture still glimmers—it is there for us to pluck at or reinvent. The shadow persists. The plenitude, and the revelations, are in the work.

Toward a New Yiddish

NOTE

"Toward a New Yiddish" was delivered at the Weizmann Institute in Rehovoth, Israel, in the summer of 1970, as a talk entitled "America" in a series of cultural Dialogues designed to facilitate intellectual exchange between Jewish Americans and Israelis. It was conceived, in part, as a reply to George Steiner, who had appeared under the same auspices two years earlier. I include it here because it is not bound by its occasion or by any period, though I am conscious of how certain events are caught in its texture like insects in amber—how long-ago and remote are these references to the New Left, Yippies, Indian headbands, "lifestyle," Chicago street demonstrations! They teach one to distrust urgency; in the end, nothing needs footnoting more than the latest thing. (And yet the Emersonian grain of the "Movement"—so it is still called by its aging inheritors—continues to reverberate, with its emphasis on sensation, in the national self-consciousness.)

A dozen years have gone by since the evolution of these ideas. They have already been thoroughly subjected to criticism and objection; they have even been charged with the sociological sin of the "visionary." And I am no longer so tenderly disposed to the possibil-

ity of a New Yiddish—which was, anyhow, an invention, a literary
conceit calculated to dispel pessimism. Gentile readers, should this
essay invite any, may or may not be surprised at this self-portrait of
a third-generation American Jew (though the first to have been
native-born) perfectly at home and yet perfectly insecure, perfectly
acculturated and yet perfectly marginal. I am myself sometimes
taken aback by these contradictions, but what I do *not* feel uneasy
about is the thesis of American pluralism, which, I think, calls for
a mood vividly different from that of Saint Paul in the ancient world.
Paul's tactical "Be all things to all men" cannot apply; my own
striving is to be one thing all the time, and to everyone; to speak in
the same voice to every interlocutor, Gentile or Jew; not to have one
attitude or subject matter (or imagining or storytelling) for one kind
of friend and another for another kind. To be inwardly inhibited
from this openness is mental abasement. Intellectual and spiritual
freedom means to be peacefully all of a piece always, no matter who
is being addressed. Anything else is parochialism.

"Toward a New Yiddish," notwithstanding (or perhaps because
of) its historical focus, is, it seems to me, the opposite of parochial
—though I am, as I have said, no longer greatly attached to its
conclusions.*

---

*For one thing, I no longer believe that the project of fashioning a Diaspora literary
culture, in the broadest *belles-lettres* sense, can be answered by any theory of an indispensable language—i.e., the Judaization of a single language used by large populations of Jews.
The enrichment of any existing language is of course not to be despised, and if English
is widened and further nourished through the introduction of Jewish concepts, mores,
sensibility, and terminology (the last being the most prevalent and influential and yet the
most trivial), that can only be its good fortune. English has already had the historic good
luck (derived from historic bad luck: many invasions) to be richer than other languages.
English, in fact, is perhaps the luckiest language with regard to "richness," and we English
speakers are, as writers, probably the luckiest language-inhabitors, simply because English
is really two languages, Germanic and Latinic: so that there are at least two strains of
nuance for every noun, fact, feeling, or thought, and every notion owns a double face.
  Hebrew is a lucky language in another way: it was the original vessel for the revolution
of human conscience, teaching the other languages what it early and painfully acquired:
moral seriousness. Because of the power of scriptural ideas, there is hardly a language left
on the planet that does not, through the use of its own syllables and vocabulary, "speak
Hebrew." Though the genius of Abraham and Moses and the Prophets runs like mother-
milk through the lips of Hebrew, all languages have a Hebrew-speaking capacity, as the
literatures of the world have somewhat tentatively, yet often honorably, demonstrated.
Language is the wineskin, thought the wine: this of course is the point of "Toward a New

How, by the way, do we recognize the parochial? It is the point of view that invented the ugly and intolerable term "ethnic." It is the point of view that dismisses as parochial a civilization not one's own. And it is, sometimes, the point of view that characterizes Jews who, for whatever reasons, personal or political, are not much interested in Jewish ideas. Such persons (unlike most Gentiles who have severed any serious connection with Christianity) call themselves "universalists." It is striking to observe that universalism of this sort is, however, the ultimate Jewish parochialism. It is mainly Jews who profess it.

Yiddish." Yet all that is required of any language for it to carry a fresh and revolutionary idea—the Jewish recoil from idols remains such an idea—is for the language in question to will itself not to be parochial.

Toward a New Yiddish

Two years ago an illustrious man of letters came out of Diaspora to
this place and offered Exile as a metaphor for the Essential Jew, and
himself as a metaphor of Exile. He came, he said, as a visitor. Now
immediately I would distinguish between a visitor and a pilgrim:
both will come to a place and go away again, but a visitor arrives,
a pilgrim is restored. A visitor passes through a place; the place passes
through the pilgrim. A visitor comes either to teach or to learn, or
perhaps simply and neutrally to observe; but a pilgrim comes on
purpose to be taught renewal. And so, as self-defined "guest" and
ideological outsider, this visitor I speak of designated, with all authenticity, his personal mode, mien, and consciousness as exilic;
then, less authentically, he characterized Exile as an arena for
humankind's finest perceptions, free of "lunatic parochialism"; and
finally—questionably—he concluded that to be most exiled is to be
most exalted, that a sensibility most outside the commonalty of Jews
is most within the "genius of Judaism." "Yes," he said, "I *am* a
wanderer, a *Luftmensch.* . . . But I have made of my harrying . . .
a creative impulse so strong that it has recast much of the politics,
art and intellectual constructs of the age." Far from being cultural

Published in *Judaism,* Summer 1970.

disaster, outsideness becomes cultural opportunity. "Marx lies in Highgate and Freud in Golders Green. . . . Einstein's ashes were scattered off New Jersey." Think also of Trotsky, Kafka, Lévi-Strauss, Chomsky, Spinoza, Heine. Homelessness is the virtue of being disarmed, and powerlessness has at least the power to slay without weaponry the serpent Nationalism, whose secret name is Atavistic Tribalism. By declaring himself marginal man, wanderer and guest, the visitor pronounced himself "unto the elements . . . free." Impressively in command of the lyrical and the moral imagination, he put both at the service of his perception of universalism, and called this the genius of Judaism. Diaspora, then, is the rootless though paradoxically fruitful soil of the Essential Jew (explained the visitor), and my own envisioning sensibility, born of my precarious tenure there (explained the visitor), is the genius of Judaism. Diaspora, *c'est moi:* what *I* am, he in effect told us, is what a Jew ought to be—thereby elevating his individual and personal satisfactions to a general theory—in fact to a behavioral ideal.

Now my intention here is not to fall into a polemical struggle with an absent luminary. I am on another line, and am lured by a seizure of history more deeply ancient than any local debate in a corner of our current Dispersion. George Steiner justifies his vision of Diaspora partly by his own achievements and reputation, partly through contemplation of the achievements and reputation of other Jews. What I want to question—the vocation and leash of these speculations—is whether the accomplishments of Jews in Diaspora are in fact *Jewish* accomplishments; and further, whether it matters that they are or are not. When George Steiner speaks of universalism and calls it Jewish, for instance, I agree that universalism is of course a Jewish impulse—but not as he conceives it. Jewish universalism emphasizes that the God of Israel is also the God of mankind-in-general. It does not claim that mankind-in-general must be the god of Israel. To celebrate what the "harrying" of Diaspora does for the Jew is somehow also to celebrate the harrying. You cannot praise the consequence without having some of your praise stick to its brute instrumentality. An idol is a-thing-that-subsists-for-its-own-sake-without-a-history; significantly, that is also what a poem is; and even universalism can become tainted if it is turned into an idol or a poem.

In short, even if Diaspora is credited with begetting, or reinforcing, the universalist mentality, it remains a perverse criterion.

By contrast, then, I come to this place as a pilgrim, to speak in dispraise of Diaspora: I include specifically the Diaspora of freedom. Now it is well known that dispraise of Diaspora is an obvious and popular stance among some Israelis. And indeed it could not be otherwise, since Zionism is an inspiration with two parents: the memory of home its warm mother, revulsion against Exile its stern father. But lately we have seen—particularly at the time of the Eichmann trial we saw—how Israeli rejection of Diaspora becomes not a revulsion against the millennial victimization of the *galut* (exile) experience, but a revulsion against the victimized Jew himself—his preoccupations, his manners and mores, the very shape of his body. The distastefulness of the portrait, its emphasis on pettiness and cowardice, coincides remarkably with that of the classic anti-Semite —also, more pathetically, with that of the classic Jewish anti-Semite. It is a description frequently in the mouths of some English and American Jews as well, and it might have been partly to counteract such unhappy distortions that George Steiner drew his opposite portrait of the Jew as *Luftmensch*, ennobled by otherness, universalized through wandering, gifted in his homelessness by exceptional sight and judgment, made free by unbelonging. If George Steiner has special praise for the human consequences of the two thousand years between Israel and Israel, some Israelis would negate and disvalue that same period as if it never was. Both the praise and the dispraise are partial renderings of root situations—but they are superficial because they are largely social responses: they are told in the language of a kind of rhetoricized sociology. My dispraise of Diaspora means to take another direction: it is centered on a revulsion against the values—very plainly I mean the beliefs—of the surrounding culture itself: a revulsion against Greek and pagan modes, whether in their Christian or post-Christian vessels, whether in their purely literary vessels, or whether in their vessels of *Kulturgeschichte*. It is a revulsion—I want to state it even more plainly—against what is called, strangely, Western Civilization.

I have this in common with Steiner: like him, I want to offer myself as a metaphor of Diaspora. Steiner finds his construct of

Diaspora appropriate to some aspects of himself; so do I. I say with him, Diaspora, *c'est moi:* only the view darkly differs. For one thing, I am the ordinary Diaspora animal, and this makes me a better, or at least a more useful because worse, example. Let me tell you what I do and how I live. I am a writer, slow and unprolific, largely unknown, the most obscure of all the writers who have, so far, whether as visitors or pilgrims, addressed this conference. Obscurity is here doubly and triply pertinent, for to be a writer is to be almost nothing; the writer is not a religious thinker, or a philosopher, or a political scientist, or a historian, or a sociologist, or a philologist. To be a writer is to be an autodidact, with all the limitations, gaps, and gaucheries typical of the autodidact, who belabors clichés as though they were sacral revelations. Especially as a Jew I am an autodidact: the synagogue at present does not speak to me, and I have no divine shelter other than reading; at the moment print is all my Judaism, and I crawl through print besotted with avaricious ignorance, happening here and there upon a valley of light. My reading has become more and more urgent, though in narrower and narrower channels. I no longer read much "literature." I read mainly to find out not what it is to be a Jew—my own life in its quotidian particulars tells me that—but what it is to *think* as a Jew. Novels and poems no longer appear to address me; even our celebrated Jewish novelists, though I read them all, appear to be in the grip of a sociology more or less gross, more or less revealing; the only Jewish novelist who seems to me purely and profoundly ideational is Saul Bellow—so I sit alone in a wastepile of discarded artists, reading one novelist. But one is not enough to make what we always hear called a Literary Renaissance among American Jews. Until very recently, my whole life was given over to the religion of Art, which is the religion of the Gentile nations—I had no other aspiration, no other commitment, was zealous for no other creed. In my twenties I lived the life of the elderly Henry James. In my thirties I worshiped E. M. Forster for the lure of his English paganism. Fifteen years went into a silent and shadowed apprenticeship of craft and vision. When at last I wrote a huge novel I meant it to be a Work of Art—but as the years ground through that labor, it turned, amazingly and horribly, into a curse. I discovered at the end that I had cursed the world I lived in, grain by grain. And I did not know why. Furthermore, that immense and silent and obscure labor had little response—my work did not speak to the Gentiles, for whom it had been begun, nor to the Jews, for whom it had been finished. And I did not know why. Though I had yearned to be famous in the religion of Art, to become so to speak a saint of Art, I remained obscure. —Diaspora, *c'est moi:* remember that I speak of myself metaphorically only, and so I do not use the word "obscurity" as having anything to do with personal reputation, but with shadow, with futility, with vanity, frivolity, and waste. I include in this hopeless destiny of obscurity persons of splendid achievement, eminent writers who have performed brilliant summarizing work. I include George Steiner, and Walter Kaufmann who spoke here last year in impassioned disparagement of nationalism; I include the spectacular Leslie Fiedler and the marvelously gifted Philip Roth, who were here seven years ago. At that time Philip Roth said: "I am not a Jewish writer; I am a writer who is a Jew." I do not know whether he would hold this view today. Nevertheless Philip Roth's words do not represent a credo; they speak for a doom. I will come back to them shortly.

But first a brief anthropological excursion through Diaspora: Diaspora, *c'est moi*—I was telling you how I, a metaphor, live. I live in Diaspora, I work in it, I nurture my child in it, and undoubtedly I shall die in it. Having complained of sociology, I now find a large tract of it lying before me. It is full of humps, but I suppose they must be gotten over. I will tell you about my street and how I live in it; or do not live in it. Far from being universalist, with the capacity to peer over boundaries and shrink oceans between Cambridge and Cambridge, I spend an unvisionary life in a house among houses. On my street mine is the Jewish house: there is an Italian house, a Lithuanian house, a German house, a Scotch-Irish house. Luggiaro, Pozha, Koechlein, Cochran. The names make music but the harmony is superficial. The blacks are seven streets away in a separate enclave, invisible and shut off; when on occasion a black child roams by on a bicycle, stares of anxiety follow him. Still, there is peace. But it is not the trusting peace of universalism or even of pluralism—it is the pragmatic peace of truce. The ordinary Diaspora animal lives side-by-side, not over-and-above. My marginality is not a source of my liberation, but rather a worrisome buzz in the back of the mind. When the neighbor's mower noisily cuts his grass, I suppose he watches the grass fly up and thinks about that. When I cut my grass I tunnel through the buzz and think of the earth beneath the grass —the grass flies up over something sweet and deep, but borrowed, transient. I will not let myself love the clover too much; not even the clover is allowed to deceive me. Diaspora does not nourish my universalist impulse. Just the opposite: it segments it. Marginality does not free me to the rich subversions of the ironic spirit. Just the opposite: it makes me tuck them away when the neighbor's Stars and Stripes smothers his porch on Flag Day. I happen not to own a flag; in silence my neighbor notices my omission; in silence I observe his silence. All this—my neighborly silence, I mean—is the ugly accommodation of cowardice. And the reason I am cowardly, I tell myself, is not because I am *at bottom* cowardly, but because I want to save my powers for the Real Thing, the life of what I once called Art. Read, read, read, and read quickly; write, write, write, and write urgently—before the coming of the American pogrom! How much time is there left? The rest of my life? One generation? Two?

No Jew I know is shocked at this pessimism, though many disagree with it. They will tell me that I exhibit the craven ghetto mentality of the *shtetl;* "America is different." I go to the public library and I find a book by three clergymen—in America it is always three clergymen—a minister, a priest, and a rabbi, and the rabbi's chapter is called "America Is Different." The rabbi is the author of a study of the French Enlightenment, an authoritative and exhaustive history showing how even Voltaire was not different. The rabbi's chapter is full of fear masking as hope. Calling it "America Is Different" is probably very polite, but it is about the same as rushing out to buy a flag to even up the street. If you feel the necessity always to be on guard as to your keeping a civil tongue, you are hardly free. Even a rabbi, even a historian, can be the ordinary Diaspora animal.

But my less nervous friends say: Oh, that is the disease of middle age: America is different *now,* look at the young. And I look at the young—especially at those young Jews who are so disproportionately represented in the New Left. See? my less nervous friends say

—see, no flags for them, except to burn and tear: they have the
courage of universalism in the face of your selfish ghetto cravenness.
They are obsessed by a vision of peace. But I see in these bright-
beaded and garlanded children a ghetto legacy as deep as any of my
own, a legacy obsessed not so much by peace as by enmity—the
certainty that government is the enemy. This they swallowed whole,
though unawares, out of their great-grandfathers' bellies: it was not
to be found in the Reform Sunday Schools that bred their creed. And
so, like me, they dream old nightmares of the czars—but without
knowing that they dream these nightmares *because they are Jews*. My
Russian-born father had a plain word to signify a certain brand of
moral anesthesia: *Amerikaner-geboren*. I translate it without elaboration as having been autolobotomized out of history, which describes,
for instance, our Jewish Yippies. They are a subspecies of the Diaspora animal, but all the same instantly recognizable. The ironies the
Yippies yell are ironic in a way they know not of: they think they
are the first generation to revile government. Their parents do not,
or dare not, revile government; their parents spend the ten dollars
for a flag, meanwhile paying dues to the Reform Sunday School to
promote the teaching of Jewish universalism. Exhilarated by insur-
rectionist and treasonable invective, the young imagine themselves
to be profoundly new, unheard-of, romantically zany and strange,
the first of their kind. Whereas they are only the de-Judaized shadows of their great-grandfathers in the Pale, whom they have excised
from memory. *"Nikolay, Nikolay, oif dayn kop ikh shpay"* was my
grandmother's lullaby to me—Czar Nicholas, I spit on your head.
—Not only fear but fearlessness makes the Diaspora animal: show
the flag or burn it, cowardice or bold revulsion, it's all the same in
exile.

The conspiracy trial of the Chicago Seven was a spectacle in two
senses: on the part of the law under whose provisions the trial was
brought, it was a spectacle of the whipping-down of civil liberties
in the United States. But on the part of the Yippies, Jerry Rubin and
Abbie Hoffman among others, it was a spectacle in its fully aesthetic
meaning. The New Left is sometimes taken as a "Jewish" movement, largely because it seems to be about social justice. But in reality
it is less a social or a prophetic movement than an aesthetic one,

especially in its Yippie aspects. Allen Ginsberg said of his role as witness in Chicago: "I have not written a poem about the experience of the trial because my testimony itself was the poem."* That poem is apparent in what is nowadays called "lifestyle."† Up to now I have been talking, as I warned, the language and themes of sociology—these are preoccupying but not critical. What *is* critical is "lifestyle": and what is even more critical is poetry. For lifestyle is the exact point of pressure whereat sociology turns into aesthetics; where demonstration becomes description and phenomena are transmogrified into values; where at last we enter into the ancient and eternal rift between the Jewish idea and the world-at-large. In America at the moment the concept of lifestyle is expressed extrinsically in a certain gaudiness of costume and vocabulary, full of the charms of novel shock and novel openness. Explaining to the court what a "human be-in" was—the event in a park near the Democratic Convention that resulted in the conspiracy trial—Ginsberg said that its purpose was "to show some different new lifestyle than was going to be shown to the younger people by the politicians who were assembled; to present different ideas for making the society more sacred and less commercial." Intrinsically lifestyle implies a hope for revolution to be effected through a community of manners. Manners are endemically and emphatically in the realm of poetry and outside the realm of acts: the poem is the incarnation of the deed, the romance of belief stands for the act. Manners are gesture, gesture is theater and magic. The revolution, then, is really a thrust, first and foremost, of taste and of poetry. The old sex-words, for instance, demythologized of their secrecy taboo, have acquired a half-comical, half-gallant, new mythos of public poetry; their use is sacramental. In Ginsberg's poetry their use is sacramental. But revolutionary lifestyle incorporates very literally a eucharistic, not a Jewish, urge. What Ginsberg in his testimony called "psychedelic consciousness" is what the Christian used to call grace. At the be-in, a group of ministers and rabbis elevated a ten-foot cross high into a cloud of tear

---

*In answer to a question at a P.E.N. meeting, New York, June 3, 1970. I record it from memory.

†In 1970 this word was not so familiar, and therefore not so comically debased, as it now seems.

gas thrown by rioting police. When Ginsberg saw this he turned to his friend and said: "They have gassed the cross of Christ." Perhaps for the first time since Rome an elevated cross was on the receiving end of a pogrom, but the fact remains that for the rabbis who carried it and for Ginsberg who pitied it the cross had been divested of its historical freight. It had been transubstantiated from a sign of the real acts of a community into the vehicle of a moment rich in aesthetic contrast, Christian grace, psychedelic consciousness, theatrical and poetical magic—like that moment in our national anthem when the Star-Spangled Banner waves gloriously through a smoky night of shellfire.

I do not think Ginsberg would object to this Ku Kluxish equation of Cross with Flag: each is a poem, and a poem has no history. That is why he can recite the mantras, love the cross, and speak of hasidism in the same breath: "allee samee," he says of all the religions of the world—all the same. He makes no exception of Judaism because—having misread hasidism, and mistaking the hasidic part for the historic whole—he imagines the Jewish vision to be an ecstasy without a history. But you cannot comprehend Sinai and still say "allee samee." Sinai does not speak out against ecstasy, but against cultishness; it commands deed, conduct, act, and says No to any impulse that would impede a community of justice. Yet ecstasy belongs to cultishness, and cultishness transcends conduct, which is what Isaiah knew when he condemned our feasts and new-moon celebrations and referred us to the Sinaitic commandments. Allen Ginsberg retains the Jewish passion for peacefulness, mercy, and justice, but he imagines that by transcending its Jewish character he will be better empowered to infuse it into all men: an acutely Christian formulation. In transcending the Jewish *behavioral* character of the vision, he transcends the social vision itself, floating off into various modes of release and abandonment. He recapitulates the Hellenization of Jewish Christianity. He restates the justification-by-faith that is at the core of Pauline Protestantism. In dethroning the separate Oneness of God—the God of Thou Shalt and Thou Shalt Not—he goes farther than little Christianity, even in its Roman plural-saint version. He wades into the great tide of the Orient, where gods proliferate and nature binds all the gods together and the self's ideal is to drown in holy selfhood until nature blots out man and every act is annihilated in the divine blindness of pure enlightenment. Monism is the negation of monotheism. Ecstasy belongs to the dark side of personality, to the mystical unknowingness of our "psychedelic consciousness," to the individual as magical repository, instrument, medium and mediator of the sacral. When man is turned into a piece of god he is freed from any covenant with God. The Yippie revolutionaries revive the Indian headband not only because it is redolent of woods and freedom, but because it suggests rite, strange lost religions, occult encampments, divine orgy. It signifies not simply the forest but the darkness of the forest. Poetry is the center, as it was in the Greek religions, as it was in the cult of Osiris, as it is in all cults untouched by the Jewish covenant. Hence the flattery and menace and popularity of astrology, a religion without a role for will or commandment. Hence the random ecstasy of drugs. There is no need for a covenant with God if God can enter flesh. What is going on now in the streets of America is what, in different costume and vocabulary, has always been going on in the churches of America. It is a reënactment, not a revolution. And by no means a new revelation. And by no means Jewish. It is the religion of Art, and just as a Jew feels alien to the aesthetic paganism of a churched America, so now he feels alien to the aesthetic paganism of the streets. Formerly at least the streets were neutral. Now they too are churched.

As in the streets, so in literature. We ought to have suspected it would come when, thirty years ago, literary idealism was captured by the band styled as New Critics. These were largely Christian Karaites who would allow no tradition to be attached to a text. The history, psychology, even the opinions, of a writer were declared irrelevant to the work and its word. A ritual called *explication de texte* was the sacrament of this movement. It died out, killed by the power and persuasiveness of biography, but also because of the rivalry and exhaustion of its priests. For the priests of that sect the text had become an idol; humanity was left out. (Some of the best critics of that time and afterward, Lionel Trilling, Philip Rahv, Alfred Kazin and Irving Howe, were Jews; they did not conform, and put humanity back in.) Now again, after a period of vagueness and confusion following the dissolution of the New Criticism, the text has become an idol, though in another form. Now it is the novel that has been aestheticized, poeticized, and thereby paganized. I will try to seize these complexities in the briefest way, by grabbing hold only of the points that stick out the most. The most flagrant point is this: the nineteenth-century novel has been pronounced dead. Since the nineteenth-century novel is essentially *the* novel, some conclude that the novel itself is dead. Critics now talk of "exhausted forms" —narrative is played out, psychology is played out, and so forth. So what is left? Two possibilities: parody of the old forms, Tolstoyan mockeries such as Nabokov's; and a new "form" called language, involving not only parody, but game, play, and rite. The novel is now said to be "about itself," a ceremony of language. This is currently the only sort of fiction receiving the practical attention of serious literary intellectuals in America. How to describe the genesis of this new breed of novel? Its father is the Frenchman Robbe-Grillet, its mother is the impressive American aesthetician Susan Sontag; its diligent foster uncles are two de-Judaized American critics, Kostelanetz and Gilman. Its practitioners are by and large not Jews. Where so many Jews are writers of fiction, this has a certain significance as to temperament: Roth, Bellow, and Malamud, the most celebrated of the Jewish writers, are all accused of continuing to work in "exhausted forms."

But this is not the real burden of the accusation; modes of technique are not the real issue. What is regarded as exhausted in nineteenth-century fiction is not simply the worked-out vein of characterization and storytelling, but something beyond mere devices: call it History, call it Idea. The novel at its nineteenth-century pinnacle was a Judaized novel: George Eliot and Dickens and Tolstoy were all touched by the Jewish covenant: they wrote of conduct and of the consequences of conduct: they were concerned with a society of will and commandment. At bottom it is not the old novel as "form" that is being rejected, but the novel as a Jewish force. The "new" novel, by contrast, is to be taken like a sacrament. It is to be a poem without a history—which is to say an idol. It is not to judge or interpret. It is to *be*; it is not to allow anything to *happen* or *become*. "Happen" implies history, "become" implies idea; both

imply *teshuvah,* a turning. But the new fiction is to be the literary
equivalent of the drug culture, or of Christianity. It is to be self-
sustaining, enclosed, lyrical and magical—like the eucharistic moment, wherein the word makes flesh. "Life," one of the most praised
of these practitioners writes, "is not the subject of fiction."* Fiction,
he says, "is where characters, unlike ourselves, freed from existence,
can shine like essence, and purely Be"—and he quotes from Ortega
y Gasset in a passage despising those who will not "adjust their
attention . . . to the work of art; instead they penetrate through it
to passionately wallow in the human reality which the work of art
refers to." But it is above all the Jewish sense-of-things to "passionately wallow in the human reality." Covenant and conduct are above
decoration. The commandment against idols, it seems to me, is
overwhelmingly pertinent to the position of the Jewish fiction-
writer in America today. If he feels separate from the religion of Art
in the streets, he can stay out of the streets. But if the religion of Art
is to dominate imaginative literature entirely, and I believe it will in
America for a very long time, can he stay out of American literature?

If he wants to stay Jewish, I think he will have to. Even as a writer,
especially as a writer, he will have to acknowledge exile. If what I
have called aesthetic paganism is to be a long-range thesis of American culture, then it is not the kind of literary or social culture he can
be at home in. The problem of Diaspora in its most crucial essence
is the problem of aesthetics. This no doubt sounds very abstract,
despite those social particulars I have tried to illustrate with. But it
is not abstract. The German Final Solution was an aesthetic solution:
it was a job of editing, it was the artist's finger removing a smudge,
it simply annihilated what was considered not harmonious. In daily
life the morality of Germans continued as before, neighbors were
kindly, who can deny it? From the German point of view, getting
rid of the Jew had nothing to do with conduct and everything to do
with art. The religion of Art isolates the Jew—only the Jew is
indifferent to aesthetics, only the Jew wants to "passionately wallow
in the human reality." Among the ancients it was the Greeks, not
the Jews, who contemplated pure form. Even now, in the whole

*William H. Gass, "The Concept of Character in Fiction," *New American Review* 7.

planet of diverse cultures, the Jew is the only one who stands there naked without art. The Jewish writer, if he intends himself really to be a *Jewish* writer, is all alone, judging culture like mad, while the rest of culture just goes on *being* culture. Earlier I quoted George Steiner's view that the Jew has "recast much of the politics, art and intellectual constructs of the age." No. He has recast nothing, least of all art. He has judged what he found. If he does not judge what he finds, if he joins it instead, he disappears. Those Diaspora Jews who survive and transcend alien cultures—Steiner cites, among others, Freud and Kafka—are precisely those who judge what they find. Critics, interpreters, summarizers of culture who are Jews can at least breathe, if only transiently, in Diaspora. If they are giants, like Freud and Kafka, they may endure, though one becomes less and less assured of the long-term survival even of Freud.

But for those who are less than giants—and culture is what happens every day, culture is normality, culture is dependent for its sustenance not on its major but on its minor figures—for those Jewish summarizers and literary and cultural critics and observers who do not tower over but, rather, hope merely to sustain, history promises little. The culture they buzz round like honeybees drops them. They become nonexistent. This is not because they are minor figures to begin with; as I have said, a culture is fed chiefly by its diligent second rank. But the diligent second rank, when it is Jewish, does not survive even as minor. Compare Chesterton and Israel Zangwill. Both were of what we now call a "minority faith," one a Catholic, one a Jew; born ten years apart, they had, in a literary way, similar careers. But everybody knows that Chesterton is an English writer and that Zangwill is not. Chesterton is not much read, except in school assignments. Zangwill is not read at all, and the last place you would expect to find him is in a textbook. Chesterton is a minor English literary figure and is noted as such among specialists. Zangwill is only a Jew who lived in England. For some Jewish historians he survives as a producer of documents, or as himself a document. For English culture he does not survive at all.

But go further and consider those who do *not* intend to be Jewish. Consider Isaac D'Israeli and his contemporary, Charles Lamb. Both are gifted minor writers, of rather similar charm. But everyone knows Charles Lamb, and if anyone has ever heard of Isaac D'Israeli it is because he is the father of a Jewish Prime Minister. Yet Isaac D'Israeli was the perfect English man-of-letters, easily comparable to, in America now, Lionel Trilling. He was not notably Jewish in his concerns, as, of course, Zangwill was. In literature his fate is the same as Zangwill's—no, worse. Even Jewish specialists find him uninteresting. He does not exist, even as a document. Lamb survives, Hazlitt survives, De Quincey survives, Leslie Stephen survives, George Saintsbury survives—all minor. But Isaac D'Israeli is wiped out of the only culture he was able to breathe in, as if he never breathed at all.

One can move through history from culture to culture and discover equal dooms. In the Italy of the Renaissance, cultivated Jews, like others, wrote sonnets in Italian in imitation of Petrarch. They did not endure even in a minor way—not as a minor note in Jewish culture, not as a minor note in Italian culture. In the so-called Golden Age of Spain, which—as Richard Rubinstein pointed out at an earlier Dialogue—is considered Golden only by Jews, was there not some gifted Jew of Toledo who wrote verses in Spanish? If so, try to find his name. So if Philip Roth still wants to say "I am not a Jewish writer; I am a writer who is a Jew," the distinction turns out to be wind; it is precisely those who make this distinction whom Diaspora most determinedly wipes out.

And it is especially to the point that one has to look to minor writers for historical examples. There are no major Jewish writers, unless you insist on including two French half-Jews, Montaigne and Proust. The novel at its height in the last century was Judaizing in that it could not have been written without the Jewish Bible; in America especially, Hawthorne and Melville and Whitman are Biblically indebted; but there never yet lived a Jewish Dickens. There have been no Jewish literary giants in Diaspora. Marx and Freud are vast presences, but they are, as I observed earlier, analyzers and judges of culture—they belong to that awkward category known as "the social sciences." Imaginative writers, by contrast, are compelled to swim in the medium of culture; literature is an instrument of a culture, not a summary of it. Consequently there are no major works of Jewish imaginative genius written in any Gentile language,

sprung out of any Gentile culture. Talmud speculates that when the
Jews went into exile, God too was exiled. Is this a metaphor of
incapacity? The literature of the Bible—very nearly our only major
literature—issued from out of the Land. When we went into exile,
did our capacity for literature abandon us also? Why have our various Diasporas spilled out no Jewish Dante, or Shakespeare, or Tolstoy, or Yeats? Why have we not had equal powers of hugeness of
vision? These visions, these powers, were not hugely conceived.
Dante made literature out of an urban vernacular, Shakespeare spoke
to a small island people, Tolstoy brooded on upper-class Russians,
Yeats was the kindling for a Dublin-confined renascence. They did
not intend to address the principle of Mankind; each was, if you will
allow the infamous word, tribal. Literature does not spring from the
urge to Esperanto but from the tribe. When Carl Sandburg writes
in a poem "There is only one man, and his name is Mankind," he
is unwittingly calling for the end of culture. The annihilation of
idiosyncrasy assures the annihilation of culture. It *is* possible to write
"There is only one ant, and its name is Antkind"; anthood is praised
thereby. The ants are blessed with the universal brotherhood of
instinct. But they have no literature. Whenever we in Diaspora make
a literature that is of-the-nations, relying on what we have in common with all men, what we fashion turns out to be a literature of
instinct, not of singularity of culture; it does not deserve perpetua-
tion. What is there of culture in Shylock's cry "Hath not a Jew
hands, organs, dimensions, senses, affections passions"? Very liberal
of Shakespeare to grant this, very socialist of him, and humanitarian,
and modern, and priest/minister/rabbi-American of him—nevertheless what Shylock's formulation signifies is that Shakespeare
even at his moral pinnacle does not see the Jew as *a man*, but only
as Mankind—which is to say as Ant, natural creature rather than
culture-making creature. In our modern Diasporas we have consistently followed Shakespeare in this diminution of our civilizing qualities: as makers-of-literature we have by and large been possessed
of organs and dimensions rather than of culture. We are all Shy-
locks proclaiming our resemblances: "allee samee," we say, insuring
the obliteration of our progeny.

The fact is that nothing thought or written in Diaspora has ever been able to last unless it has been centrally Jewish. If it is centrally Jewish it will last for Jews. If it is not centrally Jewish it will last neither for Jews nor for the host nations. Rashi lasts and Yehudah Halevi lasts: one so to speak a social thinker, the other a poet: they last for Jews. Leivick will last, and Sholem Aleichem: for Jews. Isaac D'Israeli did not last for Jews or for anyone; neither did that putative Jew of Toledo who wrote good Spanish poetry; neither will Norman Mailer. "Our cultural account in the Diaspora," Bialik said, "is all debit and no credit." Even a Heine does not right the balance. After so long a sojourn among Germans, didn't the Jews owe Germany at least a poet? For a while Heine pretended he was a German poet, though his private letters repeatedly said something else. But Germany would not keep him; Hitler struck him from the ledger and returned Heine permanently to the Jewish people. If he lasts, he lasts for us.

By "centrally Jewish" I mean, for literature, whatever touches on the liturgical. Obviously this does not refer only to prayer. It refers to a type of literature and to a type of perception. There is a critical difference between liturgy and a poem. Liturgy is in command of the reciprocal moral imagination rather than of the isolated lyrical imagination. A poem is a private flattery: it moves the private heart, but to no end other than being moved. A poem is a decoration of the heart, the art of the instant. It is what Yehudah Halevi called flowers without fruit. Liturgy is also a poem, but it is meant not to have only a private voice. Liturgy has a choral voice, a communal voice: the echo of the voice of the Lord of History. Poetry shuns judgment and memory and seizes the moment. In all of history the literature that has lasted for Jews has been liturgical. The secular Jew is a figment; when a Jew becomes a secular person he is no longer a Jew. This is especially true for makers of literature. It was not only an injunction that Moses uttered when he said we would be a people attentive to holiness: it was a description and a destiny.

When a Jew in Diaspora leaves liturgy—I am speaking now of the possibilities of a Diaspora literature—literary history drops him and he does not last.

By "last" I mean, very plainly, *sub specie aeternitatis*. If it is enough for any novelist or poet to have the attention of three decades and then to be forgotten, I am not speaking to him. But no committed writer seriously aims to be minor or obscure. I offer a tragic American exemplar of wasted powers and large-scale denial. Why, for instance, does Norman Mailer, born in the *shtetl* called Brooklyn, so strenuously and with little irony turn himself into Esau? Because he supposes that in the land of Esau the means to glory is Esau's means. Having failed through inadequate self-persuasion to write the novels of Esau, Mailer now swings round to interpretive journalism, a minor liturgical art: with old Jacob's eye he begins to judge Gentile culture. But even while judging he is allured, and his lust to be Esau grows. One day he will become a small Gentile footnote, about the size of H. L. Mencken. And the House of Israel will not know him. And he will have had his three decades of Diaspora flattery. Esau gains the short run, but the long run belongs to Jacob.

How do these admittedly merciless reflections—history confers realism, not consolation—affect the position of Jewish culture in the American Diaspora?

I spoke earlier, in that sociological hump I had to get over, of fear of an American abattoir. This may stem from the paranoia of alienation; or from a Realpolitik grasp of scary historical parallels. Never mind. Let us say it will never happen, or not for a long time. And that despite every other kind of domestic upheaval the Jews of America have a good space of future laid out before them. What then? Will cultural news come out of American Jewry?

I have a curious vision, transient but joyous. It has to do with two deeply obvious circumstances. The first is that of all Jews alive today, 45 percent live in America, and perhaps 50 percent have English for their mother tongue. This is not so much a datum as an opportunity, and I will return to it. The second is that there has been, from America, no Ingathering of Jews into the Land of Israel. But why not? What are our reasons, our actual and truthful reasons? Is it that we don't want to leave our houses, jobs, cars, yards, fences, language, fleshpots? Yes. Is it that despite occasional dark frights we are in love with the American idea, and trust it after all? Also yes. "This is a good Diaspora," I heard someone say the other day, "as Diasporas go." So is it that in the meantime we are nevertheless living spectacularly productive and reasonably happy lives? Also yes. These are all our true reasons: reasons in praise of the American Diaspora: reasons of antlike instinct rather than culture. But sometimes I wonder whether there is not another reason too—not *our* reasons, but history's. The Nazi period teaches us how not to be disposed of; also how not to dispose of ourselves. We always note how in Germany we wanted to be German. In America something else is happening. By now I have probably uttered the word "history" a hundred times; it is a Jewish word. But turn now to Joseph Brenner, who in a furious essay called "Self-Criticism" spits it out like a demon-shriek—

> History! History! [he cries.] But what has history to tell? It can tell that wherever the majority population, by some fluke, did not hate the Jews among them, the Jews immediately started aping them in everything, gave in on everything, and mustered the last of their meager strength to be like everyone else. Even when the yoke of ghetto weighed most heavily upon them—how many broke through the walls? How many lost all self-respect in the face of the culture and beautiful way of life of the others! How many envied the others! How many yearned to be like them!

All this is of course applicable to numbers of American Jews behind their silken walls. Diaspora-flattery is our pustule, culture-envy our infection. Not only do we flatter Gentiles, we crave the flattery of Gentiles. Often in America we receive it. We have produced a religious philosopher who can define himself as Jew only by means of the pressure of Christian philosophies—he cannot figure out how to be Jewish without the rivalry of polemics, because polemics produce concern and attention, and attention flatters. Our indifferent disaffected de-Judaized novelists are finally given the ultimate flattery of mimicry: a celebrated Gentile novelist writes a novel about an indifferent disaffected de-Judaized Jewish novelist. Our rabbis no longer learn or teach: they have become pastors, ersatz ministers who are flattered by invitations to serve at the White House. Jews who yearn faintly after Judaism come to Martin Buber only by way of Christian theologians: they do not start with *sh'ma yisrael,** and Buber without *sh'ma yisrael* as a premise is likely to be

---

*"Hear, O Israel," the Unitary Credo.

peculiarly misleading. We are interested in Buber because we are
flattered by the interest of Gentiles in him: the pangs of flattery throb
even in our self-discoveries. In America Exile has become a flatterer;
the fleshpots are spiritual. The reasons we do not Ingather are not
our material comforts, but our spiritual self-centeredness. Craving
flattery, we explore how to merit it, how to commit ourselves most
responsively. The Jewish community in America is obviously undistinguished, so far, in its religious achievements; but the astounding
fact is that we *define ourselves as a religious community*. This we do
ourselves; Gentiles of good will want to receive us mainly as repre-
sentatives of Mankind, not as a peculiar people. The sociological
explanations for our willingness to think of ourselves as a religious
community, though most of us profess to be agnostics at least, are
multiple, commonplace, accurate, well known—but irrelevant. Our
synagogues are empty: this too is irrelevant, because nowadays they
are only cathedrals, and we have always done without cathedrals.
But our conversations have become our synagogues. Our conversations have become liturgical. Even our professions of agnosticism
take a liturgical turn. Our sociologists measure not only our communal safety but our communal commitment, the degree of our dedication or falling-away. We talk to one another unremittingly, queru-
lously, feverishly, constantly, forever, stream after stream of Jewish
investigation. We translate Yiddish with the fury of lost love, we
publish translations of medieval Hebrew documents, we pour *piyyu-
tim* * into the air of every household. Even the enviers brood on the
propriety of their envy. Even those who crave flattery are disposed
to examine their lust. We have a fascination, not with what we are,
but with what we might become. We are not like Germany; we are
a good deal like an incipient Spain. Both ended in abattoir, but
Germany was nearly in vain. Germany and its language gave us
Moses Hess, Heine, Buber, Rosenzweig, Baeck—individuals, not a
culture or a willed peoplehood—and no literature. Spain was for a
time Jerusalem Displaced: psalms and songs came out of it. And
Jerusalem Displaced is what we mean when we say Yavneh.†

*Liturgical poetry of chiefly medieval composition.
†Yavneh was a small town where, with Roman permission after the fall of Jerusalem and
the destruction of the Temple, Rabbi Yohanan ben Zakkai and his students established

So we are not yet Ingathered; and perhaps our destiny in another place is history's reason: that America shall, for a while, become Yavneh. For a while: while the State consolidates itself against savagery. We in Diaspora are not meant by this to be insulated from the savagery: we are one people, and what happens in one part of our body is suffered in another part: when the temple is wounded, the heart slows. I do not mean that Jews in America are intended to be preserved while Jews in Israel bleed. What I mean is this: for the moment our two parts, Diaspora Israel and Jerusalem Israel, have between us the responsibility of a double reconstruction—the healers, the health-bringers, the safekeepers, in Jerusalem; the Aggadists,* the makers of literature, just now gathering strength in America. This is not to deny culture-making to the Land of Israel! The orchestras go forth; Agnon was and is and will be; painters proliferate; a poet of genius resides in the Land. Torah continues to come out of Zion, and what immensities of literary vision lie ahead is an enigma that dazzles: one does not preclude even a new Psalmist. All this is, for Israel, corollary to restoration.

For us in Diaspora cultural regeneration must be more modest: as Yiddish with all its glories, for instance, is nevertheless second to Hebrew. "Yavneh" is of course an impressionistic term, a metaphor suggesting renewal. The original Academy at Yavneh was founded after the destruction of the Temple: the new one in prospect coincides with the restoration of Zion. We are, after all, the first Diaspora in two millennia to exist simultaneously with the homeland: we are not used to it yet, we have not really taken it in, neither in America nor in Russia, and we do not yet know what the full consequence of this simultaneity can be. The informal liturgical culture rapidly burgeoning among American Jews is as much the result of the restoration of Israel as it is of the Holocaust. And yet it appears to have its own life, it is not merely an aftermath or backwash, it has an urge not to repeat or recapitulate, but to go forward—as at an earlier Yavneh Yohanan ben Zakkai plunged into the elaboration of

---

an academy. It was out of Yavneh that the definition of Jewish life as a community in exile was derived: learning as a substitute for homeland; learning as the instrument of redemption and restoration.

*Aggadah comprises the storytelling, imaginative elements in Talmud.

Aggadah and preserved Torah by augmenting it. It seems to me we are ready to rethink ourselves in America now: to preserve ourselves by a new culture-making.

Now you will say that this is a vast and stupid contradiction following all I have noted so far about the historic hopelessness of Diaspora culture. I have already remarked that "there are no major works of Jewish imaginative genius written in any Gentile language, sprung out of any Gentile culture." Then how, you will object, can there be a Yavneh in America, where all the Jews speak a Gentile language and breathe a Gentile culture? My answer is this: it can happen if the Jews of America learn to speak a new language appropriate to the task of a Yavneh.

This new language I will call, for shorthand purposes, New Yiddish. (If you stem from the Sephardic tradition, New Ladino will serve just as well.) Like old Yiddish, New Yiddish will be the language of a culture that is centrally Jewish in its concerns and thereby liturgical in nature. Like old Yiddish before its massacre by Hitler, New Yiddish will be the language of multitudes of Jews: spoken to Jews by Jews, written by Jews for Jews. And, most necessary of all, New Yiddish, like old Yiddish, will be in possession of a significant literature capable of every conceivable resonance. But since New Yiddish will be a Jewish language, the resonances will be mainly liturgical. This does not mean that all kinds of linguistic devices and techniques will not be applicable: a liturgical literature is as free as any other to develop in any mode. To speak for the moment only of the experience of old Yiddish: the Yiddish writer A. Tabatchnik reveals in an important essay that the opening-up of Yiddish poetry to modernist devices such as symbolism and impressionism not only did not obliterate the liturgical qualities of Yiddish, but in fact heightened them remarkably. There is nothing artistically confining about a liturgical literature: on the contrary, to include history is to include everything. It is the nonliturgical literatures that leave things out, that narrow themselves to minute sensuous perceptions, and commit huge indifferences. A liturgical literature has the configuration of the ram's horn*: you give your strength to the inch-hole and

*See footnote, p. 177.

the splendor spreads wide. A Jewish liturgical literature gives its strength to its peoplehood and the whole human note is heard everywhere, enlarged. The liturgical literature produced by New Yiddish may include a religious consciousness, but it will not generally be religious in any explicit sense: it will without question "passionately wallow in the human reality"; it will be touched by the Covenant. The human reality will ring through its novels and poems, though for a long time it will not be ripe enough for poetry; its first achievements will be mainly novels. These novels, the product of richly conscious literary artists, will utilize every innovative device, not excluding those now being tested in the novels of aesthetic paganism; but device will not be a self-rubbing Romantic end in itself, verbal experiment and permutation will be organic, as fingers are to the principle of the hand. Above all, the liturgical mode will itself induce new forms, will in fact *be* a new form; and beyond that, given the nature of liturgy, a *public* rather than a coterie form. Unlike the novels of aesthetic paganism, liturgical novels will be capable of genuine comic perception in contrast to the grotesqueries of despair that pass for jokes among our current Gnostics and aestheticians: compare, to see the point, the celestial *Joseph* comedies of a freely Judaized Thomas Mann with the narrow and precious inwardness of much of Barth, Barthelme, and Gass. Here I insert a warning to the trigger-happy: it is important not to confuse the liturgical novel with the catechistic novel, which is so delightful to both the Vatican and the lords of Soviet Socialist Realism. The liturgical novel, because of its special view of history, will hardly be able to avoid the dark side of the earth, or the knife of irony; the liturgical novel will not be didactic or prescriptive: on the contrary, it will be Aggadic, utterly freed to invention, discourse, parable, experiment, enlightenment, profundity, humanity. All this will be characteristic of the literature of New Yiddish. And it will characterize a new Yavneh preoccupied, not by Talmud proper, but by fresh Talmudic modes that, in our age, take the urgent forms of imaginative literature.

You will say: how can you command such a fantasy? How can you demand such a language? True, you might concede, if there *were* such a language it might produce such a literature. But who will invent this language, where will it be born? My answer is that I am speaking it now, you are hearing it now, this is the sound of its spoken prose. Furthermore, half the Jews alive today already speak it. Only 20 percent of us are Hebrew-speaking, but it is centuries now since Hebrew was anything other than the possession of a blessed minority. In the Diaspora we are condemned to our various vernaculars: even Rashi referred to French as *"bilshonenu,"* "in our language." The example of Yiddish is predominant. After all, it was not philological permutations that changed a fifteenth-century German dialect into Yiddish. The German that became Yiddish became *Jewish:* it became the instrument of our peoplehood on the European continent, and when a spectacular body of literature at last sprang out of it, it fulfilled itself as a Jewish language. I envision the same for the English of English-speaking Jews. Already English merits every condition of New Yiddish, with the vital exception of having a mature literature. But even now for Jews the English vernacular is on its way toward becoming Jewish; already there are traces (in the form of novels*) of a Jewish liturgical literature written in English. As for essays, there are dozens, and several actually contain, as in old Yiddish, numerous Hebrew words essential to their intent. And there already exists an adversary movement hostile to the language and culture of this incipient Yavneh: eminent Gentile intellectuals complain in print of "the rabbinical mind," "minority-group self-pity," "the New York intellectuals." Opposition is at least proof of reality.

When Jews poured Jewish ideas into the vessel of German they invented Yiddish. As we more and more pour not merely the Jewish sensibility, but the Jewish vision, into the vessel of English, we achieve the profoundest invention of all: a language for our need, our possibility, our overwhelming *idea.* If out of this new language we can produce a Yavneh for our regeneration within an alien culture, we will have made something worthwhile out of the American Diaspora, however long or short its duration. Besides, New Yiddish has a startling linguistic advantage over old Yiddish, which persecution pushed far from its geographic starting-point: New Yiddish can be understood by the Gentile culture around us. So we have a clear

---

*Among them, Saul Bellow's *Mr. Sammler's Planet.*

choice, to take up an opportunity or to reject it. We can do what the German Jews did, and what Isaac D'Israeli did—we can give ourselves over altogether to Gentile culture and be lost to history, becoming a vestige nation without a literature; or we can do what we have never before dared to do in a Diaspora language: make it our own, our own necessary instrument, understanding ourselves in it while being understood by everyone who cares to listen or read. If we make out of English a New Yiddish, then we can fashion a Yavneh not only for our own renewal but as a demonstration for our compatriots. From being envious apes we can become masters of our own civilization—and let those who want to call this "re-ghettoization," or similar pejoratives, look to their own destiny. We need not live like ants on the spine of the earth. In the conflict between the illuminations of liturgy and the occult darknesses of random aesthetics we need not go under: by bursting forth with a literature attentive to the implications of Covenant and Commandment—to the human reality—we can, even in America, try to be a holy people, and let the holiness shine for others in a Jewish language which is nevertheless generally accessible. We will not have to flatter or parody; we will not require flattery; we will develop Aggadah *bilshonenu*, in our own language, and build in Diaspora a permanent body of Jewish literature.

If we blow into the narrow end of the *shofar*,* we will be heard far. But if we choose to be Mankind rather than Jewish and blow into the wider part, we will not be heard at all; for us America will have been in vain.

---

*The ram's horn, an instrument blown at the New Year, is a liturgical symbol recalling the ram that substituted for Isaac.

Literature as Idol:
Harold Bloom

Over the last several years, little by little, progressively though gradually, it has come to me that the phrase "Jewish writer" may be what rhetoricians call an "oxymoron"—a pointed contradiction, in which one arm of the phrase clashes so profoundly with the other as to annihilate it. To say "Jewish writer," or "Jewish poet," or "Jewish artist" is—so it has begun to seem to me—to retell the tale of the Calico Cat and the Gingham Dog: when they have finished chewing each other over, there is nothing left.

Encountering the work of Harold Bloom tends to reinforce these still-shadowy views. Bloom, a professor at Yale (who in his own person is, in fact, the entire Department of Humanities), is a singular figure. Bred like the rest of his graduate-school generation on the New Criticism, he increasingly represents its antithesis—but no, not its antithesis after all, because a thesis can imagine its opposite, and Bloom is not so much opposite as other. Bloom represents instead a frame of mind and of reference, and a source of fantasying power, that the New Criticism could by no stretch of its position or fancy arrive at. At the age of forty-nine, he is already outside the recogniz-

Essay published in *Commentary*, January 1979.

able categories of American historical, psychological,* or textual literary criticism. The New Criticism, though it is by now more than thirty years since it *was* new, remains the model of literary text-analysis. Even when "psychology"—i.e., the writer's biography—is permitted once again to surround *explication de texte*, the habit of belief in the power of the text to mean its own meaning, which the student must pry out through word-by-word scrutiny, persists.

The New Critical formulation of how to read a page of literature was carried out against a background of nineteenth-century impressionistic "appreciation," which included not only the words of the poem, but speculations about the "mood" of the poet, with appropriate allusions to the poet's life, and often enough an account of the state of mind or spirit of the reader while under the mood-influence of the poem. The New Criticism, puritan and stringent, aimed to throw out everything that was extravagant or extraneous, everything smacking of "sensibility" or susceptibility, every deviation from biographical or psychological allegation. The idea was to look at the poem itself, rather than to generate metaphors about the poem.

The ideal of "the poem itself" has been with us for so long now, and is so bracing, that it is difficult to dislodge. Nevertheless, it is true that biography and psychology have begun to seep back into academic readings of texts, and some belletrists—one thinks immediately of William Gass—have even dared to revive the subjective style of impressionism, wherein the criticism of the text vies as a literary display with the text itself, and on a competitive level of virtuosity, even of "beauty."

The vice of the New Criticism was its pretense that the poem was a finished, sealed unit, as if nothing outside of the text could ever have mattered in the making of the poem; and further, it regarded the poem as a presence not simply to be experienced in the reading, but as an oracle to be studied and interpreted: the poem's real end was hermeneutic, its ideal state hermetic. The virtue of the New

---

*An instance of the Bloomian use of psychology: "I do not think that the psyche is a text, but I find it illuminating to discuss texts as though they were psyches, and in doing so I consciously follow the Kabbalists."

Criticism was a consequence of its vice—not only did it deny the opportunity, at least in theory, for displays of rivalrous writing ("beautiful" essays about "beautiful" poems), but in keeping out too much of the world, it also perforce kept out what was largely irrelevant to the poem and might, like a bumptious lodger with too much baggage, wreck the poem's furniture.

Into this devotedly swept and sanctified arena strode Bloom. Lacking verbal fancifulness, he was plainly no kin to the Gass school (a contemporary school of one or two, perhaps, but larger if one includes an army of literary ancestors, Virginia Woolf among them). He had little in common with the Trilling school of meticulous social understanding. He was overwhelmingly dissimilar from the early pure New Critics with their strict self-denials. He was not like any of these, yet somehow suggestive of each of them, and again light-years beyond the imaginings of all of them. Like Trilling and his students, Bloom made connections well out of the provincial text itself; like the New Critics, he paid fanatic homage to the real presence of palpable stanzas, lines, and phrases; like the most subjective and susceptible of poet-readers, he conceived of poetry-reading as a kind of poetry-writing, or rewriting. And still he resembled no one and nothing that had come before, because, though he stuck to *explication de texte* in the old way, he made connections outside of the text in a new way—and, besides, he raised the subjectivist mode of vying with the original to a higher pitch than ever before, while draining it of all self-indulgence. Meanwhile, the connections beyond "the poem itself" that he found were neither social nor psychobiographical; they were entirely new to American literary criticism; they were, in fact, theological.

The theology Bloom chose was obsessive, syncretic, but not at all random—Jewish Gnosticism (i.e., Kabbalah, or what Robert Alter has called "linguistic mysticism") strained through Freud, Nietzsche, Vico, and, of course, Gershom Scholem, whom Bloom sees as "a Miltonic figure." This theology-of-text became for Bloom a continuing invention through four books of prophetic evolution: *The Anxiety of Influence, A Map of Misreading, Kabbalah and Criticism, Poetry and Repression: Revisionism from Blake to Stevens*—volumes that reinforce one another even as they enlarge, through fresh illustrations, allusions, paradoxes, and widening sources, the arena of the Bloomian stride.

In a brief passage remarkable not only for its renewing the issue of Hellenism-versus-Hebraism as the central quarrel of the West, but also for its implicit claim that paganism—i.e., anti-Judaism—is the ultimate ground for the making of poetry, Bloom writes: "Vico understood, as almost no one has since, that the link between poetry and pagan theology was as close as the war between poetry and Hebrew-Christian theology was perpetual." And again: "Vico says that 'the true God' founded the Jewish religion 'on the prohibition of the divination on which all the gentile nations arose' "—this after Bloom has already made it clear that he agrees with Vico in equating the earliest poetry-makers with pagan diviners.

Now the New Criticism, while keeping clear of theology proper, had always had a soft spot for the Gentile sacral, and was never known for philo-Judaism (given its heroes and seers, Pound and Eliot), so in itself this equation of the origins of poetry with anti-Judaism would not have been enough to shake the academy. It was not simply in their seeking out a theological connection that Bloom's four volumes, each coming with astonishing speed on the heels of the one before, outraged one department of English after another, including his own at Yale. The real shock of Bloom was that he overturned what the academy had taken for granted for a good number of graduate-school generations: that if you analyze a poem closely enough, and with enough dogged attention to the inherent world of accessible allusion locked into every phrase, you will at length find out what the poem truly means. This New Critical premise had so much become received doctrine that it had, by now, entirely escaped questioning, and for the most recent graduate students it was there in a nameless way, like air or money: a heritage urged and used without contemplation, presumed to be both natural and permanent.

Bloom, then, came on this scene of unalterable precedent as a shatterer,* to show that the very critical medium that had seemed to

---

*Bloom, though the most provocative, is not the only successor-rebel in reaction against the New Critics. I here propose to leave the cupboard bare of the others, but for a

work so well, both for the assimilation of literature and for exchanging its terms, was incomplete and beside the point. "Few notions," Bloom observed,

> are more difficult to dispel than the "commonsensical" one that a poetic text is self-contained, that it has an ascertainable meaning or meanings without reference to other poetic texts. Something in nearly every reader wants to say: "*Here* is a poem and *there* is a meaning, and I am reasonably certain that the two can be brought together." Unfortunately, poems are not things but only words that refer to other words, and *those* words refer to still other words, and so on, into the deeply populated world of literary language. Any poem is an inter-poem, and any reading of a poem is an inter-reading. A poem is not writing, but *rewriting,* and though a strong poem is a fresh start, such a start is a starting-again.

"Such a start is a starting-again." This idea, original when applied to literature, is brilliantly borrowed from the history of religion. The "strong" poet is like Paul, or Mohammed, or the Buddha; as visionaries, these were all revisers, not innovators. All the varieties of Christianity and Islam are inconceivable without the God of the Jews, and all the varieties of Buddhism are inconceivable without their Hindu base of Atman and Brahma. Kabbalah, in turn, revises Scripture by making it up again through the expansion of its language. For Bloom, analogously, Milton becomes a kind of Moses, Wordsworth perhaps a Joshua, and Blake (in whom Bloom reads Milton) an Isaiah, or even the Psalmist. Bloom is interested in both Genesis, the Beginning, and in Beginning Again, to which Genesis is indispensable. He divides poets into "precursors" and "ephebes," or revisers; and he defines revision as purposeful misinterpretation, or "misprision." The "strong" poet, in Bloom's view, makes use of his precursor, and the "tropes" or telltale traces of the precursor can be detected in the latecomer-poet. Further, the underlying problem of poetry-making, according to Bloom, is that Milton and Words-

---

discussion of Bloom in conjunction with Northrop Frye, Paul de Man, Stanley E. Fish, Geoffrey Hartman, J. Hillis Miller, Angus Fletcher, and—among influential foreigners —Jacques Derrida and Roland Barthes, see Irene H. Chayes, "Revisionist Literary Criticism," *Commentary,* April 1976.

worth, Emerson and Whitman have already appeared and played their notes of grandeur; and the grandeur remains. Any poet born afterward is born into Miltonic and Emersonian shadows and illuminations; any poet born afterward is born into the condition of "belatedness," which he fights by wresting not the flame of the precursor, which cannot be taken, but the power to remake the flame. Invention is replaced by interpretation.

> The meaning of a poem can only be another poem.
>
>   .   .   .
>
> Every strong poem, at least since Petrarch, has known implicitly what Nietzsche taught us to know explicitly: that there is only interpretation, and that every interpretation answers an earlier interpretation, and then must yield to a later one.
>
>   .   .   .
>
> Poets' misinterpretations or poems are more drastic than critics' misinterpretations or criticism, but this is only a difference in degree and not at all in kind. There are no interpretations but only misinterpretations, and so all criticism is prose poetry.

In the Bloomian scheme, interpretation is a process nearly analogous to a process in physics; to describe and summarize it, Bloom has developed a kind of physics of rhetoric, a terminology concisely and meticulously calculated to account for each stage in the conduct of "belatedness."

> We are studying a kind of labor that has its own latent principles, principles that can be uncovered and taught systematically.

Poems are, Bloom says, *"acts of reading"* (the emphasis is Bloom's own), and the description of how a poem comes into being out of its reading of an earlier poem, i.e., out of its own "swerving" from the influence of a powerful precursor-poem, Bloom names a "dialectic of revisionism." It would be unfair to try to paraphrase or condense Bloom's exposition of his "principles"; each of his four theoretical books is, in his own sense, a retelling or reinterpretation or revision of his starting insight, and each of the later three is a starting-again, a reinvigoration of the earliest. *Kaballah and Criticism,* for instance, restates the Bloomian concern in still another dress, this time the dress of Cordovera and Luria. The ingenuity of the restate-

ments themselves testify to Bloom's artistic intelligence, his supernal
—even infernal—erudition, his architectural powers, both massive
and rococo, his quick appetite for telling and then telling again in
fresh garb. The tapestry is always changing, the critical fabrication
is always new; but the obsessive narrative of the Bloomian drama
beats unflaggingly below—the drama of giants who once walked the
earth, and turned "originality" into an acrobatic labor for those who
came after. Through misreadings, evasions, defenses, repressions, all
the canny devices of "misprision" under the pressure of "influence,"
the strong newcomer at last converts the materials of the precursor
into substitute, sometimes antithetical, matter. It is a story of purga-
tion and renewal. Above all, it is a story of a contest for power, in
which the competitors struggle for the possession of context;
in which context *is* contest. And finally, it is a mode of Gnosticism,
wherein, through the toil of attaining knowledge of the Sublime
Maker, the searcher himself *becomes* that Maker.

Through all of this, Bloom has invented, and continues to invent,
a vocabulary of concision, which he begins now to call a "shorthand." Here, for instance, is his "mapping" of "the pattern of ratios"
in Whitman's *Song of Myself:*

Sections:	1– 6	*Clinamen,* irony of presence and absence
	7–27	*Tessera,* synecdoche of part for whole
	28–30	*Kenosis,* metonymy of emptying out
	31–38	*Daemonization,* hyperbole of high and low
	39–49	*Askesis,* metaphor of inside vs. outside
	50–52	*Apophrades,* metalepsis reversing early and late

These inventions are later augmented by Kabbalistic terminology,
as well as by vocabulary borrowings taken from Freud—without,
however, subscribing in any way seriously to the Freudian scheme.
(In fact, he sees Freud as still another interesting datum of revisionist
criticism.) Revisionism, Bloom explains, "as a word and as a notion
contains the triad of re-seeing, re-esteeming, and re-aiming, which
in Kabbalistic terms becomes the triad of contraction, breaking-of-
the-vessels, and restitution, and in poetic terms the triad of limita-
tion, substitution, and representation."

It is possible that this fabricated and borrowed terminology may put off a reader of poetry as easily as a medical textbook may put off a philosopher; and just as anatomical taxonomy seems far from philosophy (though the philosopher himself may be no more than a sausage filled with all those named parts), so does the vocabulary Bloom has devised seem far from "normal" criticism, and still farther from poetry itself. Listed nakedly, the Bloomian glossary has the ring of engineers' shoptalk. But this is to miss—because of the smoke it gives out—a chance of sighting the burning bush. The glossary is the girandole—the scaffolding out of which the Bloomian fireworks erupt. And what the fiery wheel writes on the sky is, after all, a single idea: discontinuity. What Bloom means by "revisionism" is a breaking off with the precursor; a violation of what has been transmitted; a deliberate offense against the given, against the hallowed; an unhallowing of the old great gods; the usurpation of an inheritance by the inheritor himself; displacement. Above all, the theft of power. These themes—or, rather, this chorus chanting a uniform theme—Bloom expresses through a nervy prowess accompanied by all the voices of inspiration that a capacious and daring mind, richly packed, can bring to bear on a ruling fascination. The jeweled diversity of Bloom's expanding and self-paraphrasing glossary is the consequence of an intoxication with the beauty and persuasiveness of the bewitchment it serves—a bewitchment by force, power, seizure, rupture; the dream of storming, looting, and renovating heaven.

Bloom's appropriation, in the third book of the series, not simply of Kabbalistic terminology, but, going beyond analogy and metaphor, of Kabbalahlike vaultings of imagination in applying that terminology, has begun, it would seem, to win him a "Jewish" reputation. Not that Bloom, with his celebrated command of the Romantics, is perceived as a Jewish critic; but his unprecedented incursions into Hebrew—what other American critic is at home with *shevirat ha-kelim?*—has at least suggested that Jewish sources imply Jewish insights—or, if not that, then surely a Jewish "stance."

Professor Alvin Rosenfeld, for instance, in an essay in *The Southern Review* called "Notes on the Antithetical Criticism of Harold Bloom," points out that the "strain of revisionary defiance" represented by Kabbalah "was greatly feared by the rabbis, who correctly understood its antinomian impulses. For to the Gnostic, knowledge is always knowledge of origins, ultimately *a rival claim* upon origins, which in human terms inevitably means an attempt to transform man into God"—and yet, having shown in two sentences how Bloom jumps past Jewish claims, Rosenfeld ends by asking Bloom to be more "balanced," to stress "preservation" and "continuation" as much as "rebellion" and "loss." Rosenfeld concludes: "If [Bloom] can now adjust his critical stance in a way that will allow for restitution [through "balance"], a new power may be his." But this is to shout "Go West!" to a comet flying eastward. The "equilibrium," the "vitalizing tension . . . between . . . tradition and innovation" that Rosenfeld calls for in Bloom, is precisely what Bloom, all along the way, has schemed to destroy. Rosenfeld notes:

> Bloom's devotion to the Hebrew Bible has often been expressed in his writings. For instance, in *A Map of Misreading*, he identifies himself "as a teacher of literature who prefers the morality of the Hebrew Bible to that of Homer, indeed who prefers the Bible aesthetically to Homer . . ." If present signs hold, one expects to see more, not less, emphasis on biblical thinking and exegesis in his work.

This would appear to promise a stronger Jewish element to come, stronger even, and possibly more central, than Bloom's Kabbalistic concerns—but the fact is opposite. Kabbalah is Gnosticism in Jewish dress; still, it is not the Jewish dress that Bloom is more and more attracted by—it is the naked Gnosticism. To "prefer the morality of the Hebrew Bible to that of Homer" is not to make a choice at all —there is no morality, of the kind Bloom means, in Homer. And simply to speculate whether one might prefer the Bible "aesthetically" to Homer is itself, of course, already to have chosen the Greek way: the Jewish way, confronting Torah, does not offer such a choice.

If, then, one intends to reflect on Bloom's work from a Jewish point of view, it is necessary to take him at his Gnostic word when he utters it. ("In the beginning was the Word, and the Word was with God, and the Word was God.") And if one means to find in Bloom a Jewish utterance, it must be in the utterance itself, not in the prospect or the hope of an utterance. The *fait accompli* of Bloom's work judges the Jewish Bloom. If Bloom, with Vico, equates the origins of poetry with pagan divination—i.e., with anti-Judaism—and is persuaded of the "perpetual war" between poetry and Judaism, then it is inescapable that Bloom, in choosing poetry, also chooses anti-Judaism. Bloom's gifts, and the structures that derive from them, yield a clue to what those awesome architectural masters who devised the cathedrals must have been like; but the cathedrals were wanting, one might say, in Jewish content.

For myself, I believe Bloom to be engaged in the erection of what can fairly be called an artistic anti-Judaism. This does not place him with Pound and Eliot, who are simply anti-Semitic in the commonplace sense, nor yet with the New Critics, whose austere faculty for "tradition" was confined to Christianity. Bloom is neither anti-Jewish nor, as his incursions into Kabbalah prove, parochial in the usual way of English-speaking literary intellectuals. Bloom is no ordinary literary intellectual. Within the bowels of the Bloomian structure there lives, below all, the religious imagination: sibylline, vatic, divinatory—in short, everything that the Sinaitic force, bent on turning away from god-proliferation, denies. Bloom's four theorizing volumes vault beyond criticism toward their destination—which is a long theophanous prose-poem, a rationalized version of Blake's heroic Prophetic Books. Not unlike Blake, Bloom means to stand as a vast and subtle system-maker, an interrupter of expectations, a subverter of predictability—the writer, via misprision, of a new Scripture based on discontinuity of tradition. In this he is pure Kabbalist. Contrary to Jesus, whom the Gospels report to have declared, "Till heaven and earth pass, one jot or one tittle shall in no wise pass from the law" (a statement vividly anti-misprision, and one that those less stiff-necked interpreters, the rabbis of the Talmud who were Jesus's contemporaries, never made), Bloom invents subversion after subversion, until he comes at last to the job of idol-making.

Idol-making: I posit this not figuratively, not metaphorically, not what Bloom might call "metaleptically," but literally. And I choose for Bloom the more drastic term "idol-maker" over "idolator" because the idolator, having no self-consciousness, is a kind of innocent conformist. The idol-maker, by contrast, has the highest self-consciousness of all, and should be prepared philosophically, con-

scientiously, for the consequences of the pervasive idolatry in which
he has, in effect, a vested interest.

Here, lifted out of the astonishing little volume called *Kabbalah
and Criticism,* is a severe (a favorite adjective of Bloom's) representation of an idol:

> What then does an idol create? Alas, an idol *has* nothing, and *creates*
> nothing. Its presence is a promise, part of the substance of things
> hoped for, the evidence of things not seen. Its unity is in the good will
> of its worshiper.

Now a confession. Following one of Bloom's techniques in his
reading of Nietzsche and Freud, I have substituted one word for
another. Bloom wrote "poem," not "idol"; "reader," not "worshiper." What turns out to be an adeptly expressive description of
an idol is also, for Bloom, a useful description of a poem.

The single most useful, and possibly the most usefully succinct,
description of a Jew—as defined "theologically"—can best be rendered negatively: a Jew is someone who shuns idols, who least of all
would wish to become like Terach, the maker of idols. A Jew—so
Jews are taught to think—is like Abraham, who sees through idols.
But Bloom is both: he is both Terach and Abraham.* He is a system-
builder who is aware that a closed, internalized system is an idol, and
that an idol, without power in itself, is nevertheless a perilous, indeed
a sinister, taint in the world.

Before I offer the necessary explanations for these views, we
should, I think, reach a sophisticated understanding of idols. An idol
is obviously not only a little wooden graven image standing in the
mud. Nor is an idol merely a false idea. An idol can be, and usually
is, remarkably made, wonderfully persuasive in its parts, and in its
parts often enough wonderfully true. An idol can have, above all, a

---

*According to a *midrash,* Terach was a maker and seller of idols. One day he left the boy
Abraham to watch the shop. After remonstrating with one customer after another,
Abraham picked up an ax and smashed all the idols but one—the biggest. When Terach
returned, he angrily asked for an explanation. Abraham replied: "Father, the idols were
hungry, and I brought them food. But the big god seized your ax, killed the other gods,
and ate all the food himself." "Abram," said Terach, "you are mocking me. You know
well that idols can neither move, nor eat, nor perform any act." Abraham said: "Father,
let your ears hear what your tongue speaks." *The Rabbis' Bible* (Behrman House, 1966).

psychological realism that is especially persuasive and seductive. And beyond this, an idol can be seen to *work*. (To illustrate most reductively: the Egyptian cat god tells us a great deal about cats, and something also about the mind of the Egyptian who worshiped it, and even more about the ingeniously imaginative mind that created it. Furthermore, it did its job in its time as a working divinity: it demanded awe and accommodation.)

The chief characteristic of any idol is that it is a system sufficient in itself. It leads back only to itself. It is indifferent to the world and to humanity. Like a toy or like a doll—which, in fact, is what an idol is—it lures human beings to copy it, to become like it. It dehumanizes. When we see a little girl who is dressed up too carefully in starched flounces and ribbons and is admonished not to run in the dirt, we often say, "She looks like a little doll." And that is what she has been made into: the inert doll has become the model for the human child, dead matter rules the quick. That dead matter will rule the quick is the single law of idolatry.* Scripture tells us that the human being is made in the image of God, and since we do not know how to adumbrate God, we remain as free, as unpredictable, as unfated in our aspirations as quicksilver. But when we make ourselves into the image of an image, no matter how flexible the imagination of aspiration, we are bound, limited, determined, constrained; we cannot escape the given lineaments, and no matter how multitudinous are the avenues open to us, they all come, as in a maze, to a single exit.

A second important characteristic of any idol is that it is always assumed to pre-exist the worshiper.† An idol always has the authority of an ancestor or a precursor, even if it has just come fresh from

---

*This law of idolatry is again and again expressed with great precision by Bloom. Writing on the "revisionary ratio" he names "*Apophrades*, or The Return of the Dead," Bloom reflects, "But the strong dead return, in poems as in our lives, and they do not come back without darkening the living. . . . The precursors flood us, and our imaginations can die by drowning in them, but no imaginative life is possible if such inundation is wholly evaded."

†The *midrash* mentioned earlier also has Abraham asking the age of a man who has come to buy an idol to protect his house. "I am fifty years old," says the customer, "and have been a soldier for more than thirty years." "You are fifty," Abraham scoffs, "whereas this idol was carved by my father only last week. And though you are a seasoned warrior, you ask protection from it!"

the maker's carpentry bench or brain-shop. In Rome, a just-hacked-out model of Venus has all the authority of a seven-hundred-year-old shrine to Astarte, because both rest on the precursor-goddess, the moon, which rules the tides of both sea and menstruation. Every idol is by nature an ideal, an image-known-before. Every idol is a precursor, and every idolator is a Johnny-come-lately, absorbing old news to refurbish for his instant needs.

A third characteristic of any idol is that, because it is inert, it cannot imagine history. It is always the same, no matter how multiform its appearances. It cannot create or alter history. When the God of the Jews said to Abraham, *lech l'cha*, Go forth, history was profoundly made, and continues to be made; the words *lech l'cha*, first heard five thousand years ago, at this moment agitate presidents, prime ministers, oil sheikhs, hawks and doves. But an idol, which cannot generate history, can be altered by it: from-the-sublime-to-the-ridiculous is the rule of every idol. Hadrian was a ferocious oppressor of Jews, and declared himself a god to be worshiped in statuary of mammoth beauty. Digging in the sand for old coins a few years ago, an American tourist in Israel drew up the great curly bronze head of the Emperor. He, the god, is reduced to curio.

A fourth characteristic of any idol is perhaps the most universally repugnant, because it demonstrates how the power of the (power-less) idol—i.e., the powerful imaginations of its devotees—can root out human pity. From this uniquely Jewish observation flows the Second Commandment. The Commandment against idols is above all a Commandment against victimization, and in behalf of pity. Pity, after all, is not "felt," as if by instinct or reflex. Pity is taught; and what teaches it is the stricture against idols. Every idol is a shadow of Moloch, demanding human flesh to feed on. The deeper the devotion to the idol, the more pitiless in tossing it its meal will be the devotee. Moloch springs up wherever the Second Commandment is silenced. In the absence of the Second Commandment, the hunt for victims begins. The Second Commandment is more explicit than the Sixth, which tells us simply that we must not kill; the Second Commandment tells us we must resist especially that killing which serves our belief. In this sense, there are no innocent idols. Every idol suppresses human pity; that is what it is made for. When art is put in competition, like a god, with the Creator, it too is turned into an idol; one has only to recall the playing of Mozart at the gates of Auschwitz to see how the muses can serve Moloch—the muses, like the idols they are, have no moral substance or tradition. What the Second Commandment, in its teaching against victimization and in behalf of pity, also teaches, is the fear of godhood. And the "fear of godhood," Bloom unequivocally writes, "is a fear of poetic strength, for what the ephebe enters upon, when he begins his life cycle as a poet, is in every sense a process of divination." The strivings of divination—i.e., of God-competition—lead away from the Second Commandment, ultimately contradict it, and crush the capacity for pity.

These four essential characteristics of idolatry—that an idol can lead only to itself and has no meaning other than itself; that an idol always has an ideal precursor on which to model its form; that an idol can have no connection to human deed and human history-making; that an idol crushes pity—these are also the characteristics that, in Bloom's scheme, mark the way of poems. Bloom tells us that every poem born into the world is, so to speak, the consequence of an idolatry, and has been made in the image of an older poem, a precursor-poem at whose feet the new poem has worshiped. And just as an idolator takes away from his contemplation of the idol whatever his psychological hungers require, so does the new poem take from the older poem whatever *it* needs for its life. Moreover, even when Bloom's structures, unlike the actual Molochs of ancient, recent, and current history, appear to be socially harmless and gossamer, they nevertheless dream of a great swallowing and devouring. Even Bloom's superficially bloodless "interpretation" turns out to be annihilation. (Cf., once again, *kenosis* and *shevirat ha-kelim.*) The sacrificial victim is endemic to the Bloomian system, and links it ineluctably with the pagan sacral.

So far I have been describing Bloom as Terach, the maker of idols. But I said earlier that he is also Abraham, who sees through the hollowness and human uselessness of idols. Like Abraham, Bloom recognizes that Terach is courting perversity, that Terach in his busy shop has put himself in competition with the Creator, luring away customers by means of loss leaders, that Terach refuses to accept Creation as given, and has set up counter-realities in the form of instant though illusory gratifications—namely, immediate answers to riddles. The answers may or may not be lies. Often enough the answer an idol gives is a workable answer. Doubtless fertility goddesses have been as responsible for as many births as any current fertility drug manufactured by Upjohn or Lederle. But they are exceptionally poor at urging the moral life, because to understand the moral life, one must know how to pay attention to, and judge, history—and at this idols are no good at all.

In a brief passage in his breathtaking albeit iconolatrous book *The Anxiety of Influence,* Bloom acknowledges how idols and icons—i.e., poems—are no good at all in urging the moral life. It seems to me this passage is the most significant commentary on Bloom's system; in it he becomes Abraham and chases all the customers out of Terach's shop. Above all, it is a statement that calls into question the entire volume that surrounds it, and all the subsequent volumes:

> If the imagination's gift comes necessarily from the perversity of the spirit, then the living labyrinth of literature is built upon the ruin of every impulse most generous in us. So apparently it is and must be —we are wrong to have founded a humanism directly upon literature itself, and the phrase "humane letters" is an oxymoron. . . . The strong imagination comes to its painful birth through savagery and misrepresentation. The only humane virtue we can hope to teach through a more advanced study of literature than we have now is the social virtue of detachment from one's own imagination, recognizing always that such detachment made absolute destroys any individual imagination.

"The social virtue of detachment from one's own imagination"— this splendidly humane sequence, set in a paragraph of clarified self-comprehension, expresses precisely the meaning of the Second Commandment. The "strong imagination," born out of a "savagery and misrepresentation" neither yoked nor undone by the Second Commandment, created the earliest Moloch, the furnace-god, and encouraged mothers to throw their babies into the fire. The savagery is plain; the misrepresentation is the general conviction that throwing children into furnaces is a social good. Since, as we have seen, idols always imitate their precursor-ideals, it can be no surprise that the post-Enlightenment Moloch of the Nazis reproduced the very Moloch recounted in the Bible—not simply in the furnace (here "misprision" was introduced in the form of technological substitutions, perhaps), but also in the ideal of a service to society.

Based on Bloomian premises, it comes down to this: no Jew may be idolator or idol-maker; poems are the products of "strong imaginations," and poets are dangerously strong imaginers, vampirishly living on the blood of earlier imaginers, from Moloch to Moloch; no Jew ought to be a poet.

One might want to intervene here with the reasonable reflection that "Tintern Abbey" is not yet Moloch. Quite. But push, push "Tintern Abbey" a little farther, and then a little farther, push the strong imagination of Nature a little farther, and one arrives finally at Moloch. "Tintern Abbey" assumes that the poet, in contemplating his own mind and seeking his own mood, inspired by a benign landscape, will be "well pleased to recognise / In nature and the language of the sense / . . . [the] soul / Of all my moral being." But the ecstatic capacity, unreined, breeds a license to uncover not only joy, love, and virtue, but a demon. The soul's license to express everything upon the bosom of a Nature perceived as holy can beget the unholy expression of savagery. It is not a new observation that the precursors of the Hitler Youth movement were the *Wandervögel,* young madcap bands and bards who wandered the German landscape looking for a brooding moodiness to inspire original feeling.

Still another passage from *The Anxiety of Influence* (this one on Terach's side) introduces in detail one of the ingenious terms of Bloom's special analytic vocabulary:

> *Kenosis,* or "emptying," at once an "undoing" and an "isolating" movement of the imagination. I take *kenosis* from St. Paul's account of Christ "humbling" himself from God to man. In strong poets, the *kenosis* is a revisionary act in which an "emptying" or "ebbing" takes place *in relation to the precursor.* This "emptying" is a liberating discontinuity, and makes possible a kind of poem that a simple repetition of the precursor's afflatus or godhood could not allow. "Undoing" the precursor's strength *in oneself* serves also to "isolate" the self from the precursor's stance. . . .

Historically, morally, theologically, one cannot be a Jew and stand by this passage.

To recapitulate the idea-germ that exploded into the brilliant hugeness and huge brilliance of the Bloomian system of analysis: a recognition that all of us are disconsolate latecomers; that we are envious and frustrated inheritors; that there have been giants on the earth before us; and what therefore shall we puny latecomers do, how shall we steal the fire that the great ones before us, our fortunate Promethean precursors, have already used up for their own imaginings? The answer comes through modes of discontinuity—*kenosis*, in the term Bloom borrows from Saint Paul, and *shevirat ha-kelim*, the "breaking of the vessels," in the term he borrows from Kabbalah. But the discontinuity does not imply iconoclasm, the Abrahamitic shattering of the idol. On the contrary: it means reinvigorating the ideal of the idol in a new vessel, as Astarte begets Venus, as Rome, through Venus, feels itself possessed by its own goddess.

The notion of "'undoing' the precursor's strength" has no validity in normative Judaism. Jewish liturgy, for instance, posits just the opposite; it posits *recapturing without revision* the precursor's stance and strength when it iterates "our God, and God of our fathers, God of Abraham, Isaac, and Jacob." Nearly every congeries of Jewish thought is utterly set against the idea of displacing the precursor. "Torah" includes the meanings of *tradition* and *transmittal* together. Although mainstream Judaism rejected the Karaites in favor of an interpretive mode, interpretation never came to stand for disjunction, displacement, ebbing-out, isolation, swerving, deviation, substitution, revisionism. Transmittal signifies the carrying-over of the original strength, the primal monotheistic insight, the force of which drowns out competing power systems. That is what is meant by the recital in the Passover Haggadah, "We ourselves went out from Egypt, and not only our ancestors," and that is what is meant by the *midrash* that declares, "All generations stood together at Sinai," including present and future generations. In Jewish thought there *are* no latecomers.

Consequently the whole notion of "modernism" is, under the illumination of Torah, at best a triviality and for the most part an irrelevance. Modernism has little to do with real chronology, except insofar as it means to dynamite the continuum. Modernism denotes discontinuity: a radical alteration of modes of consciousness. Modernism, perforce, concerns itself with the problem of "belatedness." But modernism and belatedness are notions foreign and irrelevant to the apperceptions of Judaism. Modernism and belatedness induce worry about being condemned to repeat, and therefore anxiously look to break the bond with the old and make over, using the old as the governing standard—or influence—from which to learn deviation and substitution. The mainstream Jewish sense does not regard a hope to recapture the strength, unmediated, of Abraham and Moses as a condemnation. Quite the opposite. In the Jewish view, it is only through such recapture and emulation of the precursor's stance, unrevised, that life can be nourished, that the gift of the Creator can be received, praised, and fulfilled. Jewish thought makes much of its anti-antinomian precursors as given, and lacks both the will and the authority to undo or humble or displace them, least of all to subject them to purposeful misprision. A scribe with the Torah under his hand will live a stringent life in order not to violate a single letter. There is no competition with the text, no power struggle with the original, no envy of the Creator. The aim, instead, is to reproduce a purely transmitted inheritance, free of substitution or incarnation.

But the idol-maker envies the Creator, hopes to compete with the Creator, and schemes to invent a substitute for the Creator; and thereby becomes satanic and ingrown in the search and research that is meant to prise open the shells holding the divine powers. This is the work of "misprision," the chief Bloomian word. Misprision is to Bloom what Satan is to Milton. It is not an accident that the term —before Bloom exercises revisionary misprision upon it—denotes "felony," "wrongdoing," "violation." These definitions proffer a critical judgment of reality; they point, simply, to an Abrahamitic or, better yet, Sinaitic "shalt not." But when Bloom utters "misprision," it is the spirit of Terach that orders it.

Bloom, then, is a struggler between Terach and Abraham. He knows, mutedly, what Abraham knows, but he wants, vociferously, what Terach wants. "To revise is not to fulfill," he is heard to murmur in *Poetry and Repression,* in a voice transfixed by Jewish transmittal. But in all four Prophetic Books one hears, far louder than that, Terach's transfiguring chant: *clinamen, tessera, kenosis, daemonization, askesis, apophrades*. And in the end it is Terach who chiefly claims Bloom. Like Terach, like Freud, like Marx, like the Gnostics, like the classical Christian theologians who are the inheritors of the Gnostics, like the Kabbalists and the hasidim who are similarly the inheritors of the Gnostics, like all of these, the Bloomian scheme of misprision of the precursor is tainted by a variety of idol-making.

Bloom, giving us Vico's view in quotation, plainly gives his own: "The making that is poetry is god-making, and even the ephebe or starting-poet is as much demon as man or woman." An idol, the product of the demonic *yetzer ha-ra,* * is an internalized system that allows no escape from its terms; and if one tries to escape, the escape itself is subject to interpretation as being predictable within the system. All the avenues of a maze, both the traps and the solutions, belong to the scheme of the maze.

Or think instead of a great crystal globe, perilously delicate yet enduring, with a thousand complex working parts visible within, the parts often exceedingly ingenious and the whole a radiant bauble: an entire man-made world beautiful, above all rational, and complete in itself. But it draws one to intellectual slavery. It signifies bondage to the wheel of self-sufficient idolatry.

The most enduring configurations of Jewish religious idiom are not unfamiliar with Bloom's inventions; they were considered and discarded as long ago as Abraham, and again in Egypt, and again in confrontation with the Hellenizers, and now again in confrontation with so-called modernism, which is only Gnostic syncretism refurbished.

Literature, one should have the courage to reflect, is an idol. We are safe with it when we let the child-part of our minds play with poems and stories as with a pack of dolls; then the role of imaginative literature is only trivial. But what Bloom, anxiously influenced, has done, is to contrive a system of magic set in rational psychological

---

*The impulse toward evil, related also to the creative capacity; the desire to compete with the Creator in ordering being and reality.

terms, and requiring (as the Jewish religious idiom never will) a mediator. For Freud the mediator or medium is the unconscious. For Bloom the mediator or medium is the precursor-poem. But for each, imagination has devised an inexorable, self-sufficient, self-contained magic system, the most magical aspect of which is the illusion of the superbly rational.

Bloom himself has seen that he began as a desperately serious critic of literature and ended as one inflamed by Cordovero and Luria. Perhaps the trouble—it is every writer's trouble—is that he should not have been serious about literature in the first place; seriousness about an idol leads to the misprision that is violation. As Bloom the system-maker, in book after book, more and more recognizes that what he has invented is magic, i.e., "practical Kabbalah," he turns to the magic system of the actual and historic Kabbalah for confirmation. It is as if Harold Bloom suddenly woke up one morning to discover that he had concocted Kabbalah on his own; only it was already *there.* That is like Venus opening her eyes in a dawning Rome to learn that she is Astarte reborn. Astarte will always be reinvented. In the absence of the Second Commandment idolatry will always be reconstituted—if not in wood or stone, then in philosophical or political concept; if not in philosophical or political concept, then in literature.

Through his placing the critic in competition with the creator, Bloom is often regarded as having committed an act of artistic hubris; but those who look askance at Bloom's belief that the poem's interpretation is as much the poem's life as the "original" ought to be more troubled by the hubris of the poet, which the whole body of Bloom's work strives to emphasize and even enlarge. The Bloomian transmutation of critic into poet, after all, is not so innovative as it might seem; it is no news that a critic may feel himself to be in a clandestine contest with the creative artist by understanding himself to be still another creative artist. It is true that Bloom has significantly altered the meaning of what it is to be "original"; but whether or not his conclusions are found to be attractive or persuasive, what he has made his originals *do* can stop the breath. He has vouchsafed them the temerity to usurp the Throne of Heaven.

Now none of this is to accuse or blame Bloom's position because it is on the side of this grandest usurpation of all. The Second Commandment runs against the grain of our social nature, indeed against human imagination. To observe it is improbable, perhaps impossible; perhaps it has never been, and never will be, wholly observed. But the Second Commandment is nevertheless expressive of one of the essential ideals of Judaism, and like most of the essential ideals of Judaism—consider in this light the institution of the Sabbath—it is uniquely antithetical to the practices and premises of the pre-Judaic and non-Judaic world. In short, it is the Jewish idiom— with regard to art as well as other matters—that is in its deepest strain dissenting, contradictory, frequently irreconcilable, and for Bloom and others to think of his system as "antithetical" is a sizable mistake. What is antithetical goes against the grain of the world at large, while to work at idol-making is not only not to go against the world's grain, but to consort with it in the most ancient, intimate, sibylline, and Delphic way. Bloom stands for the most part as defense counselor for those eternally usurping diviners against whom Zechariah inveighed: "For the idols have spoken vanity, and the diviners have seen a lie, and have told false dreams; they comfort in vain."

But if there *can* be such a chimera as a "Jewish writer," it must be the kind of sphinx or gryphon (part one thing, part another) Bloom himself is, sometimes purifying like Abraham, more often conjuring like Terach, and always knowing that the two are icily, elegiacally, at war. Bloom as Terach: "The Kabbalists read and interpreted with excessive audacity and extravagance; they knew that the true poem is the critic's mind, or as Emerson says, the true ship is the shipbuilder." Bloom as Abraham: "The Talmud warns against reading Scripture by so inclined a light that the text reveals chiefly the shape of your own countenance."

In an essay called "The Sorrows of American-Jewish Poetry," Bloom writes: "There is no recovery of the covenant, of the Law, without confronting again, in all deep tribulation, the God of the Fathers, Who is beyond image as He is beyond personality, and Who can be met only by somehow again walking His Way."

These words, I think, constitute still another call for misprision; but there is no way they can speak against themselves, or be creatively misread. The recovery of Covenant can be attained only in the living-out of the living Covenant; never among the shamanistic toys of literature.

Alas, like all the others, we drift toward the shamans and their toys.

The Riddle of the Ordinary

Though we all claim to be monotheists, there is one rather ordinary way in which we are all also dualists: we all divide the world into the Ordinary and the Extraordinary. This is undoubtedly the most natural division the mind is subject to—plain and fancy, simple and recondite, commonplace and awesome, usual and unusual, credible and incredible, quotidian and intrusive, natural and unnatural, regular and irregular, boring and rhapsodic, secular and sacred, profane and holy: however the distinction is characterized, there is no human being who does not, in his own everydayness, feel the difference between the Ordinary and the Extraordinary.

The Extraordinary is easy. And the more extraordinary the Extraordinary is, the easier it is: "easy" in the sense that we can almost always recognize it. There is no one who does not know when something special is happening: the high, terrifying, tragic, and ecstatic moments are unmistakable in any life. Of course the Extraordinary can sometimes be a changeling, and can make its appearance in the cradle of the Ordinary; and then it is not until long afterward that we become aware of how the visitation was not, after all, an ordinary one. But by and large the difference between special times

---

Essay published in *Moment*, July/August 1975.

and ordinary moments is perfectly clear, and we are never in any doubt about which are the extraordinary ones.

How do we respond to the Extraordinary? This too is easy: by paying attention to it. The Extraordinary is so powerful that it commands from us a redundancy, a repetition of itself: it seizes us so undividedly, it declares itself so dazzlingly or killingly, it is so deafening with its LOOK! SEE! NOTICE! PAY ATTENTION!, that the only answer we can give is to look, see, notice, and pay attention. The Extraordinary sets its own terms for its reception, and its terms are inescapable. The Extraordinary does not let you shrug your shoulders and walk away.

But the Ordinary is a much harder case. In the first place, by making itself so noticeable—it is around us all the time—the Ordinary has got itself in a bad fix with us: we hardly ever notice it. The Ordinary, simply by *being* so ordinary, tends to make us ignorant or neglectful; when something does not insist on being noticed, when we aren't grabbed by the collar or struck on the skull by a presence or an event, we take for granted the very things that most deserve our gratitude.

And this is the chief vein and deepest point concerning the Ordinary: that it *does* deserve our gratitude. The Ordinary lets us live out our humanity; it doesn't scare us, it doesn't excite us, it doesn't distract us—it brings us the safe return of the school bus every day, it lets us eat one meal after another, put one foot in front of the other. In short, it is equal to the earth's provisions; it grants us life, continuity, the leisure to recognize who and what we are, and who and what our fellows are, these creatures who live out their everydayness side by side with us in their own unextraordinary ways. Ordinariness can be defined as a breathing-space: the breathing-space between getting born and dying, perhaps; or else the breathing-space between rapture and rapture; or, more usually, the breathing-space between one disaster and the next. Ordinariness is sometimes the *status quo*, sometimes the slow, unseen movement of a subtle but ineluctable cycle, like a ride on the hour hand of the clock; in any case the Ordinary is above all *what is expected.*

And what is expected is not often thought of as a gift.

The second thing that ought to be said about the Ordinary is that

it is sometimes extraordinarily dangerous to notice it. And this is
strange, because I have just spoken of the gratitude we owe to the
unnoticed foundations of our lives, and how careless we always are
about this gratitude, how unthinking we are to take for granted the
humdrum dailiness that is all the luxury we are ever likely to know
on this planet. There are ways to try to apprehend the nature of this
luxury, but they are psychological tricks, and do no good. It is
pointless to contemplate, only for the sake of feeling gratitude, the
bitter, vicious, crippled, drugged, diseased, deformed, despoiled, or
corrupted lives that burst against their own mortality in hospitals,
madhouses, prisons, all those horrendous lives chained to poverty
and its variegated spawn in the long, bleak wastes on the outer
margins of Ordinariness, mired in the dread of a ferocious Extraor-
dinariness that slouches in insatiably every morning and never departs even in sleep—contemplating this, who would deny gratitude
to our own Ordinariness, though it does not come easily, and has its
demeaning price? Still, comparison confers relief more often than
gratitude, and the gratitude that rises out of reflection on the extraordinary misfortune of others is misbegotten. —You remember how
in one of the Old English poets we are told how the rejoicing hosts
of heaven look down at the tortures of the damned, feeling the
special pleasure of their own exemption. The consciousness of Ordinariness *is* the consciousness of exemption.

That is one way it is dangerous to take special notice of the
Ordinary.

The second danger, I think, is even more terrible. But before I am
ready to speak of this new, nevertheless very ancient, danger, I want
to ask this question: if we are willing to see the Ordinary as a treasure
and a gift, what are we to *do* about it? Or, to put it another way, what
is to be gained from noticing the Ordinary? Morally and metaphysically, what are our obligations to the Ordinary? Here art and philosophy meet with a quizzical harmony unusual between contenders.
"Be one of those upon whom nothing is lost," Henry James advised;
and that is one answer, the answer of what would appear to be the
supreme aesthetician. For the sake of the honing of consciousness,
for the sake of becoming sensitive, at every moment, *to* every mo-

ment, for the sake of making life as superlatively polished as the most sublime work of art, we ought to notice the Ordinary.

No one since the Greek sculptors and artisans has expressed this sense more powerfully than Walter Pater, that eloquent Victorian whose obsession with attaining the intensest sensations possible casts a familiar light out toward the century that followed him. Pater, like Coleridge before him and James after him, like the metaphysicians of what has come to be known as the Counterculture, was after all the highs he could accumulate in a lifetime. "We are all under sentence of death," he writes, ". . . we have an interval, and then our place knows us no more. Some spend this interval in listlessness, some in high passions, the wisest . . . in art and song. For our only chance lies in expanding that interval, in getting as many pulsations as possible into the given time. Great passions may give us this quickened sense of life. . . . Only be sure it is passion—that it does yield you this fruit of a quickened, multiplied consciousness. . . . Of this wisdom, the poetic passion, the desire for beauty, the love of art for art's sake, has most; for art comes to you professing frankly to give nothing but the highest quality to your moments as they pass, and simply for those moments' sake." And like a Zen master who seizes on the data of life only to transcend them, he announces: "Not the fruit of experience, but experience itself, is the end."

What—in this view, which once more has the allegiance of the *Zeitgeist*—what is Art? It is first noticing, and then sanctifying, the Ordinary. It is making the Ordinary into the Extraordinary. It is the impairment of the distinction between the Ordinary and the Extraordinary.

The aestheticians—the great Experiencers—can be refuted. I bring you a Hebrew melody to refute them with. It is called "The Choice"; the poet is Yeats; and since the poem is only eight lines long I would like to give over the whole of it. It begins by discriminating between essence and possession: life interpreted as *doing* beautiful things or *having* beautiful things:

> The intellect of man is forced to choose
> Perfection of the life, or of the work,

And if it take the second must refuse
A heavenly mansion, raging in the dark.
When all that story's finished, what's the news?
In luck or out the toil has left its mark:
That old perplexity an empty purse,
Or the day's vanity, the night's remorse.

Our choice, according to Yeats, is the choice between pursuing the life of Deed, where acts have consequences, where the fruit of experience is more gratifying than the experience itself, and pursuing the life of Art, which signifies the celebration of shape and mood. Art, he tells us, turns away from the divine preference, and finishes out a life in empty remorse; in the end the sum of the life of Art is nothing. The ironies here are multitudinous, for no one ever belonged more to the mansion of Art than Yeats himself, and it might be said that in this handful of remarkable lines Yeats condemned his own passions and his own will.

But there is a way in which the Yeats poem, though it praises Deed over Image, though it sees the human being as a creature to be judged by his acts rather than by how well he has made something—there is a way in which this poem is after all *not* a Hebrew melody. The Jewish perception of how the world is constituted also tells us that we are to go in the way of Commandment rather than symbol, goodness rather than sensation: but it will never declare that the price of Art, Beauty, Experience, Pleasure, Exaltation is a "raging in the dark" or a loss of the "heavenly mansion."

The Jewish understanding of the Ordinary is in some ways very close to Pater, and again very far from Yeats, who would punish the "perfection of the work" with an empty destiny.

With David the King we say, "All that is in the heaven and the earth is thine," meaning that it is all there for our wonder and our praise. "Be one of those upon whom nothing is lost"—James's words, but the impulse that drives them is the same as the one enjoining the observant Jew (the word "observant" is exact) to bless the moments of this world at least one hundred times a day. One hundred times: but Ordinariness is more frequent than that, Ordinariness crowds the day, we swim in the sense of our dailiness; and yet there is a blessing for every separate experience of the Ordinary.

Jewish life is crammed with such blessings—blessings that take note of every sight, sound, and smell, every rising-up and lying-down, every morsel brought to the mouth, every act of cleansing. Before he sits down to his meal, the Jew will speak the following: "Blessed are You, O Lord our God, Ruler of the Universe, whose Commandments hallow us, and who commands us to wash our hands." When he breaks his bread, he will bless God for having "brought forth bread from the earth." Each kind of food is similarly praised in turn, and every fruit in its season is praised for having renewed itself in the cycle of the seasons. And when the meal is done, a thanksgiving is said for the whole of it, and table songs are sung with exultation.

The world and its provisions, in short, are *observed*—in the two meanings of "observe." Creation is both noticed and felt to be sanctified. Everything is minutely paid attention to, and then ceremoniously praised. Here is a Talmudic saying: "Whoever makes a profane use of God's gifts—which means partaking of any worldly joy without thanking God for it—commits a theft against God." And a Talmudic dispute is recorded concerning which is the more important Scriptural utterance: loving your neighbor as yourself, or the idea that we are all the children of Adam. The sage who has the final word chooses the children-of-Adam thesis, because, he explains, our common creatureliness includes the necessity of love. But these celebrations through noticing are not self-centered and do not stop at humanity, but encompass every form of life and non-life. So there are blessings to rejoice in on smelling sweet woods or barks, fragrant plants, fruits, spices, or oils. There is a blessing on witnessing lightning, falling stars, great mountains and deserts: "Blessed are You . . . who fashioned Creation." The sound of thunder has its praise, and the sight of the sea, and a rainbow; beautiful animals are praised, and trees in their first blossoming of the year or for their beauty alone, and the new moon, and new clothing, and sexual delight. The sight of a sage brings a blessing for the creation of human wisdom, the sight of a disfigured person praises a Creator who varies the form of his creatures. From the stone to the human being, creatureliness is extolled.

This huge and unending shower of blessings on our scenes and habitations, on all the life that occupies the planet, on every plant and animal, and on every natural manifestation, serves us doubly: in the first place, what you are taught to praise you will not maim or exploit or destroy. In the second place, the categories and impulses of Art become the property of the simplest soul: because it is all the handiwork of the Creator, everything Ordinary is seen to be Extraordinary. The world, and every moment in it, is seen to be sublime, and not merely "seen to be," but brought home to the intensest part of consciousness.

Come back with me now to Pater: "The service of philosophy," he writes, "of speculative culture, toward the human spirit is to rouse, to startle it into sharp and eager observation. Every moment some form grows perfect in hand or face; some tone on the hills or the sea is choicer than the rest; some mood of passion or insight or intellectual excitement is irresistibly real and attractive to us—for that moment only." And now here at last is Pater's most celebrated phrase, so famous that it has often been burlesqued: "To burn always with this hard, gemlike flame, to maintain this ecstasy, is success in life."

But all this is astonishing. An idolater singing a Hebrew melody? I call Pater an idolater because he is one; and so is every aesthetician who sees the work of art as an end in itself. Saying "Experience itself is the end" is the very opposite of blessing the Creator as the source of all experience.

And just here is the danger I spoke of before, the danger Yeats darkly apprehended—the deepest danger our human brains are subject to. The Jew has this in common with the artist: he means nothing to be lost on him, he brings all his mind and senses to bear on noticing the Ordinary, he is equally alert to Image and Experience, nothing that passes before him is taken for granted, everything is exalted. If we are enjoined to live in the condition of noticing all things—or, to put it more extremely but more exactly, in the condition of awe—*how can we keep ourselves from sliding off from awe at God's Creation to worship of God's Creation?* And does it matter if we do?

The difference, the reason it matters, is a signal and shattering one: the difference is what keeps us from being idolators.

What is an idol? Anything that is allowed to come between ourselves and God. Anything that is *instead of* God. Anything that we call an end in itself, and yet is not God Himself.

The Mosaic vision concerning all this is uncompromisingly pure and impatient with self-deception, and this is the point on which Jews are famously stiff-necked—nothing but the Creator, no substitute and no mediator. The Creator is not contained in his own Creation; the Creator is incarnate in nothing, and is free of any image or imagining. God is not any part of Nature, or in any part of Nature; God is not any man, or in any man. When we praise Nature or man or any experience or work of man, we are worshiping the Creator, and the Creator alone.

But there is another way of thinking which is easier, and sweeter, and does not require human beings to be so tirelessly uncompromising, or to be so cautious about holding on to the distinction between delight in the world and worship of the world.

Here is a story. A Buddhist sage once rebuked a person who excoriated an idolator: "Do you think it makes any difference to God," he asked, "whether this old woman gives reverence to a block of wood? Do you think God is incapable of taking the block of wood into Himself? Do you think God will ignore anyone's desire to find Him, no matter where, and through whatever means? All worship goes up to God, who is the source of worship."

These are important words; they offer the most significant challenge to purist monotheism that has ever been stated. They tell us that the Ordinary is not merely, when contemplated with intensity, the Extraordinary, but more, much more than that—that the Ordinary is also the divine. Now there are similar comments in Jewish sources, especially in Hasidism, which dwell compassionately on the nobility of the striving for God, no matter through what means. But the striving is always toward the Creator Himself, the struggle is always toward the winnowing-out of every mediating surrogate. The Kotzker Rebbe went so far in his own striving that he even dared to interpret the command against idols as a warning not to make an idol out of a command of God. —So, in general, Jewish thought balks at taking the metaphor for the essence, at taking the block of wood as symbol or representation or mediator for God, despite the fact that the wood and its worshiper stand for everything worthy of celebration: the tree grew in its loveliness, the carver came and fashioned it into a pleasing form, the woman is alert to holiness; the tree, the carver, the woman who is alert to holiness are, all together, a loveliness and a reason to rejoice in the world. But still the wood does not mean God. It is instead of God.

It is not true, as we so often hear, that Judaism is a developmental religion, that there is a progression upward from Moses to the Prophets. The Prophets enjoined backsliders to renew themselves through the Mosaic idea, and the Mosaic idea is from then to now, and has survived unmodified: "Take heed to yourselves, that your heart be not deceived, and ye turn aside, and serve other gods, and worship them." (Deut. 11:16.) This perception has never been superseded. To seem to supersede it is to transgress it.

So it is dangerous to notice and to praise the Ordinariness of the world, its inhabitants and its events. We want to do it, we rejoice to do it, above all we are commanded to do it—but there is always the easy, the sweet, the beckoning, the lenient, the *interesting* lure of the *Instead Of:* the wood of the tree instead of God, the rapture-bringing horizon instead of God, the work of art instead of God, the passion for history instead of God, philosophy and the history of philosophy instead of God, the state instead of God, the shrine instead of God, the sage instead of God, the order of the universe instead of God, the prophet instead of God.

There is no Instead Of. There is only the Creator. God is alone. That is what we mean when we utter the ultimate Idea which is the pinnacle of the Mosaic revolution in human perception: God is One.

The child of a friend of mine was taken to the Egyptian galleries of the Museum. In a glass case stood the figure of a cat resplendent in the perfection of its artfulness—long-necked, gracile, cryptic, authoritative, beautiful, spiritual, autonomous, complete in itself. "I understand," said the child, "how they wanted to bow down to this cat. I feel the same." And then she said a Hebrew word: *asur*—forbidden—the great hallowed No that tumbles down the centuries from Sinai, the No that can be said only after the world is no longer taken for granted, the No that can rise up only out of the abundant celebrations and blessings of Yes, Yes, Yes, the shower of Yeses that praise fragrant oils, and wine, and sex, and scholars, and thunder, and new clothes, and falling stars, and washing your hands before eating.

Remembering Maurice Samuel

When exactly this took place I cannot now recall. I see a plain wood table, a full water pitcher, a small bright space; a lofty Viking of a man; a squarish, briefer man. There is an audience for this so-called "symposium," and I, in my hungry twenties, am in that moment enduring the first spasms of a lasting blow; afterward the blow will be recognizable as an ambush by the Idea of a Jewish history.

It is more than a mere lacuna, it is a poverty, not to be sure of the place. In those years I used to follow Maurice Samuel from lectern to lectern, running after whatever it was I thought I might get from him. I ran after others too: poets, story-writers, novelists, everyone who might be in possession of a volcanic pen. I supposed the pen itself made volcanoes; I had a perfect faith, common to the literary young, that imaginative power is contained in the mastery of words.

The place, after all, may have been the art gallery of the Ninety-second Street Y in New York—a compromise-hall. If the audience is not large enough to fill the Y's auditorium, the speakers and their loyal little flocks are packed into the smaller hall, to huddle on metal

Appeared as the Foreword to *The Worlds of Maurice Samuel: Selected Writings* (Jewish Publication Society of America, 1977).

folding chairs and pretend they are a crowd. For speaker and for audience there is always something slightly (and secretly) diminishing about the more modest room; it is as if those two elements of the scheme, teller and told, have together failed of permanence and eminence and are designated, even before the first word falls, to the evanescence of a puny event.

The event was not puny. There they stood, the courtly pair, beginning with the same obsession: the history of the Jewish people. One of the two was Erwin Goodenough, the Yale scholar; the other was Maurice Samuel—an uncategorizable presence, thickly though unsatisfactorily labeled: essayist, novelist, activist, thinker, historian, polemicist, (not least) public lecturer. Nor is "Yale scholar" good enough for Goodenough: stand before the row of his books and you ponder a library. Something in his figure suggested the high monument of his work: the great learning, the ordering, erudite, deeply honest brilliance—the mind, say, of George Eliot sans the novelistic surge.

These two had come together as "discussants," not as antagonists; but afterward they parted in a state of—how to describe it?—metaphysical separation. Not that they disagreed; they did not disagree. What was clear history for the Yale monument was clear history also for the public lecturer. What the noble Gentile scholar, unfolding the centuries, saw, the steady Jewish thinker, though implicated in those dense unreeling scrolls, saw with an equal eye. Eloquence for eloquence, they were a match; grandeur for grandeur, sensibility for sensibility, mind for mind, wit for wit. The room—whatever place this was, Y or other place—swelled to the size of an endless peopled meadow. Before that, and especially afterward, I would find myself a molecule in vaster audiences than this, halls as wide as some Roman plaza: as the years passed, throngs came to witness the fabled speaking fame of Maurice Samuel. All the same, it was in this narrower space that the huge Idea opened.

I do not now remember how the argument came to its crux, by what turnings or challenges; but now, thinking back on it, I see how like a clash of a pair of archangels it was—secular archangels—each intent on hammering out the meaning (or unmeaning) of Jewish history.

"The history of the Jews," Goodenough began, "is what the Jews have done, and what has been done to them."

"The history of the Jews," Samuel said, "is that. And something else."

"There *is* no something else," Goodenough said. "There is only what has been. The history of any people is coextensive with that people."

"The history of the Jewish people is coextensive with the Idea of the Covenant," Samuel said.

Then Goodenough: "The Covenant is *ought*. For history, *is* is all there is."

Then Samuel: "For Jewish history, *ought* is all that matters. Without the Covenant there is no Jewish people."

Goodenough: "Jewish history is history made by Jews."

Samuel: "The Covenant made Jewish history. If a Jew worships an idol, is that Jewish history?"

Goodenough: "Yes."

Samuel: "No. If a Jew worships an idol, that is one Jew worshiping an idol, but it is not Jewish history."

Goodenough: "And if a thousand Jews worship an idol?"

Samuel: "Then that is a thousand Jews worshiping an idol, but it is not Jewish history."

Goodenough: "History is the significance of data."

Samuel: "History is the significance of data. And more."

Goodenough: "History is what has happened. Nothing else."

Samuel: "History is what has happened. And also a judgment on what has happened."

And so on. Obviously I have made up the words of this dialogue, but I have not invented their direction. When the debate halted, it was plain that Goodenough had won it on the ground of "logic." But Samuel had won it on lesser, or maybe higher, ground: on the ground of stiff-neckedness, which has something to do with the way Jews receive the struggling light of holiness. What had come between them was not the force of fact, but this small persistent flame.

What flew up out of that archangelic exchange was Samuel's buried theme—the covenantal nature of the Jew. It was a buried theme because so far as his hearers and readers can tell he never again referred to it overtly. It was a volcanic theme because it taught that idea and imagination are the same; and that the imagination of an idea can successfully contradict what is truly known.

Yet Samuel's subject, by and large, was what is truly known—flat history, history exactly as Goodenough would have it: a record left by a people, not an afflatus divinely breathed, still less a Voice. Samuel was on the side of the pragmatic and the concrete: the "real." He was not in the prophetic line, in however minor a fashion; he gave public lectures to uneven audiences (every age, every "level"), and he did it, in fact, for a living. He was called, and did not mind calling himself, a *maggid*—an itinerant preacher. But he was no more a *maggid* than he was a contemporary lesser prophet; he did not preach, or exhort, or redeem; perhaps, now and then, he reminded. Even his reminders were informational, not clerical. He was learned, but he had taught himself. He was scholarly, but the excuse for this was a fevered need to know. He revered language, but he loved idea more. He was meticulous, but his range kept widening. He was, in short, not a closed system. If, as a public speaker, he had no title and arrived on every scene without an official description or affiliation, and was neither preacher nor professor, and not quite performer either, what exactly did he *do?*

His métier was thinking: thinking aloud. In his autobiography Samuel distinguishes between "reciters"—cautious types who declaim a fixed text—and genuine lecturers like himself, who evolve, or discover, a text. But perhaps there has never been another lecturer as daring as Maurice Samuel. He set out like a climber negotiating a ledge; he hit on a point, sometimes an obstacle, sometimes a gratifying piece of good fortune; whatever it was, he assessed it, grappled with it, took his victory, and sprang on to the next peak. Along the way he tossed in his talismans of erudition, irony, and above all the long view. He was quick, he was fleet, he was dogged, he made connections. And still, when all this has been described, nothing has been described. What did he do? What was his job?

His job was to address a generation and to explain. In essence he was an argumentative explainer. This is different from *maggid*, prophet, sage, teacher—they all, in their several degrees and guises, have the kind of authority that emanates from their persons. They are *beings*, voices, conscious of speech and the effect of speech, conscious of themselves as representing value, tradition, core. They know they are there to *be;* and that by being, they will transmit. But an explainer is out to give an explanation, not a tenet. The explainer thinks aloud; he is not thinking of his role; he has no expected, usual, given role. An explainer hurls himself into his story. He becomes the story. How does he do this? By joining himself with its elements, by taking sides with its various parts. By sorting out. By setting aside error and misapprehension—only after first entering into their spirit.

In brief: through polemics. Polemics is the chief instrument, the illustrious and ancient mode, of the explainer. Through polemics, as through no other means, an idea can be beaten out. Polemics is a hammering, a hacking into the flanks of imagination. It has the furious relation of stone to sculpture; there is no serenity in its progress. It begins with what is deformed, and only after the ringing and the smashing does it lead to grace. But the aesthetic analogy does not go far enough. Polemics is thinking in the furnace of antithesis. Polemics sees the adversary as an outrage, but also as an advantage. One reason it is inappropriate to define Maurice Samuel as *maggid,* or prophet, or sage, or teacher, is that not one of these avatars commands the antiphonal as a *necessity.* Wisdom-teaching, whatever its devices, goes in a straight line; it knows what it knows and is not really required to look over its shoulder at what does not pertain. In that sense it may be more correct for tradition to have assigned Moses the epithet "our polemicist" instead of "our teacher." "Thou shalt not" is as concerned with the antagonistic culture as it is with the ideal culture and is perpetually looking over its shoulder at alien practices: to shun is to see.

Maurice Samuel is above all a polemicist, assuredly the best of our time. Leo Baeck is a consummate polemicist, but only once (though that once is a pinnacle), in his essay "Romantic Religion." Walter Kaufmann, Baeck's translator and the author of *Critique of Religion and Philosophy,* is a more consistent polemicist, though more often from the standpoint of idiosyncratic, rather than Jewish, thought. But Samuel is a polemicist from beginning to end: which is to say an unrelenting critic of thought—and always from the Jewish standpoint. For Samuel the Jewish view is almost never yielded up through simple declaration or exposition; it is wrested out of the engagement with, and finally a disengagement from, an alternative world view. *The Gentleman and the Jew* and *The Professor and the Fossil* are only the most emphatic of such demonstrations.

Nothing serves Samuel's powers better than Arnold Toynbee's misrepresentations, errors, and contradictions. It will not do to say that if Professor Toynbee had not existed, Maurice Samuel would have had to invent him: given the actual history of the West, there is no way for Professor Toynbee *not* to have existed. He is the classic anti-Semite in scholar's clothing, as was Apion (died 45 C.E.) before him. The same can be said of the configuration of the "gentleman." There is no way, given the actual history of Europe, for the "gentleman" idea, with its code of honor, heroism, and valor based on bloodshed, *not* to have manifested itself in contradistinction to the Jewish code of moral decorum—*mitzvah.* But in both instances the polemicist must have not merely significant mastery but complete mastery of the code, cult, culture, and overriding concepts of his antagonist. Indeed, he must *include* in himself his antagonist. A polemicist must first embody that which he hopes to expel. It must be a version of self he casts out.

Without a Manchester childhood devoted to the consumption of English schoolboy novels, without a period of rejection of, or at least indifference to, parental heritage, without a phase of passionate allegiance to "universalism" (the kind that de-Judaizes)—without, in short, having brought himself up as an ideal Englishman—Samuel could not have taken on Toynbee, or the principle of the "gentleman," or the opponents of the Zionist idea. If Moses, nurtured in Pharaoh's palace, was as much polemicist as lawgiver, it was because he knew the priests who administered the idols firsthand, and knew how to beat these royal magicians at their own game. And the case for Theodor Herzl, the Viennese journalist and boulevardier, is of course open and shut: the modern State of Israel was founded on the tongue of an imaginative polemicist. Maurice Samuel did not come from so far over on the other side—he is closer to his Uncle Berel the tailor than he is to the English playing fields—but for a time he traveled toward the allure of what he later called "the brilliance and attractiveness of . . . a frivolous world," and he was drawn in that direction early enough to understand profoundly, and from the inside, what it was he ultimately opposed.

"He was the teacher of a generation," the people who were in his audiences say of him, remembering the rigorous lectures—they were not entertainments—and the remarkable radio dialogues with Mark Van Doren. "He is my teacher," his readers say, preserving both the sense of individual possession and the present tense—readers' privileges. But both memory of the lectures (corruptible though instructive) and familiarity with the books (continuing and renewable) offer finally a static sort of homage if they address themselves only to Samuel as teacher. It will not do—not simply because, unlike a teacher, he did not primarily intend to shape any of us. Sitting rapt among his hearers, observing how (in those "question periods" that follow public lectures) he did not suffer fools gladly, I was struck, even then, with the recognition that he hardly cared whether his voice touched fools or gods. He was grappling not with *us* but with certain footholds, difficult to ascend to, just above his line of sight; impossible to posit rationally that the footholds are *there.* That strange wrestling in a small space with the scholar of Yale remains a paradigm of Samuel as writer, thinker, imaginer. What he was after was the Idea that would separate itself out from all other ideas, as a single hammer can go to work on all the flanks of so many stones; the stones split, the hammer beats on. He neither wrote nor spoke wholly for our sake, as prophets and teachers and *maggidim* do. Instead, much of it was for the sake of that hammer—the one that knocks to pieces idols and other well-made falsehoods. Polemicist's hammer: steadily it breaks, just as steadily it builds.

I. B. Singer's Book of Creation

Some time ago, when Isaac Bashevis Singer first mounted the public platform to speak in English, he was asked whether he really believed in *sheydim*—in imps and demons, ghosts and spirits. The response, partly a skip and partly a glint, followed considerable playful pondering and ended in a long shrug: "Yes and no." The rebuke of an imp guarding secrets, one might judge—but surely a lesser imp, capable mainly of smaller mischiefs: the knotting of elflocks in the audience's hair, perhaps.

Years pass; the astonishing stories accumulate; the great Nobel is almost upon Singer, and the question reliably recurs. Now the answer is direct and speedy: "Yes, I believe there are unknown forces." This is no longer the voice of a teasing imp. Never mind that its tone clearly belongs to an accustomed celebrity who can negotiate a Question Period with a certain shameless readiness; it is also a deliberate leaning into the wind of some powerful dark wing, fearsomely descried.

Whether the majesty of the Nobel Prize for Literature has since altered Singer's manipulation of this essential question, I do not

---

The Collected Stories of Isaac Bashevis Singer (Farrar, Straus & Giroux, 1981).
Published in *The New York Times Book Review*, March 21, 1982.

know. Nevertheless the question remains central, though not quite so guileless as it appears. Should we believe that Singer believes in the uncanny and the preternatural? Is there ever a trustworthy moment when a storymonger is not making things up, especially about his own substance and sources? Doesn't an antic fancy devoted to cataloguing folly always trifle with earnest expectation? And what are we to think of the goblin cunning of a man who has taken his mother's given name—Bashevis (i.e., Bathsheba)—to mark out the middle of his own? Singer's readers in Yiddish call him, simply, "Bashevis." A sentimental nom de plume? His is anything but a nostalgic imagination. Does the taking-on of "Bashevis" imply a man wishing to be a woman? Or does it mean that a woman is hiding inside a man? Or does Singer hope somehow to entangle his own passions in one of literature's lewdest and nastiest plots: King David's crafty devisings concerning the original Bathsheba? Or does he dream of attracting to himself the engendering powers of his mother's soul through the assumption of her name? Given the witness of the tales themselves, we are obliged to suspect any or all of these notions, as well as others we have not the wit of fantasy to conjure up.

Accordingly, nearly every one of the forty-seven stories in *The Collected Stories of Isaac Bashevis Singer* is a snail-whorl narrative grown out of similar schemings, impersonations, contrivances, devices, and transmutations. The story of David and Bathsheba is, without fail, one that Singer's plot-fecundity might have churned up, though it would likely be a demon that dispatches Uriah the Hittite. The story of a woman taking on the semblance of a man, Singer has in fact already invented, in "Yentl the Yeshiva Boy," a remarkable fable about a girl who lusts after scholarship. In "The Dead Fiddler," coarse Getsel, in the form of a dybbuk, hides inside a woman, causing the delicate Liebe Yentle to swig and swear. As for the acquisition of names that confer eccentric or arrogant ambitions, there is Zeidel Cohen, a descendant of the exegete Rashi, who prepares to become Zeidlus the First, Pope of Rome; and Alchonon the teacher's helper, a plain fellow who succeeds in passing himself off, in "Taibele and Her Demon," as the lecherous Hurmizah, stepnephew of Asmodeus, King of the Demons.

On one flank Singer is a trickster, a prankster, a Loki, a Puck. His themes are lust, greed, pride, obsession, misfortune, unreason, the oceanic surprises of the mind's underside, the fiery cauldron of the self, the assaults of time and place. His stories offer no "epiphanies" and no pious resolutions; no linguistic circumscriptions or Hemingwayesque self-deprivations. Their plenitudes chiefly serve undefended curiosity, the gossip's lure of what-comes-next. Singer's stories have plots that unravel not because they are "old-fashioned" —they are mostly originals and have few recognizable modes other than their own—but because they contain the whole human world of affliction, error, quagmire, pain, calamity, catastrophe, woe: things happen; life is an ambush, a snare; one's fate can never be predicted. His driven, mercurial processions of predicaments and transmogrifications are limitless, often stupendous. There are whole fistfuls of masterpieces in this one volume: a cornucopia of invention.

Because he cracks open decorum to find lust, because he peers past convention into the pit of fear, Singer has in the past been condemned by other Yiddish writers outraged by his seemingly pagan matter, his superstitious villagers, his daring leaps into gnostic furies. The moral grain of Jewish feeling that irradiates the mainstream aspirations of Yiddish literature has always been a kind of organic extension of Talmudic ethical ideals: family devotion, community probity, *derekh erets*—self-respect and respect for others—the stringent expectations of high public civility and indefatigable integrity, the dream of messianic betterment. In Singer, much of this seems absent or overlooked or simply mocked; it is as if he has willed the crashing-down of traditional Jewish sanity and sensibility. As a result, in Yiddish literary circles he is sometimes viewed as—it is the title of one of these stories—"The Betrayer of Israel."

In fact, he betrays nothing and no one, least of all Jewish idealism. That is the meaning of his imps and demons: that human character, left to itself, is drawn to cleanliness of heart; that human motivation, on its own, is attracted to clarity and valor. Here is Singer's other flank, and it is the broader one. The goblin cunning leads straight to this: Singer is a moralist. He tells us that it is natural to be good, and unholy to go astray. It is only when Lilith creeps in, or Samael, or Ketev Mriri, or the sons of Asmodeus, that evil and impurity are kindled. It is the inhuman, the antihuman, forces that are to blame for harms and sorrows. Surely these imps must be believed in; they may have the telltale feet of geese—like Satan, their sire—but their difficult, shaming, lubricious urges are terrestrially familiar. Yet however lamentably known they are, Singer's demons are intruders, invaders, no true or welcome part of ourselves. They are "psychology"; and history; and terror; above all, obsessive will. If he believes in them, so, unwillingly but genuinely, do we.

And to understand Singer's imps is to correct another misapprehension: that he is the recorder of a lost world, the preserver of a vanished sociology. Singer is an artist and transcendent inventor, not a curator. His tales—though dense with the dailiness of a God-covenanted culture, its folkways, its rounded sufficiency, especially the rich intensities of the yeshiva and its bottomless studies—are in no way documents. The Jewish townlets that truly were are only seeds for his febrile conflagrations: where, outside of peevish imagination, can one come on the protagonist of "Henne Fire," a living firebrand, a spitfire burning up with spite, who ultimately, through the spontaneous combustion of pure fury, collapses into "one piece of coal"? Though every doorstep might be described, and every feature of a head catalogued (and Singer's portraits are brilliantly particularized), parables and fables are no more tied to real places and faces than Aesop's beasts are beasts.

This is not to say that Singer's stories do not mourn those murdered Jewish townlets of Poland, every single one of which, with nearly every inhabitant, was destroyed by the lords and drones of the Nazi Gehenna. This volume includes a masterly memorial to that destruction, the broken-hearted testimony of "The Last Demon," which begins emphatically with a judgment on Europe: "I, a demon, bear witness that there are no more demons left. Why demons, when man himself is a demon?" And sums up:

> I've seen it all . . . the destruction of Poland. There are no more Jews, no more demons. The women don't pour out water any longer on the night of the winter solstice. They don't avoid giving things in even numbers. They no longer knock at dawn at the antechamber of the synagogue. They don't warn us before emptying the slops. The rabbi was martyred on a Friday in the month of Nissan. The commu-

nity was slaughtered, the holy books burned, the cemetery desecrated. *The Book of Creation* has been returned to the Creator. . . . No more sins, no more temptations! . . . Messiah did not come for the Jews, so the Jews went to Messiah. There is no further need for demons.

This tenderness for ordinary folk, their superstitions, their folly, their plainness, their lapses, is a classical thread of Yiddish fiction, as well as the tree trunk of Singer's own hasidic legacy—love and reverence for the down-to-earth. "The Little Shoemakers" bountifully celebrates the Fifth Commandment with leather and awl; the hero of "Gimpel the Fool," a humble baker, is endlessly duped and stubbornly drenched in permanent grace; the beautiful story "Short Friday" ennobles a childless old couple who, despite privation and barrenness, turn their unscholarly piety into comeliness and virtue. Shmuel-Leibele's immaculate happiness in prayer, Shoshe's meticulous Sabbath meal, shine with saintliness; Singer recounts the menu, "chicken soup with noodles and tiny circlets of fat . . . like golden ducats," as if even soup can enter holiness. Through a freakish accident—snow covers their little house and they are asphyxiated— the loving pair ascend in death together to paradise. When the demons are stilled, human yearning aspires toward goodness and joy. (Singer fails to note, however, whether God or Samael sent the pure but deadly snow.)

In Singer the demons are rarely stilled, and the luminous serenity of "Short Friday" is an anomaly. Otherwise pride furiously rules, and wild-hearted imps dispose of human destiny. In "The Unseen," a prosperous and decent husband runs off with a lusty maidservant at the urging of a demon; he ends in destitution, a hidden beggar tended by his remarried wife. "The Gentleman from Cracow" corrupts a whole town with gold; he turns out to be Ketev Mriri himself. In "The Destruction of Kreshev," a scholar who is a secret Sabbatian and devil-worshiper induces his wife to commit adultery with a Panlike coachman. Elsewhere, excessive intellectual passion destroys genius. An accomplished young woman is instructed by a demon to go to the priest, convert, and abandon her community; the demon assumes the voice of the girl's grandmother, herself the child of a Sabbatian. A rabbi is "plagued by something new and terrifying: wrath against the Creator," and struggles to fashion himself into an atheist. Character and motive are turned inside out at the bidding of imps who shove, snarl, seduce, bribe, cajole. Allure ends in rot; lure becomes punishment.

This phantasmagorical universe of ordeal and mutation and shock is, finally, as intimately persuasive as logic itself. There is no fantasy in it. It is the true world we know, where we have come to expect anguish as the consequence of our own inspirations, where we crash up against the very circumstance from which we had always imagined we were exempt. In this true world suffering is endemic and few are forgiven. Yet it may be that for Singer the concrete presence of the unholy attests the hovering redemptive holy, whose incandescence can scatter demons. *Yes, I believe in unknown forces.*

Not all the stories in this collection emerge from the true world, however. The eerie authority of "The Cabbalist of East Broadway" is a gripping exception, but in general the narratives set in the American environment are, by contrast, too thin. Even when intentionally spare—as in the marvelous "Vanvild Kava," with its glorious opening: "If a Nobel Prize existed for writing little, Vanvild Kava would have gotten it"—the European settings have a way of turning luxuriantly, thickly coherent. Presumably some of these American locales were undertaken in a period when the fertile seed of the townlets had begun to be exhausted; or else it is the fault of America itself, lacking the centrifugal density and identity of a yeshiva society, the idea of community as an emanation of God's gaze. Or perhaps it is because many of these American stories center on Singer as writer and celebrity, or on someone like him. It is as if the predicaments that fly into his hands nowadays arrive because he is himself the centrifugal force, the controlling imp. And an imp, to have efficacy, as Singer's genius has shown, must be a kind of dybbuk, moving in powerfully from outside; whereas the American narratives are mainly inside jobs, about the unusual "encounters" a famous writer meets up with.

The Collected Stories is supplied with a sparse Author's Note (misleadingly called an Introduction on the book jacket), but it is unsatisfyingly patched, imbalanced, cursory; anyone trusting imps will fail to trust the Note. Apparently Singer thinks fiction is currently under a threat from "the zeal for messages." I wish it were possible to list every translator's name, from Saul Bellow, Isaac Rosenfeld, Dorothea Strauss, Mirra Ginsburg, and Joseph Singer to the less renowned Ruth Schachner Finkel, Evelyn Torton Beck, Herbert Lottman, Rosanna Gerber, Elizabeth Schub, and all the rest. It is interesting that there are so many, and that there are always new ones. Singer has not yet found his Lowe-Porter or Scott Moncrieff. Still, the voice is steady and consistent, as if there were only one voice; undoubtedly it is the imposition of Singer's own. After all these years, the scandalous rumors about Singer's relation to his changing translators do not abate: how they are half-collaborators, half-serfs, how they start out sunk in homage, accept paltry fees, and end disgruntled or bemused, yet transformed, having looked on Singer plain. One wishes Singer would write their frenzied tale, set it in Zamość, and call it "Rabbi Bashevis's Helpers." In any event, his helpers cannot reach the deep mine and wine of Singer's mother tongue, thronged (so it was once explained to me by a Tel Aviv poet accomplished in Hebrew, Yiddish, and English) with that unrenderable Hebrew erudition and burnished complexity of which we readers in English have not an inkling, and are permanently deprived. Deprived? Perhaps. *The Collected Stories,* when all is said and done, is an American master's Book of Creation.

The Phantasmagoria
of Bruno Schulz

Thirty-five years ago, Bruno Schulz, a fifty-year-old high-school art teacher in command of one of the most original literary imaginations of modern Europe, was gunned down by a Jew-hunting contingent of SS men in the streets of an insignificant provincial town in eastern Galicia. On the map of Poland the town hides itself from you; you have to search out the tiniest print to discover Drogobych. In this cramped crevice of a place Schulz too hid himself—though not from the Nazis. Urged on by a group of writers, the Polish underground devised a means of escape—false papers and a hiding place. Schulz chose to die unhidden in Drogobych. But even before the German storm, he had already chosen both to hide and to die there. He knew its streets, and their houses and shops, with a paralyzed intimacy. His environment and his family digested him. He was incapable of leaving home, of marrying, at first even of writing. On a drab salary, in a job he despised, he supported a small band of relatives, and though he visited Warsaw and Lvov, and once even went as far as Paris, he gave up larger places, minds, and lives for the sake of Drogobych—or, rather, for the sake of the gargoylish and astonishing map his

Bruno Schulz, *The Street of Crocodiles* (Penguin Books, 1977).
Published in *The New York Times Book Review*, February 13, 1977.

imagination had learned to draw of an invisible Drogobych contrived entirely out of language.

In English there is virtually no biographical information to be
had concerning Schulz. It is known that his final manuscript, a
novel called "The Messiah," was carried for safekeeping to a
friend; both friend and manuscript were swallowed up by the sacrificial fires of the Europe of 1942. All of Schulz's letters, and two-
thirds of the very small body of his finished work—two novels, one
novella—remain untranslated and, so far, inaccessible to American
readers. It is a powerful omission. Think what our notion of the
literature of the Dark Continent of Europe would be like if we had
read our way so late into the century without the most renowned
of the stories in *Red Cavalry,* or without "Gimpel the Fool," or
without *The Metamorphosis.* A verbal landscape stripped of Babel
or Singer or Kafka is unimaginable to us now, and it may turn out,
in the wake of *The Street of Crocodiles,* that Schulz can stand naturally—or unnaturally—among those writers who break our eyes
with torches, and end by demonstrating the remarkable uses of a
purposeful dark.

In this dark the familiar looms freakish, and all of these—Babel as
Cossack Jew, Singer purveying his imps and demiurges, Kafka with
his measured and logical illogic—offer mutations, weird births, es-
sences and occasions never before suspected. *The Street of Crocodiles,*
at one with that mythic crew, is a transmogrified Drogobych: real
town and real time and real tasks twisted and twisted until droplets
of changed, even hateful, even hideous, beauty are squeezed out of
bolts of cloth, ledgers, tailors' dummies, pet birds, a row of shops,
a puppy, a servant girl. As in Kafka, the malevolent is deadpan; its
loveliness of form is what we notice. At the heart of the malevolent
—also the repugnant, the pitiless—crouches the father: Schulz's own
father, since there is an inviolable autobiographical glaze that paints
over every distortion. The father is a shopkeeper, the owner of a
dry-goods store. He gets sick, gives up work, hangs around home,
fiddles with his account books, grows morbid and sulky, has trouble
with his bowels, bursts out into fits of rage. All this is novelist's
material, and we are made to understand it in the usual way of
novels.

But parallel with it, engorging it, is a running flame of amazing imagery—altogether exact and meticulous—that alters everything. The wallpaper becomes a "pullulating jungle . . . filled with whispers, lisping and hissing." Father "sitting clumsily on an enormous china chamberpot" turns into a prophet of "the terrible Demiurge," howling with "the divine anger of saintly men." Father shrinks, hides in closets, climbs the curtains and perches there like a baleful stuffed vulture, disappears "for many days into some distant corner of the house." Schulz's language is dense with disappearances, losses, metamorphoses. The dry-goods shop is flooded by a "cosmogony of cloth." Crowded streets become "an ultra-barrel of myth." The calendar takes on a thirteenth month. Rooms in houses are forgotten, misplaced. A bicycle ascends into the zodiac. Even death is somehow indefinite; a murk, a confusion. Father "could not merge with any reality and was therefore condemned to float eternally on the periphery of life, in half-real regions, on the margins of existence. He could not even earn an honest citizen's death." Father, alive, lectures on manikins: "There is no dead matter . . . lifelessness is only a disguise behind which hide unknown forms of life." A dog represents "the most essential secret of life, reduced to this simple, handy, toy-like form." Wallpapers become bored; furniture, "unstable, degenerate," breaks out into rashes. The maid rules the master with ominous and magisterial positions of her fingers—she points, waggles, tickles. She is a kind of proto-Nazi. Father takes up ornithology and hatches a condor like "an emaciated ascetic, a Buddhist lama," an idol, a mummy—it resembles father himself. (A fore-echo of Kosinski, another Pole obsessed by fearful birds.) Father loathes cockroaches, violently pursues them, and is transformed, undertaking at last their "ceremonial crawl."

> He lay on the floor naked, stained with black totem spots, the lines of his ribs heavily outlined, the fantastic structure of his anatomy visible through the skin; he lay on his face, in the grip of an obsession of loathing which dragged him into the abyss of its complex paths. He moved with the many-limbed, complicated movements of a strange ritual in which I recognized with horror an imitation of the ceremonial crawl of a cockroach.

In Kafka's myth, it is the powerless son who turns into a cockroach; here it is the father who has lost control. Everything is loosened; it is not that the center does not hold; there never *was* a center. "Reality is as thin as paper and betrays with all its cracks its imitative character." "Our language has no definitions which would weigh, so to speak, the grade of reality." Given these hints, it may be misleading to anticipate *The Street of Crocodiles* with so "normal" a signal as *novel:* it is a thick string of sights and sinuosities, a cascade of flashes, of extraordinary movements—a succession of what television has taught us to call "film clips," images in magnetic batches, registered storms, each one shooting memories of itself into the lightnings of all the others. What is being invented in the very drone of our passive literary expectations is Religion—not the taming religion of theology and morality, but the brute splendors of rite, gesture, phantasmagoric transfiguration, sacrifice, elevation, degradation, mortification, repugnance, terror, cult. The religion of animism, in fact, where everything comes alive with an unpredictable and spiteful spirit-force, where even living tissue contains ghosts, where there is no pity.

Such metaphysical specters have their historical undersides. Home shifts, its forms are unreliable, demons rule. Why should these literary Jews of twentieth-century Slavic Europe—Babel, whose language was Russian, two years younger than Schulz; Kafka, who wrote in German, seven years older; Singer, a Yiddish writer, a dozen years younger; and finally (one is tempted to enter the next generation) the American Kosinski—why should these cultivated Slavic Jews run into the black crevices of nihilism, animalism, hollow riddle? Why, indeed, should these writers be the very ones almost to *invent* the literary signposts of such crevices? Gogol came first, it is true; but it is the Slavic Jews who have leaped into the fermenting vat. The homelessness and ultimate pariahship felt by Schulz—an assimilated, Polish-speaking Jew, not so much a Jew as a conscious Pole—in the years before the fiery consummation of the Final Solution may explain why the real Drogobych took on the symbolic name Crocodile Street, and became the place where "nothing ever succeeds . . . nothing can ever reach a definite conclusion."

Out of the Flames:
The Recovery of Gertrud Kolmar

NOTE

Gertrud Kolmar, a reclusive German Jewish poet whose lonely and rigorous intensities have been compared to the crystal severities of Paul Celan and Nellie Sachs, was born in Berlin in 1894. The critic Walter Benjamin was her cousin. In 1940, having written in German all her life, she began to teach herself Hebrew; and by 1941, when she was seized for forced labor by the Nazis, she was already experimenting with poetry in Hebrew. She was murdered in Auschwitz in 1943, at age forty-eight.

> Thus saith the Lord God: Come from the four winds, O breath, and breathe upon these slain, that they may live . . . and the breath came into them, and they lived, and stood up upon their feet, an exceeding great army. Then he said: . . . these bones are the whole house of Israel. . . . Behold, O my people, I will open your graves, and cause you to come up out of your graves . . . into the house of Israel.
>
> EZEKIEL 37:9–12

A dream of reversal, of reconstruction: who has not, in the forty years since the European devastation, swum off into this dream? As if the reel of history—and who does not see history as tragic cinema? —could be run backward: these mounds of ash, shoes, teeth, bones, all lifted up, healed, flown speck after speck toward connection, toward flowering, grain on grain, bone on bone, every skull blooming into the quickness of a human face, every twisted shoe renewed on a vivid foot, every dry bone given again to greening life. Ezekiel's vision in the valley of bones.

An imagining with the immensity of "an exceeding great army." Who rises up, what? Populations; a people; a civilization. And everything unmade, undone, unwritten, unread. The children did not live to do their sums, the carpenters did not live to cut the doors to fit the houses that the architects and engineers left in midair, in midmind. Unwritten alphabets clog the breath of this dream like so many black hosts of random grit—letters still inchoate, not yet armied into poems, novels, philosophies. Torrents of black letters fill the sky of this imagining like a lost smoke. And singular voices, lost.

Published as a Foreword to *Dark Soliloquy: The Selected Poems of Gertrud Kolmar* (The Seabury Press, A Continuum Book, 1975).

Every now and then, though, the dream becomes enfleshed: a voice comes up out of its grave, the living mind resumes its dialogue with history. Anne Frank, most famously; Emanuel Ringelblum's Warsaw Ghetto diaries; Yitzhak Rudashevski's Vilna Ghetto diaries, begun when he was fifteen. But these recovered voices yield direct records of the harrowings. Ezekiel's vision wonders something else: how would the historian Ringelblum have written that history had that history not riven him? What would the mature Anne Frank's novels—she *would* have become a novelist—have turned out to be?

The marvelous recovery of Gertrud Kolmar's poetry signifies the redemption of just such a ripened art.

Gertrud Kolmar died in Auschwitz at age forty-eight; she was given time to become herself, though no time for her name to grow; until this moment, she must be considered unknown. She was published and reviewed barely eight weeks before *Kristallnacht,* that infamous country-wide pogrom called the Night of the Breaking Glass—after which her external precincts narrowed and narrowed toward death. Not so the open cage of her spirit: she felt herself "free in the midst of . . . subjugation." A forced laborer in a Berlin factory, she continued to make poetry and fiction. Ghettoized in a tenement, she began to study Hebrew, and her last—lost—poems were written, most remarkably, defiantly, and symbolically, in the language of the house of Israel.

What has been recovered is not the record of the harrowings—though there is this besides—but the whole blazing body of her poetry, unconsumed. The American poet she is most likely to remind us of is Emily Dickinson—and not so much for her stoic singleness, the heroism of a loneliness teeming with phantasmagorical seeing, as for the daring pressure she puts on language in order to force a crack in the side of the planet, letting out strange figures and fires: she is a mythologist. To fathom this, one must turn finally to the Blake of the *Four Zoas,* or perhaps merely to German folklore: Kolmar too invents fables and their terrible new creatures, intent on tearing out of the earth of the Dark Continent of Europe its controlling demons.

How the devils cry, oh how the deserts cry!

The Biological Premises of
Our Sad Earth-Speck

We were born to die; we were born to endure, on the way to death, sorrow—sorrow in manifold shapes. We are denizens of an abundant, versatile, astonishing, beautiful, and unhappy planet—unhappy because the entitlement to life is the guarantor of death; unhappy because we are divided into tormentors and tormented.

Who assigned this division? Nature? To nature, looking dispassionately on the panther with its teeth in the breast of the ewe, the creature who is tormenting and the creature who is tormented are both innocent parties to a reasonable act. Prey is one possible design of life; perhaps on other planets, circling other stars, there are different schemes and contracts. But prey is ours: we are made according to the principle of hunger. On this planet, we feed.

All the wars that have to do with the claims and confusions of tribe and territory rest on this contract: they are wars of Feeding, and in that sense belong to the planet's overall scheme. Wars, invented and organized by the highest available consciousnesses (do the worms go to war? do the fish? do the paramecia?), are the planet's chief source and cause of torment. Yet even here, all is congruent; there is no contradiction, no loose strand; though maimings and murders

---

Essay published in *Confrontation*, Fall/Winter 1978.

mount, Feeding is ultimately served; and, as long as our planet's governing principle is salient, nothing is mysterious.

Nothing is mysterious, that is, until we come to what has been called Spirit. When Spirit enters, everything we have learned to think of as "nature" is routed, and all the planet's rules appear to be contravened; then up rears monstrousness. Spirit—or Imagination, which means Image-making, which is to say Idolatry—puts gods into bizarre and surprising places: into stones, plain or hewn; into rivers and trees; into human babies born under significant stars; into tyrants; into kings or carpenters; into dry bread and wet wine. Into, in short, the familiar stuff and matter of the planet itself.

And when what is called Spirit introduces the idolatry of matter (nearly a tautology: Spirit always argues for the divinity of matter, and is, in fact, matter's best advocate), the impulse for killing changes. Now, under Spirit's reign, wars are grounded not in na-ture's own scheme of prey, not, that is, in Feeding—Feeding, at least, while it may express itself in greed, is founded in need—but rather in some matter-centered ideal: such as those long-ago wars fought between the adherents of transubstantiation and the loyalists of in-substantiation, who argued over whether a piece of baked dough turned, when certain words were addressed to it, literally into God, or whether it only harbored God invisibly (as an iron, heated or cool, looks the same from the outside). Such wars cannot be "justified" by the ubiquitous law of Feeding. No law or scheme or principle or contract applies to the wars of Spirit. They are straight butchery.

It is only what is called Spirit—i.e., Idolatry—that produces this kind of butchery. Idolatrous killing does not come out of need, nor even out of greed; and it feeds no one and nothing: only matter itself. Idolatry can perceive only matter; its job is to transmute matter from one form into another form, and all for the sake of the adoration of matter itself; idolatry adores personifications and incarnations. Sometimes it puts God into the form of a man; sometimes, in its economy of hygiene, it suggests that a whole people personifies evil, or, rather, the evils that vermin breed. In either case it traffics, ultimately, in corpses. And whatever deals in corpses grows fond and fonder yet of torment.

Four decades ago the Jews of Europe were rounded up at various convenient points, and were compelled to stand naked, whole families together, at the edges of pits, hills, ravines, or graves they had dug themselves; then they were shot, and tumbled dead into the waiting void. When this proved to be inefficient (mere thousands could be dispatched by so technologically primitive a method), the remaining Jews of Europe—millions—were locked into freight cars, stacked standing together there like cordwood, some dying as they stood, the rest awash in a muck of excrement, urine, menstrual blood, and the blood of violence. When the transport reached its destination, the Jews were herded into a nearby wood, stripped naked, and made to gallop into so-called shower chambers, where they were gassed by an effective insecticide. Then their corpses were burned in commodious and serviceable furnaces designed explicitly for this purpose. Specially selected properties of their corpses were transmuted into other matter: baled human hair for bolsters and pillows; gold teeth for the war effort; eyeglasses for recycling; artificial limbs for the value of their materials; and so on. (On one occasion a woman of artistic originality converted human skin into lampshades; but that is conceded as too frivolous a use of matter to serve as true idolatry.)

The advocates of Spirit who conceived, directed, and engaged in these transformations of one form of matter into another—living bodies into corpses, corpses into bone meal, and all in the course of less than an hour—were indeed recognizable as members of one of the civilized nations of the West; they were idolatrous Germans who had formulated an ideal of matter termed "race." These Germans were not the only idolators of personification and incarnation: they were aided in their cult by thousands upon thousands of other Europeans, who, with the exception of the Danes, uniformly assisted in the roundup of the Jews. They were abetted also by the leadership of their enemies, all of them fully informed of the process of transmutation of Jews into bone meal, but reluctant to intercept it.

Now the planet whereon we live and die decrees the rule of prey (or, to say it plainly, the ingestion of one creature by another) for the benefit of the planet itself: that it may multiply in all its diversity and teem with ever-renewing plenitudes of kind and of form. In this scheme—salubrious for the species, melancholy for the individual—

matter is continuously in a state of conversion from one form into another: this, as we have seen, we call hunger, and it is according to the planet's nature.

But the conversion of matter that takes place under the reign of Idolatry—human bone meal for the sake of human bone meal—is *not* according to the planet's nature. It is a monstrosity—an abnormality, a deformity, a contortion and a mutilation so stupendous and disordering that it must somehow result in consequences for the ordinary regulation of the planet. It is not surprising that these consequences are still inchoate and unable to be foreseen. A disturbance in nature leads no one can tell where. When mutations suddenly abound, evolution occurs. Yet it was impossible to predict, when the first fish stepped out upon his fins onto dry land, what would happen either to the fish or to the land. Now it is true that we usually tend to think of evolution as positive—as motion, however aberrant, on the way toward complexities of "improvement"; but can anyone know what these mutations of Idolatry may signify for the post-Auschwitz planet? The German aberration murdered millions of human beings—among them some six million Jews, one-third of all Jews—not according to any design of nature (e.g., prey), but according to an original design of Spirit incarnated as "racial purity," as "the Aryan ideal": proof of that incarnation being those millions of corpses of Jews. The notion of incarnation is always imposture: but nature knows what is natural, and the planet is undeceived. The malady of the Germans and their helpers—though it may, superficially, parody the normal excesses of a war of ingestion —fails to exemplify prey and its necessary afflictions (Feeding, need, greed). Instead, the German malady points to something not well understood, something that runs against the planet's grain, though now and again our unhappy world has been host, on a smaller scale, to such aberration.

The Holocaust—the burnt offering of the Jewish people in the furnace of the German Moloch—is an instance of aberration so gargantuan that it cannot leave wary nature (which understands its prerogatives and guards them against facile mutation) unshaken. Killing for the pangs of hunger, nature always celebrates; killing out of rage or fear or lust, nature often claims; but killing for Spirit, on behalf of the adoration of death, nature abhors. It is for the sake of life that nature allows its creatures to become instruments of death. Jewish bone meal is a slur on a planet given over to life: a disorder that contradicts nature's means and calumniates its ends.

What other mutation of the last fifty years has swarmed out of history in order to confront the biological premises of our sad earth-speck?

Innovation and Redemption:
What Literature Means

I. INNOVATION

A while ago, freed by a bout of flu from all responsibility, I became one of those nineteenth-century leisured persons we hear about, for whom the great novels are said to have been written. In this condition I came, for the first time, to the novels of Thomas Hardy. I began with *Tess of the D'Urbervilles,* and discovered this: it is possible first to ask the question "What is this novel *about?*" and then to give an answer. Hardy writes about—well, *life* (nowadays we are made to hesitate before daring seriously to employ this word); life observed and understood as well as felt. A society with all its interminglings and complexities is set before us: in short, knowledge; knowledge of convention and continuity; also knowledge of something real, something *there*. *Tess,* for instance, is thick with knowledge of Cow. What is a cow, how does it feel to lean against, how do you milk, what is the milkshed like, what is the life of a milker, who is the milker's boss, where does the milk go? To touch any element of Cow intimately

Conflated from: "Some Antediluvian Reflections," *American Journal,* Vol. 1, No. 1 (December 1, 1971). "Where Are the Serious Readers?," *Salmagundi,* Summer-Fall 1978. "What Literature Means," *Partisan Review,* Vol. 49, No. 1 (1982).

and concretely is to enter a land, a society, a people, and to penetrate into the whole lives of human beings.

The world of Cow, or its current equivalents, is now in the possession of writers like Leon Uris and Harold Robbins—shadows of shadows of Hardy. Post-Joyce, the "real" writers have gone somewhere else. And though we may not, cannot, turn back to the pre-Joycean "fundamentalist" novel, it is about time it was recognized that too much "subjectivity" has led away from mastery (which so-called "experimental" novelist tells us about Cow?) and from seriousness (to which black-humorist or parodist would you entrust the whole lives of human beings?).

What is today called "experimental" writing is unreadable. It fails because it is neither intelligent nor interesting. Without seriousness it cannot be interesting, and without mastery it will never be intelligent.

The idea of the experimental derives from the notion of generations: a belief in replacement, substitution, discontinuity, above all repudiation. Who invented "generations," and when did they come into being? John Hollander, reflecting on children's literature, notes that the idea of "children" as a classification of fresh innocence is itself a remarkably short-lived fancy, squeezed into that brief pre-Freudian bourgeois moment that made Lewis Carroll possible; before the nineteenth century there *were* no children, only smaller-sized working people; and then Freud arrived to take the charm, and the purity, out of Victorian childhood.

There are, in fact, no "generations," except in the biological sense. There are only categories and crises of temperament, and these crisscross and defy and deny chronology. The concept of generations, moreover, is peculiarly solipsistic: it declares that because I am new, then everything I make or do in the world is new.

When I was a quite young child, just beginning to write stories, I had an odd idea of time. It seemed to me that because writing signified permanence, it was necessary to address not only everyone who might live afterward, but also everyone who had ever lived before. This meant one had to keep one's eye on the ancient Greeks in particular, to write for *them* too; and, knowing no ancient Greek, I got around the difficulty by employing the most archaic language

the Green, Yellow, Blue, Red, and Violet Fairy Books had to offer.
Now if this belief that everything counts forever, both backward
and forward, is a kind of paradisal foolishness, it is no more nonsensi-
cal than the belief that nothing counts for long—the credo that the
newest generation displaces the one before it. The problem with
believing in generations is not only the most obvious one—that you
excise history, that you cut off even the most immediately usable past
—but the sense of narrow obligation it imposes on the young, a kind
of prisoner's outlook no less burdensome than all the following dicta
taken together:

1. That each new crop of mass births must reinvent culture.
2. That models are unthinkable.
3. That each succeeding generation is inherently brighter and
   more courageous than the one before.
4. That "establishments" are irreversibly closed.
5. That whatever has won success is by definition stale.
6. That "structurelessness"—i.e., incoherence—must be understood as a paradox, since incoherence is really coherence.
7. That "experiment" is endlessly possible, and endlessly positive,
   and that the more "unprecedented" a thing is, the better it is.
8. That "alternative forms" are salvational.
9. That irrational (or "psychedelic") states represent artistic
   newness.

I could make this list longer, but it is already long enough to
demonstrate the critical point that more useful cultural news inhabits
the Fifth Commandment than one might imagine at first glance.

The sources of these statements are of course everywhere—they
are the bad breath of the times. At best, "experimental" fiction aims
for parody: it turns the tables on the old voices, it consists of allusion
built upon allusion, it is a choreography of ridicule and satire. It goes
without saying that no literature can live without satire; satire
nourishes and cleanses and resuscitates. The great satires that have
survived are majestic indictments. Our attention now is assaulted by
ephemeral asterisks claiming to be satire: when you follow the dim
little star to its destination, what you find is another littleness—
parody. Parody without seriousness, without, in the end, irony. If
the writer does not know what to do with the remnants of high

culture, he parodies them; if he does not know what to do with kitsch, he simply invites it in. Twenty years hence, the American fiction of parody is going to require an addendum—complete citations of the work and tone and attitude it meant to do in. Whatever seems implicit now because of its currency as memory or tradition will have to be made explicit later, for the sake of comprehension, when tradition is forgotten and memory is dead. (Compare any annotated copy of "The Rape of the Lock.") And meanwhile, the trouble with parody is that it is endlessly reflective, one parody building on a previous parody, and so on, until eventually the goal becomes ingenuity in the varieties of derivativeness, and one loses sight of any original objective notion of what literature can be about, of the real sources of literature. Redundance is all—and in the name of escape from the redundance of convention.

One of the great conventions—and also one of the virtues—of the old novel was its suspensefulness. Suspense *seems* to make us ask "What will happen to Tess next?," but really it emerges from the writer's conviction of social or cosmic principle. Suspense occurs when the reader is about to learn something, not simply about the relationship of fictional characters, but about the writer's relationship to a set of ideas, or to the universe. Suspense is the product of teaching, and teaching is the product of mastery, and mastery is the product of seriousness, and seriousness springs not from ego or ambition or the workings of the subjective self, but from the amazing permutations of the objective world.

Fiction will not be interesting or lasting unless it is again conceived in the art of the didactic. (Emphasis, however, on *art*.) The experimental is almost never the innovative. The innovative imagines something we have never experienced before: think of Tolstoy's imagining the moment of dying in "The Death of Ivan Ilych." The experimental fiddles with what has gone before, precisely and exclusively with what has gone before; it is obsessed by precedent and predecessors. The innovative, by contrast, sets out to educate its readers in its views about what it means to be a human being—though it too can fiddle with this and that if it pleases, and is not averse to unexpected seizures and tricks, or to the jarring gifts of vitality and cunning. Innovation cannot be defined through mere *method;* the experimental can be defined no other way. And innovation has a hidden subject: coherence.

An avatar of "alternative kinds of literary coherence"* asks us to note how

> the criteria for measuring literacy change in time, so that the body of information and ideas that seemed "literate" in the forties may, because of the sheer increase of knowledge, seem only semi-literate now. Moreover, unless older writers' minds are open enough to recognize that what a young poet learns today may be quite different from what his predecessors know, they may miss evidences of his learning . . . very rare is the literary gent over forty who can recognize, for instance, such recent-vintage ideas as say, feedback, information theory and related cybernetic concepts. This deficiency partially explains why, try as hard as we might, it is often so frustrating, if not impossible, to conduct an intelligent dialogue with older writers, the most dogmatic and semi-literate of whom are simply unable to transcend their closed and hardened ways of thought and learning. Not only do the best educated young minds seem much better educated than older intellectuals were at comparable ages, but also what a well-informed young writer knows is likely to be more relevant, not just to contemporary understanding, but also to the problems of creating literary art today.

(Surely the authors of *The Waste Land* and *Finnegans Wake,* literary and intellectual heroes of the forties, would count as "older writers"—instances, no doubt, of semi-literacy and hardened ways.)

Mindful that youth alone may not altogether make his argument, and relying on the McLuhanite vocabulary current a decade ago, the same writer offers still another variant definition of "coherence":

> A truth of contemporary avant-garde esthetics is that "formless art" is either a polemical paradox or an impossible contradiction in terms,

---

*Richard Kostelanetz, "Young Writers in North America," *The American Pen,* Fall 1971. Mr. Kostelanetz illustrates what he means by "alternative kinds of coherence," and perhaps also by literacy, in part with the following:

> Errect, do it, do it again
> Errect, o take me, have me, let Yourself out
> Errect, o yes, o yess, yesss i'm Out

for any work that can be defined—that can be characterized in any way—is by definition artistically coherent. It follows that just because a work fails to cohere in a linear fashion need not mean that it cannot be understood; rather, as recent literature accustoms us to its particular ways of organizing expression, so we learn to confront a new work with expectations wholly different from those honed on traditional literature.

Or, history is bunk.

And just here is the danger and the grief—those "wholly different" expectations. If apprentice writers are trained to define away plain contradictions, bringing us at last to a skilled refinement of Orwellian doublethink (incoherence is coherence), if standardized new "information"—though no one doubts that "feedback, information theory and related cybernetic concepts" are the Cow of our time —is to take the place of the idiosyncratic cadences of literary imagination and integration, if "the criteria for measuring literacy" lead to the dumping of both cognition and recognition, if focus and possession are to be dissipated into the pointless distractions and distractabilities of "multimedia" and other devices, if becoming "wholly different" means the tedium of mechanical enmity toward and mechanical overthrow of "older writers," and if all this is to be programmed through hope of instantaneous dissolutions, then not only literature but *the desire to have a literature* will be subverted.

Culture is the continuity of human aspiration—which signifies a continuity of expectations. Innovation in art is not rupture. Innovation in art is not the consequence of the implantation of "wholly different" expectations. Innovation in art means the continuity of expectations.

Every new sentence, every new fragment of imaginative literature born into the world, is a heart-in-the-mouth experiment, and for its writer a profound chanciness; but the point of the risk is the continuation of a recognizably human enterprise. "Wholly different" means unrecognizable; unrecognizable means the breaking-off of a culture, and its supplanting. It cannot be true that the end of a culture is the beginning of art. When cultural continuity is broken off—as in the Third Reich—what happens is first the debasement, then the extirpation, of any recognizable human goals. First the violation of art (Mozart at the gas chamber's door), then the end of art.

Innovation in art is not the same as innovation in the human psyche; just the opposite. Innovation in art has as its motivation the extension of humanity, not a flow of spite against it. The difference between barbarian and civilized expectations is the difference between the will to dominate and the will toward regeneration. To dominate you must throw the rascals out; to regenerate, you have to take them with you. Spite vandalizes. Innovation redeems.

As for who the rascals are: there is no predicament that cures itself so swiftly as that of belonging to "the young." Alice, nibbling at the mushroom, shrank so quickly that her chin crashed into her shoe: *that* fast is how we go from twenty-three to fifty-four, and from fifty-five to eighty-six. *Vita brevis!* If writers are to have a program, it ought not to be toward *ressentiment,* but toward achronology. Younger writers who resent older ones will, before they are nearly ready for it, find themselves hated by someone astonishingly recently out of the pram. Older writers who envy younger ones have a bottomless cornucopia to gorge on: the baby carriages are packed with novelists and poets. The will to fashion a literature asserts the obliteration of time. The obliteration of time makes "experiment" seem a puff of air, the faintest clamor of celestial horselaugh.

2. REDEMPTION

At a party once I heard a gifted and respected American writer— a writer whose prestigious name almost everyone would recognize —say, "For me, the Holocaust and a corncob are the same." The choice of "corncob"—outlandish, unexpected, askew—is a sign of the strong and daring charge of his imagination, and so is its juxtaposition with the darkest word of our century. What he intended by this extraordinary sentence was not to shock the moral sense, but to clarify the nature of art.

He meant that there is, for art, no such element as "subject matter"; for art, one sight or moment or event is as good as another—

there is no "value" or "worth" or "meaning"—because all are equally made up of language, and language and its patterns are no different from tone for the composer or color for the painter. The artist as citizen, the writer explained, can be a highly moral man or woman—one who would, if the Nazis came, hide Jews. But the artist as artist is not a moral creature. Within literature, all art is dream, and whether or not the artist is or is not in citizenly possession of moral credentials is irrelevant to the form and the texture of the work of art, which claims only the territory of the imagination, and nothing else.

For that writer, a phrase such as "a morally responsible literature" would be an oxymoron, the earlier part of the phrase clashing to the death with the latter part. To be responsible as a writer is to be responsible solely to the seizures of language and dream.

I want to stand against this view. The writer who says "For me, the Holocaust and a corncob are the same" is putting aside the moral sense in art, equating the moral impulse only with the sociologically real, or perhaps with the theologically ideal. In literature he judges the moral sense to be an absurd intrusion. He is in the stream that comes to us from Greece, through Walter Pater and Emerson: art for its own sake, separated from the moral life. He is mainly Greek.

For me, with certain rapturous exceptions, literature *is* the moral life. The exceptions occur in lyric poetry, which bursts shadowless like flowers at noon, with the eloquent bliss almost of nature itself, when nature is both benevolent and beautiful. For the rest—well, one discounts stories and novels that are really journalism; but of the stories and novels that mean to be literature, one expects a certain corona of moral purpose: not outright in the grain of the fiction itself, but in the form of a faintly incandescent envelope around it. The tales we care for lastingly are the ones that touch on the redemptive—not, it should be understood, on the guaranteed promise of redemption, and not on goodness, kindness, decency, all the usual virtues. Redemption has almost nothing to do with virtue, especially when the call to virtue is prescriptive or coercive; rather, it is the singular idea that is the opposite of the Greek belief in fate: the idea that insists on the freedom to change one's life.

Redemption means fluidity; the notion that people and things are

subject to willed alteration; the sense of possibility; of turning away
from, or turning toward; of deliverance; the sense that we act for
ourselves rather than are acted upon; the sense that we are responsible, that there is no *deus ex machina* other than the character we have
ourselves fashioned; above all, that we can surprise ourselves. Implicit in redemption is amazement, marveling, suspense—precisely
that elation-bringing suspense of the didactic I noted earlier, wherein
the next revelation is about to fall. Implicit in redemption is everything against the fated or the static: everything that hates death and
harm and elevates the life-giving—if only through terror at its
absence.

Now I know how hazardous these last phrases are, how they
suggest philistinism, how they lend themselves to a vulgar advocacy
of an "affirmative" literature in order to fulfill a moral mandate. I too
recoil from all that: the so-called "affirmative" is simple-minded,
single-minded, crudely explicit; it belongs either to journalism or to
piety or to "uplift." It is the enemy of literature and the friend of
coercion. It is, above all, a hater of the freedom inherent in storytelling and in the poetry side of life. But I mean something else: I mean
the corona, the luminous envelope—perhaps what Henry James
meant when he said "Art is nothing more than the shadow of humanity." I think, for instance, of the literature of *midrash*, of parable,
where there is no visible principle or moral imperative. The principle does not enter into, or appear in, the tale; it *is* the tale; it realizes
the tale. To put it another way: the tale is its own interpretation. It
is a world that decodes itself.

And that is what the "corona" is: interpretation, implicitness, the
nimbus of *meaning* that envelops story. Only someone who has
wholly dismissed meaning can boast that the Holocaust and a corncob are, for art, the same. The writers who claim that fiction is
self-referential, that what a story is about is the language it is made
out of, have snuffed the corona. They willingly sit in the dark, like
the strict-constructionist Karaites who, wanting to observe the Sabbath exactly, sat in the lampless black and the fireless cold on the very
day that is most meant to resemble paradise. The misuse of the
significance of language by writers who most intend to celebrate
the comeliness of language is like the misuse of the Sabbath by

the fundamentalist Karaites: both annihilate the thing they hope to glorify.

What literature means is meaning.

But having said that, I come to something deeply perilous: and that is imagination. In Hebrew, just as there is *t'shuva*, the energy of creative renewal and turning, so there is the *yetzer ha-ra*, the Evil Impulse—so steeped in the dark brilliance of the visionary that it is said to be the source of the creative faculty. Imagination is more than make-believe, more than the power to invent. It is also the power to penetrate evil, to take on evil, to become evil, and in that guise it is the most frightening human faculty. Whoever writes a story that includes villainy enters into and becomes the villain. Imagination owns above all the facility of becoming: the writer can enter the leg of a mosquito, a sex not her own, a horizon he has never visited, a mind smaller or larger. But also the imagination seeks out the unsayable and the undoable, and says and does them. And still more dangerous: the imagination always has the lust to tear down meaning, to smash interpretation, to wear out the rational, to mock the surprise of redemption, to replace the fluid force of suspense with an image of stasis; to transfix and stun rather than to urge; to spill out, with so much quicksilver wonder, idol after idol. An idol serves no one; it is served. The imagination, like Moloch, can take you nowhere except back to its own maw. And the writers who insist that literature is "about" the language it is made of are offering an idol: literature for its own sake, for its own maw: not for the sake of humanity.

Literature is for the sake of humanity.

My conclusion is strange, and takes place on a darkling plain. Literature, to come into being at all, must call on the imagination; imagination is in fact the flesh and blood of literature; but at the same time imagination is the very force that struggles to snuff the redemptive corona. So a redemptive literature, a literature that interprets and decodes the world, beaten out for the sake of humanity, must wrestle with its own body, with its own flesh and blood, with its own life. Cell battles cell. The corona flickers, brightens, flares, clouds, grows faint. The *yetzer ha-ra*, the Evil Impulse, fills its cheeks with a black wind, hoping to blow out the redemptive corona; but at the last moment steeples of light spurt up from the corona, and the world with its meaning is laid open to our astonished sight.

In that steady interpretive light we can make distinctions; we can see that one thing is not interchangeable with another thing; that not everything is the same; that the Holocaust is different, God knows, from a corncob. So we arrive, at last, at the pulse and purpose of literature: to reject the blur of the "universal"; to distinguish one life from another; to illumine diversity; to light up the least grain of being, to show how it is concretely individual, particularized from any other; to tell, in all the marvel of its singularity, the separate holiness of the least grain.

Literature is the recognition of the particular.

For that, one needs the corona.

The Hole/Birth Catalogue

I. THE LOGIC OF THE HOLE

It may be that almost everything that separates women from men is a social fabrication—clothing, occupations, thinking habits, temperament. It may be that when we say "woman" we are invoking a heritage of thought, a myth, a learned construct: an *idea*. But childbirth is not any of these. "Woman" can be an imagining, a convenient dream of law or economics or religion. But childbirth is an event, *the* event of the race, and only half the race undergoes it. Is it, for that half, an illimitable experience, endlessly influencing, both before and afterward, an event that dominates until death?

Everyone is born, everyone dies, and though styles of death are subject to invention and misfortune—getting a bullet through your skull feels different, presumably, from the slow drugged death of the terminal cancer victim—we all struggle out of the birth canal with the same gestures and responses. What happens immediately afterward—who cares for the infant, and how, and where—is all at once the expression of the culture. If anatomy is destiny, technology is also a kind of destiny, and the baby bottle, no less than the jet plane,

Essay published in *Ms.*, October 1972.

can alter a civilization. Beds, stirrups, hospitals, doctors, nurses, stitches, bandages, pills, pillows, all the debris of folklore that flies out after every birth with the certainty of the expulsion of the placenta—these are the social impedimenta that clutter the event. They seem almost to be the event itself.

But the person in childbirth can be alone in a forest, and still the baby's head will be driven through the hole at the bottom of her torso. It is sensible for the hole not to be covered. The baby is born entirely exposed, either with a hole of its own or with an inseminatory rod. It is attached by a string of flesh. When the string is cut, that is the end of the event.

Is it the end of the event?

How long is the event of childbirth? Several hours; it varies with the individual. How long is human life? Here the variation is greater. It is possible to die at birth, to be run over by a truck at thirty, to be bombed at forty, to live to be old. But "woman" is concretely— not mythologically—woman only for the sake of the few hours of childbirth. All the rest of the time her life and body are subject to more ordinary interruptions, by which she is distinguished very little from anyone else. Childbirth is an appointment (menstruation is the appointment calendar, listing only cancellations; like any negative calendar it requires small attention)—an appointment undertaken nine months before: which, unless nullified by abortion, must inevitably be kept.

But imagine a lucky and healthful land where a human being is likely to live peaceably until eighty. Imagine one who has experienced childbirth only twice, with the event lasting each time about six hours. For the sake of twelve hours out of a life seven hundred and one thousand two hundred and eighty hours long, this person is called "woman." For the sake of twelve hours out of a life seven hundred and one thousand two hundred and eighty hours long, this person is thrust into an ethos that enjoins rigid duties on her, almost none of them rationally related to the two six-hour events of childbirth.

Or imagine, in this lucky and healthful land, a person sixty years old. She is widowed and lives alone in a dark little flat. Consider her.

Thirty years ago she spent six hours expelling an infant out of her hole via powerful involuntary muscular contractions. She did it in a special room in a big building. It was a rod-bearing infant, which afterward grew to be somewhat under six feet in height, dressed itself in two cloth tubes cut off at the ankles, and by now has spurted semen up a number of human holes; having settled down in a house in California, it has inseminated one hole three times. The person in the dark little flat thinks of herself as the grandmother of Linda, Michael, and Karen. Which is to say: she thinks of herself as a hole; the *Ur*-hole, so to speak; and that is very interesting.

It is also very interesting to look closely at this person who thinks of herself as a hole. She is covered up by a cloth tube cut off at the knees. Why is she covered up by one cloth tube cut off at the knees, instead of two cloth tubes cut off at the ankles? Thirty years ago she expelled an infant out of her hole; that is the reason. Anatomy is destiny, and it is her destiny, because of her hole, to wear one cloth tube cut off at the knees instead of two cloth tubes cut off at the ankles.

Now look at the hair that grows on her head. Do not look for the hair in her armpits; she has clipped that. The reason she has clipped the hair in her armpits is that thirty years ago she expelled an infant out of her hole. But her head hair: look at that. It is of a certain length and is artificially curled. The reason her head hair is of that length, artificially curled, is that thirty years ago she expelled an infant out of her hole.

Watch her. She is sitting at the kitchen table sewing another cloth tube. Once in a while she rises and stirs something in a pot. The reason she is sitting at the kitchen table sewing a cloth tube (the kind cut off at the knees), the reason she gets up now and then to stir her pot, is not that she is hungry or is in need of another cloth tube. No: the reason is that thirty years ago she expelled an infant out of her hole, and ever since then she has conscientiously performed the duties that do not flow from the event.

And if the event had not taken place? She would still conscientiously perform those duties that do not flow from the event that did not happen. The hole in her body dictates her tasks, preoccupations, proprieties, tastes, character. Wondrous hole! Magical hole! Dazzlingly influential hole! Noble and effulgent hole! From this hole everything follows logically: first the baby, then the placenta, then, for years and years and years until death, a way of life. It is all logic, and she who lives by the hole will live also by its logic.

It is, appropriately, logic with a hole in it.

2. DESTINY, BIRTH, LIFE, DEATH

"Anatomy is destiny." These are Freud's words, and they have become almost as famous as his name itself. But, ah, fame is not truth; and destiny is precisely what anatomy is *not*. A hole is not destiny. A protuberance is not destiny. Even two protuberances—a pair of legs, nearly half the human body—are not destiny. If anatomy were destiny, the wheel could not have been invented; we would have been limited by legs.

Destiny is what is implicit in the very area we cannot speak of because it is not known—the sense of things beyond and apart from shape or dimension or hole or protuberance. There is an armless painter who holds the brush between his toes. Cut off two more limbs and he will use his teeth. The engineering is secondary to the vision. Anatomy is only a form of technology—nature's engineering. Destiny means, at the lowest, a modification of anatomy, and, at the highest, a soaring beyond anatomy. A person—and "person" is above all an idea—escapes anatomy. To reduce the person altogether to her anatomy is to wish the person into a nullity.

There is, first of all, the nullity of the servant.

In *Civilization and Its Discontents*, Freud posits a remarkable anatomical theory for the secondary and dependent condition of woman. The argument begins with the assertion that since fire represents the power of civilization, whoever can control fire can be dominant over civilization. By the "control" of fire, Freud explains, he means the ability to put it out at will. A man can pee on a fire from a little distance. Prevented by her anatomy, a woman cannot. Therefore man is in charge of civilization and woman cannot be.

Later in the same essay Freud identifies woman as having a "retarding and restraining influence" on civilization. This is because the tasks of civilization require "instinctual sublimations of which women are little capable."

But all this is the later Freud. *Civilization and Its Discontents* was composed after cancer had already begun to ravage Freud's face, and when Hitlerism had already begun to corrode German civilization. If he was writing, under such circumstances, with a kind of melancholy truculence, it might be instructive to see what Freud's views were at an earlier and happier time. Consider, then, Freud in love.

In love with Martha Bernays, Freud translated John Stuart Mill's essay "On the Subjection of Women" into German. He did not notice its relevance to his fiancée's position—she had committed herself to a long and chaste engagement, during which she was to idle away years in waiting for the marriage. As for the essay itself, he did not like it. For one thing, he complained of its "lifeless style." (In a footnote Freud's biographer, Ernest Jones, a Freudian disciple, explains: "In exculpation of Mill one should mention that his wife is supposed to have been the main author of the book in question." It is axiomatic that a "wife's" style is inferior.) Freud's letter about Mill, written to his fiancée, is long; but worth, one supposes, the attention due genius:

> He [Mill] was perhaps the man of the century who best managed to free himself from the domination of customary prejudices. On the other hand—and that always goes together with it—he lacked in many matters the sense of the absurd; for example, in that of female emancipation and in the woman's question altogether. I recollect that in the essay I translated a prominent argument was that a married woman could earn as much as her husband. We surely agree that the management of a house, the care and bringing up of children, demand the whole of a human being and almost exclude any earning, even if a simplified household relieve her of dusting, cleaning, cooking, etc. He had simply forgotten all that, like everything else concerning the relationship between the sexes. That is altogether a point with Mill where one simply cannot find him human. His autobiography is so prudish or so ethereal that one could never gather from it that human

beings consist of men and women and that this distinction is the most significant one that exists. In his whole presentation it never emerges that women are different beings—we will not say lesser, rather the opposite—from men. He finds the suppression of women an analogy to that of Negroes. Any girl, even without a suffrage or legal competence, whose hand a man kisses and for whose love he is prepared to dare all, could have set him right. It is really a stillborn thought to send women into the struggle for existence exactly as men. If, for instance, I imagined my sweet gentle girl as a competitor it would only end in my telling her . . . that I am fond of her and that I implore her to withdraw from the strife into the calm uncompetitive activity of my home. It is possible that changes in upbringing may suppress all a woman's tender attributes, needful of protection and yet so victorious, and that she can then earn a livelihood like men. It is also possible that in such an event one would not be justified in mourning the passing away of the most delightful thing the world can offer us—our ideal of womanhood. I believe that all reforming action in law and education would break down in front of the fact that, long before the age at which a man can earn a position in society, Nature has determined woman's destiny through beauty, charm, and sweetness. Law and custom have much to give women that has been withheld from them, but the position of women will surely be what it is: in youth an adored darling and in mature years a loved wife.

"Nature has determined woman's destiny." It is, to borrow from Jones, no exculpation of Freud to note that he was a man of his class and era, and that this letter was written before 1890. Mill's essay is dated 1869; if Freud was, at his own valuation, a judge of human affairs, he was a retrogressive judge. And if he is, at the valuation of his posterity, a genius, his is the genius of retrogression.

But also of something worse. We come now to the nullity of death.

Mill, all lucidity and sanity, is called "prudish" and "ethereal"—words meaning precisely the opposite of what Mill's essay exhibits to everyone who has ever read it attentively, with the exception of its German translator. Who is the prude—the man who sees the distinction between men and women as "the most significant one that exists," significant chiefly for reducing women to petlike dependency in "my home," or the man who refuses to turn distinctions into liabilities? Who is the ethereal thinker—the man who poetizes about tender attributes and adored darlings and miracle-working kisses, or the man who draws up a solid catalogue of palpable discriminations against women? In inventing anatomy-is-destiny, Freud justified his having a household servant all the days of his life. The letter to his fiancée (who appears to have swallowed it all) is not only prudish and ethereal, but also bleatingly sentimental—because that is what sentimentality *is:* justification, exculpation, a covering-over, a retreat from clarity, prudishness and etherealism concealing real conditions.

Still, running a household, after all, is not tantamount to death, anguish, or even waste. Decent and fulfilling lives have gone down that road, if fulfillment is counted in pies and sock-washings. And why not? Bureaucrats and dentists are equal drudges and fiddlers, jobs are cells of domesticated emotion, offices are repetitious and restrictive boxes. Both men and women practice housewifery, wherever they are. Hemingway's early stories are cookbooks. If only "the management of a house" were the whole story! But no: once invoke Nature and Destiny and you are inviting an intensified preoccupation with death. Death becomes the whole story.

This is simply because all the truth any philosophy can really tell us about human life is that each new birth supplies another corpse. Philosophy tells only that; it is true; and if the woman is seen only as childbearer, she is seen only as disgorger of corpses. What is a baby-machine if not also a corpse-maker? Philosophy—Freud is a philosopher—leads only to the inexorable cadaver, and never to the glorious So What: the life-cry.

To say anatomy-is-destiny is to misunderstand the So What, that insatiable in-between which separates the fresh birth from the cadaver it turns out to be. To say anatomy-is-destiny is to reverse the life instinct—to reverse not only the findings of Darwin, but civilization in general. If the fish had stuck to its gills there would have been no movement up to the land. Lungs came because a creature of the sea wanted to take a walk, not vice versa. When a previous abundance of water began to evaporate during the breakup of the Ice Age, the unlucky fish had either to adapt to its destiny—air—or die. Air preceded lungs. In the history of evolution, destiny always precedes anatomy, and anatomy conforms by thinking up a convenient modification. In the history of civilization, dream precedes engineering. Imagine walking on the moon, and the artifact to take you there will follow the conception.

Freud, a retrograde thinker, had it backward. Celebrated for theorizing on evanescent and gossamer dream-life, he nevertheless limited humanity to the grossest designs of the flesh. In postulating anatomy-is-destiny, he stopped at the flesh; and the flesh dies. It is no surprise that Freud came finally to "discover" what he called the "death instinct." He divided the mind between Eros and destructiveness, making death as central to his scheme as sexuality. And in choosing the centrality of death, he reinvented as instinct what the priests of the Pharaohs took to be ontology. By putting birth first, he put death before life.

This is no paradox. The life instinct, insofar as we can define it (and we cannot), is the struggle to dare higher and higher, beyond the overtly possible, and in spite of knowing we will die. "The force that through the green fuse drives the flower / Drives my green age."

In the light of Freud's assertion of the death instinct, it is absolutely no wonder that he distorted, misunderstood, and hated religion—which is to say holiness: which is to say the struggle to dare higher and higher, beyond the overtly possible. Freud's *Selbsthass* was of a piece with his hatred for his inherited faith.* He despised Judaism because it had in the earliest moment of history rejected the Egyptian preoccupation with a literal anatomy of death and instead hallowed, for its own sake, the time between birth and dying. Judaism has no dying god, no embalming of dead bodies, above all no slightest version of death instinct—"Choose life." In revenge against Judaism's declared life principle, and to satisfy the urgencies and priorities of the death instinct, Freud—this was the theme of *Moses and Monotheism*—turned Moses into an Egyptian. It meant he was

---

*He was joyous when Jung became a disciple—until then, he wrote Karl Abraham, psychoanalysis had seemed like a "Jewish national affair," but now, with a Gentile attached to it, it would gain in value.

turning himself into an Egyptian. It is no joke to notice that for mummies anatomy is all the destiny they will ever own.

3. DEATH (CONTINUED), A LETTER FROM A MADMAN, AND A PRUDISH AND ETHEREAL CONCLUSION

The being-born belongs to all of us, yet we remember nothing. In the forgetting itself lies the life principle, the glorious So What—you are here, get started, live, see, do, dream, figure a destiny, and make its mold for your little time. This is the meaning of the forgetting. And just as the being-born belongs to all of us, so the giving-birth belongs to no one. It is not a property or a lasting act. The making of the child gets done, and thereafter the child is a person, not a consequence or an ornament, and must be seen to with the diligence and generosity due all persons.

To make of the giving-birth a lifelong progression of consequences is to make a shrine of an act. It is a species of idolatry. A moment is mummified and consecrated—that very moment which the whole human race cannot remember. We are told that the capacity for childbirth makes a "woman." Woman, then, becomes the amnesia of the race. She is nullified into an absence.

But now there is a contradiction. She is not an absence; she represents, above all, the protoplasmic *thereness* of the human animal. She represents precisely what decays. She stands for dust, being dust-bringer. I took note earlier of that stupendously simple point: whoever creates the babies creates the corpses. Whoever signifies Birth signifies Death. Anatomy—in the case of woman, parturition—is destiny, the uterus is a grave, the childbearer carries death.

Freud saw woman wholly as childbearer. Seemingly apart from this perception, he came upon the notion of the death instinct. This he related to the killing of the "primal father" by the sons banded together (a curious unprovable fiction on which a great part of Freud's work rests). He, the great connector, did not connect his perception of the destructiveness and aggressiveness in human nature with the act of parturition. Logic makes the connection.

Whoever destroys, whoever is aggressive, has first to be born; the childbearer becomes Shiva the Destroyer. It is the logical product of anatomy-is-destiny. The uterus destines the woman to spew destruction.

How can this terrible logic, this ultimate *reductio* which places the whole burden of humankind's failings on the woman's uterus, be contravened?

With great simplicity. Do not define woman solely by the act of parturition, and the demonic structure dissolves. Then the woman bears the baby, but her entry into parenthood—parenthood, that brevity—does not tie off the world. Parenthood becomes a rich episode in a life struck full with diverse and multiform episodes. She is a mother, a worker, a reader, a sailor. She is a judge, a peddler, a druggist, a polisher of shoes, a pilot, a publisher, an engineer. She is any combination of anything. She chooses life. She is not mythologized by a definition: one-who-gives-birth-and-therefore-spreads-destruction-and-creates-graveyards.

Now it is time to tell about my letter. It is from a madman. The usefulness of madmen is famous: they demonstrate society's logic carried out flagrantly down to its last scrimshaw scrap.

My madman's letter is typed on four long sheets of legal-sized paper, and all in carbon. Many copies of this letter have been broadcast by the diligent fellow, typing day and night on his machine. Here and there, at some especially passionate point, he has underlined with a heavy pencil. I pity him so much labor.

The reason he has sent the letter to me is clear. I have published some pieces on woman and society. He must somehow have worked up a list (he is a master of lists, as we shall see)—a list of writers on the Woman Question, and we are his targets.

"Friend," he begins, "women will soon be the most hated and despised of all living things. It is your fanaticism for fecundity that is overpopulating the earth and ruining our ecology."

Good: my madman is not so crazy after all. He wants to save the environment. And he calls me friend. Already I like him a little.

But already I notice the Freudian turn in him. He too thinks of woman solely as childbearer.

"Years ago," he continues, "the fist was man's weapon to slay other men. Then the rock and the club were used. Spears and swords followed, with long lances. The bow and arrow preceded the rifle and six-shooter. The machine guns, artillery pieces, tanks, and aerial bombs follow. Finally, the A-bomb." Another Freudian turn. My madman has discovered the death instinct. But, though mad, he is logical (and here he has underlined with a furious blackness): *"The progress of weaponry corresponded with the output of women's wombs. That sums it up!"*

But apparently the summing-up is insufficient. There is more, much more: "Anyone who has a money-interest in population growth is apt to be against birth control and abortion." He means us to understand that it is women who are preëminently against birth control and abortions. It follows that women represent the money-interests. But now begin my madman's lists, and here is a little lapse: his catalogue of money-interests is curiously devoid of women. He lists doctors, diaper manufacturers, morticians, sellers of graveyard space, tombstones, funeral flowers, caskets, chauffeurs who drive hearses and funeral limousines, publishers of schoolbooks, auto firms that sell cars, trucks, and school buses, oil firms, tire manufacturers, road builders, realtors, contractors. "Lawyers, judges, cops, and jailers get their cut too.

"I don't mean to be harsh," he finishes kindly. "But you women will have to assess your priorities a bit better! You women, with your mania to procreate to keep the Pentagons of the world up all through the small hours night after night scheming ways to kill and maim the product of your overworked wombs. Great will be the animosity toward your overwhelming womb-output! Toward your selfish spawning! *Soon*"—now he begins to underline again, and this makes his saliva flow nastily—*"soon pregnant women will be spat on, assaulted, and even killed!"*

So much for Freud's adored darlings. The death instinct, having given up on the primal father, is ganging up on pregnant women, who always used to be sure of at least a seat on the bus.

Reductio ad absurdum. My madman is after all a madman. But he is also, observe, a *practical* logician. Further, he owns the courage of

Justice to Feminism

The two essays that follow are "out of date"—the first in the most literal way (Vietnam, civil rights, high birthrates), and both in that they are at odds with their times. Each was written against the grain of academic expectation. Though they were composed a decade apart—the very decade that saw the birth and burgeoning of the women's movement—and though they are united by a point of view that remains steady and unchanged, each essay appears to be out of phase with majority opinion at its own end of the crucial decade. Feminism as a literary issue was absent before the women's movement, and now that there is a strong women's movement consciously defining itself through deliberate segregation, it seems to me that feminism is again absent.

"No one has been serious and passionate, and certainly no one has been argumentative, concerning attitudes about women," I wrote in 1965, when there was no glimmer of a women's movement in sight. "The rebels are few." "Enlightenment has, for women, and especially by women, not yet occurred." How peculiar all that would sound only a short while later! And not simply peculiar, but offensively whimsical, like a costume not really antiquated enough to have taken on remoteness or indifference. The words grate.

But in the middle sixties, to write an essay on the exclusion (and self-exclusion) of women was an anomalous and isolating act—as anomalous and isolating as it had been for Virginia Woolf forty years earlier. Even its language (it shames me now) is strangely, unpleasantly formal. The eerie gravity of tone derives not so much from a pretense of authority as from the stiffness of the unused and the unfamiliar: a walk in new shoe-leather. The tone combines temerity and mimicry; it flaunts the sneer that fears a sneer. I was writing from a briar patch on a desert island in the middle of a bog—an uncomfortable and lonely place to be. Feminism was, in those years, a private tenet one held alone, in an archaic voice.

By 1977, when I wrote my "Dissent" from the headlong development of self-segregation in the women's movement, I was again alone. I found that the new exclusions and psychological definitions of the shapers of this movement exactly matched the old exclusions and definitions. A politics of sex had come into being only to undermine classical feminism. For writers, regression under the banner of a "new" feminism was especially saddening. In the absence of a women's movement, the term "woman writer" had shut out, damaged, and demeaned writers; with the emergence of the movement and the direction it has taken, there are now no allies anywhere against reductiveness, and the language of clarity falls more and more into rubble.

1. Previsions of the Demise of the Dancing Dog

Young women, . . . you are, in my opinion, disgracefully ignorant. You have never made a discovery of any importance. You
have never shaken an empire or led an army into battle. The
plays of Shakespeare are not by you, and you have never introduced a barbarous race to the blessings of civilization. What is
your excuse?

VIRGINIA WOOLF, *A Room of One's Own*

No comradely socialist legislation on women's behalf could ac-
complish a millionth of what a bit more muscle tissue, gratuitously offered by nature, might do. . . .

ELIZABETH HARDWICK, *A View of One's Own*

Several years ago I devoted a year to Examining the Minds of the
Young. It was a curious experience, like going into theater after
theater in a single night, and catching bits of first acts only. How will
the heroine's character develop? Will the hero turn out to be captain
of his fate or only of some minor industry? I never arrived at the
second act, and undoubtedly I will never be witness to the denoue-
ment. But what I saw of all those beginnings was extraordinary: they
were all so similar. All the characters were exactly the same age, and
most had equal limitations of imagination and aspiration. Is "the
individual," I wondered, a sacred certainty, and the human mind
infinitely diversified, as we are always being told? Examine for yourself the Minds of the Young and it is possible you will begin to think
the opposite. Democratic theory is depressingly correct in declaring

From *Woman in Sexist Society* (Basic Books, 1971).

all men equal. Just as every human hand is limited at birth by its five
fingers, so is every human mind stamped from a single, equally
obvious, pattern. "I have never in all my various travels seen but two
sorts of people, and those very like one another; I mean men and
women, who always have been, and ever will be, the same," wrote
Lady Mary Wortley Montagu in the middle of the eighteenth century. Human nature is one.

The vantage point from which I came to these not unusual conclusions was not from reading the great philosophers, or even from
reading Lady Mary—it was from a job. I was hired by a large urban
university to teach English to freshmen: three classes of nearly a
hundred young men and young women, all seventeen, some city-
born, some suburban, some well-off, some only scraping by, of every
ethnic group and of every majority religion but Hindu. Almost all
were equipped with B high-school averages; almost all were more
illiterate than not; almost all possessed similar prejudices expressed
in identical platitudes. Almost all were tall, healthy, strong-toothed,
obedient, and ignorant beyond their years. They had, of course, very
few ideas—at seventeen this can hardly be called a failing; but the
ideas they had were plainly derived not from speculation but from
indoctrination. They had identical minuscule vocabularies, made
identical errors of grammar and punctuation, and were identically
illogical. They were identically uneducated, and the minds of the
uneducated young women were identical with the minds of the
uneducated young men.

Now this last observation was the least surprising of all. Though
unacquainted with the darkest underbrush of the human mind (and
here it must be emphatically averred that deep scrutiny, at indecently
short intervals, of one hundred freshman themes is the quickest and
most scarifying method of achieving intimacy with the human mind
in its rawest state), I had never doubted that the human mind was
a democratic whole, that it was androgynous, epicene, asexual, call
it what you will; it had always seemed axiomatic to me that the minds
of men and women were indistinguishable.

My students confirmed this axiom to the last degree. You could
not tell the young men's papers from the young women's papers.
They thought alike (badly), they wrote alike (gracelessly), and they

believed alike (docilely). And what they all believed was this: that the minds of men and women are spectacularly unlike.

They believed that men write like men, and women like women; that men think like men, and women like women; that men believe like men, and women like women. And they were all identical in this belief.

But I have said, after all, that they were alike in illiteracy, undereducation, ignorance, and prejudice.

Still, to teach at a university is not simply to teach; the teacher is a teacher among students, but he is also a teacher among teachers. He has colleagues, and to have colleagues is to have high exchanges, fruitful discourses, enlightening quarrels. Colleagues, unlike students, are not merely literate but breathtakingly literary; not merely educated but bent under the weight of multitudinous higher degrees; not merely informed but dazzlingly knowledgeable; not merely unprejudiced but brilliantly questing. And my colleagues believed exactly what my students believed.

My colleagues were, let it be noted, members of the Department of English in the prestige college of an important university. I was, let it be revealed, the only woman instructor in that department. Some years before, the college had been all male. Then the coeds were invited in, and now and then in their wake a woman was admitted, often reluctantly, to the faculty. Before my own admittance, I had been living the isolated life of a writer—my occupation for some years had consisted in reading great quantities and in writing embarrassingly tiny quantities. I was, I suppose, not in that condition generally known as "being in touch with the world." I was in touch with novels, poetry, essays, enlarging meditations; but of "the world," as it turned out, I apparently knew little.

I came to the university in search of the world. I had just finished an enormous novel, the writing of which had taken many more years than any novel ought to take, and after so long a retreat my lust for the world was prodigious. I wanted Experience, I wanted to sleep under bridges—but finding that all the bridges had thickly trafficked cloverleaves under them, I came instead to the university. I came innocently. I had believed, through all those dark and hope-sickened years of writing, that it was myself ("myself"—whatever that means for each of us) who was doing the writing. In the university, among my colleagues, I discovered two essential points: (1) that it was a "woman" who had done the writing—not a mind—and that I was a "woman writer"; and (2) that I was now not a teacher, but a "woman teacher."

I was suspect from the beginning—more so among my colleagues than among my students. My students, after all, were accustomed to the idea of a "woman teacher," having recently been taught by several in high school. But my colleagues were long out of high school, and they distrusted me. I learned that I had no genuinely valid opinions, since every view I might hold was colored by my sex. If I said I didn't like Hemingway, I could have no *critical* justification, no *literary* reason; it was only because, being a woman, I obviously could not be sympathetic toward Hemingway's "masculine" subject matter—the hunting, the fishing, the bullfighting, which no woman could adequately digest. It goes without saying that among my colleagues there were other Hemingway dissenters; but their reasons for disliking Hemingway, unlike mine, were not taken to be simply ovarian.

In fact, both my students and my colleagues were equal adherents of the Ovarian Theory of Literature, or, rather, its complement, the Testicular Theory. A recent camp follower (I cannot call him a pioneer) of this explicit theory is, of course, Norman Mailer, who has attributed his own gift, and the literary gift in general, solely and directly to the possession of a specific pair of organs. One writes with these organs, Mailer has said in *Advertisements for Myself*; and I have always wondered with what shade of ink he manages to do it.

I recall my first encounter with the Ovarian Theory. My students had been assigned the reading of *Wise Blood*, the novel by Flannery O'Connor. Somewhere in the discussion I referred to the author as "she." The class stirred in astonishment; they had not imagined that "Flannery" could connote a woman, and this somehow put a different cast upon the narrative and their response to it. Now among my students there was a fine young woman, intelligent and experimental rather than conforming, one of my rare literates, herself an anomaly because she was enrolled in the overwhelmingly male College of

Engineering. I knew that her mind usually sought beyond the commonplace—she wrote with the askew glance of the really inquisitive.
Up went her hand. "But I could *tell* she was a woman," she insisted.
"Her sentences are a woman's sentences." I asked her what she
meant and how she could tell. "Because they're sentimental," she
said, "they're not concrete like a man's." I pointed out whole paragraphs, pages even, of unsentimental, so-called tough prose. "But she
sounds like a woman—she has to sound that way because she is," said
the future engineer, while I speculated whether her bridges and
buildings would loom plainly as woman's work. Moreover, it rapidly
developed that the whole class now declared that it too, even while
ignorant of the author's sex, had nevertheless intuited all along that
this was a woman's prose; it had to be, since Flannery was a she.

My second encounter with the idea of literature-as-physiology
was odder yet. This time my interlocutor was a wonderfully gentle,
deeply intellectual young fellow teacher; he was going to *prove* what
my freshmen had merely maintained. "But of course style is influenced by physical make-up," he began in his judicious graduate-
assistant way. Here was his incontrovertible evidence: "Take Keats,
right? Keats fighting tuberculosis at the end of his life. You don't
suppose Keats's poetry was totally unaffected by his having had
tuberculosis?" And he smiled with the flourish of a young man who
has made an unanswerable point. "Ah, but *you* don't suppose," I put
it to him cheerfully enough, "that being a woman is a *disease?*"

But comparing literary women with having a debilitating disease
is the least of it. My colleague, after all, was a kindly sort, and stuck
to human matters; he did not mention dogs. On the other hand,
almost everyone remembers Dr. Johnson's remark upon hearing a
woman preacher—she reminded him, he said, of a dog dancing on
its hind legs; one marvels not at how well it is done, but that it is
done at all. That was two centuries ago; wise Lady Mary was Johnson's contemporary. Two centuries, and the world of letters has not
been altered by a syllable, unless you regard the switch from dogs
to disease as a rudimentary advance. Perhaps it is. We have advanced
so far that the dullest as well as the best of freshmen can scarcely be
distinguished from Dr. Johnson, except by a bark.

And our own Dr. Johnson—I leave you to guess his name—
hoping to insult a rival writer, announces that the rival "reminds me
of nothing so much as a woman writer."

Consider, in this vein, the habits of reviewers. I think I can say in
good conscience that I have never—repeat, *never*—read a review of
a novel or, especially, of a collection of poetry by a woman that did
not include somewhere in its columns a gratuitous allusion to the
writer's sex and its supposed effects. The Ovarian Theory of Literature is the property of all society, not merely of freshmen and poor
Ph.D. lackeys: you will find it in all the best periodicals, even the
most highbrow. For example: a few years ago a critic in *The New
York Review of Books* considered five novels, three of which were by
women. And so his review begins: "Women novelists, we have
learned to assume, like to keep their focus narrow." And from this
touchstone—with no ground other than the "we have learned to
assume"—falls his praise and his censure. The touchstone, of course,
is properly qualified, as such touchstones always are, by reverent
asides concerning the breadth of George Eliot and the grasp of Jane
Austen. Ah, indispensable George and Jane! They have come into
the world, one concludes, only to serve as exceptions to the strictures
of reviewers; and they *are* exceptions. Genius always is; it is how
genius is defined. But if the exception is to be dragged into every
routine review of novelists and poets who are women, then the rule
must drop equally on all. Let every new poet, male and female, be
reviewed in the shadow of Emily Dickinson and Coleridge. Let
every unknown novelist, male and female, be reviewed in the blaze
of *Anna Karenina* and *Wuthering Heights*. If this seems like nonsense, then reviewers must take merit as their point of concentration,
not stale expectation, and not the glibbest of literary canards.

Still, the canards are, in their way, small fun, being as flexible and
fragile as other toys. A collection of canards is bound to be a gaggle
of contradictions. When, for instance, my bright engineering student identified Flannery O'Connor as "sentimental," she was
squarely in one-half of a diluvial, though bifurcated, tradition.
Within this tradition there are two hoary views of woman. One: she
is sentimental, imprecise, irrational, overemotional, impatient, un-
perseveringly flighty, whimsical, impulsive, unreliable, unmechani-

cal, not given to practicality, perilously vague, and so on. In this view she is always contrasted with man, who is, on the other hand, unsentimental, exact, rational, controlled, patient, hard-headed, mechanically gifted, a meeter of payrolls, firm of purpose, wary of impulse, anything but a dreamer. Description One accounts for why throughout her history she has been a leader neither of empires nor of trades nor of armies. But it is also declared that, her nature having failed her in the practical world, she cannot succeed in the world of invention either: she is unequipped, for example, for poetry, in that (here is Description Two) she is above all pragmatic, sensible and unsentimental, unvisionary, unadventurous, empirical, conservative, down-to-earth, unspontaneous, perseveringly patient and thus good at the minutiae of mechanical and manipulative tasks, and essentially unimaginative. In short, she will wander too much or she will wander not at all. She is either too emotional or not emotional enough. She is either too spontaneous or not spontaneous enough. She is either too sensitive (that is why she cannot be president of General Motors) or she is not sensitive enough (that is why she will never write *King Lear*).

But none of this is to imply that woman is damned, and damned from every direction. Not at all. The fact is that woman qua woman is more often celebrated. If she cannot hear the muse, says Robert Graves, what does it matter? She *is* the muse. *Man Does, Woman Is* is the title of Graves's most recent collection of poetry. If we are expected to conclude from this that woman is an It rather than a Thou (to use Martin Buber's categories), why deplore it? The Parthenon too is beautiful, passive, inspiring. Who would long to *build* it, if one can *be* it?

And even this is unfair, since it is simultaneously true that woman is frequently praised as the more "creative" sex. She does not need to make poems, it is argued; she has no drive to make poems, because she is privileged to make babies. A pregnancy is as fulfilling as, say, Yeats's *Sailing to Byzantium*. Here is an interesting idea worth examination. To begin with, we would have to know what it cost Yeats —I am speaking physically—to wring out a poem of genius. Perhaps we cannot know this. The writing of great and visionary literature is not a common experience and is not readily explorable. A. E.

Housman—a lesser poet than Yeats, to be sure, though as pure a one —said of the genesis of a poem that it affected his flesh: that if a wisp of a line came to him while he was in the middle of shaving, for instance, he could sense the bristles standing on end. Most poets, if they speak of it at all, report extreme exhaustion accompanied by supreme exaltation. Yeats himself spoke of the poet living amid whirlwinds. Virginia Woolf, a writer of a kind of prose very near poetry in tone and aspiration, was racked in the heat of composition by seizures of profoundly tormenting headaches. Isaac Babel called himself a "galley slave." Conrad was in a frenzy for weeks on end —"I turn in this vicious circle and the work itself becomes like the work in a treadmill—a thing without joy—a punishing task. . . . I am at it day after day, and I want all day, every minute of a day, to produce a beggarly tale of words or perhaps to produce nothing at all. . . . One's will becomes a slave of hallucinations, responds only to shadowy impulses, waits on imagination alone." Dostoyevsky said plainly: "*I worked and was tortured.*" Flaubert wrote, "You don't know what it is to stay a whole day with your head in your hands trying to squeeze your unfortunate brain so as to find a word." Tolstoy told a friend, "One ought only to write when one leaves a piece of flesh in the ink-pot each time one dips one's pen." For Isak Dinesen, the "great and difficult task" was pursued "without faith and without hope." And George Eliot said of the writing of *Romola* —it occupied two years—that she began it young, and finished it old.

That is what "creativity" is. Is a pregnancy like that? The fact is, given health (and one must never assume the abnormal, since being a woman is really *not* like having a disease), the condition of pregnancy is—in the consciousness—very nearly like the condition of nonpregnancy. It is insulting to a poet to compare his titanic and agonized strivings with the so-called "creativity" of childbearing, where—consciously—nothing happens. One does not will the development of the fetus; one can be as dull or as active, or as bored or as intense, as one pleases—anything else is mere self-absorption and daydream: the process itself is as involuntary and as unaware as the beating of one's own heart. Of course, it is a miracle that one's heart goes on beating, that the fetus goes on growing—but it is not a human miracle, it is Nature's miracle. If we want to talk about Nature, very well—but now we are talking about literature. To produce a new human being out of a pair of cells is a marvel, but it is not *our* marvel. Once we, male and female, have joined two disparate cells by our human wills, the rest is done for us, not by us. The woman's body is a vessel, thereafter, for a parasite. For the presence of the zygote she is thereafter no more responsible than she is for the presence of her heart and lungs. To call a child a poem may be a pretty metaphor, but it is a slur on the labor of art. Literature cannot be equated with physiology, and woman through her reproductive system alone is no more a creative artist than was Joyce by virtue of his kidneys alone, or James by virtue of his teeth (which, by the way, were troublesome). A poem emerges from a mind, and mind is, so far as our present knowledge takes us, an unknowable abstraction. Perhaps it is a compliment to a woman of no gifts to say of her in compensation, "Ah, well, but she has made a child." But that is a cheap and slippery mythology, and a misleading one. It induces the false value of self-inflation in mediocre women. It is scarcely our duty to compliment the mediocre for their mediocrity when we are hardly employed enough in celebrating the gifted for their gifts, wrung out by the toil of desire and imagination. It takes something away from Yeats to compare a mediocre child—and most children, like most parents, *are* mediocre—with *Sailing to Byzantium*. But it is just as irrelevant to compare a brilliant child with a brilliant poem. Biology is *there:* it does not need our praise, and if we choose to praise it, it is blasphemous to think we are praising not God but ourselves.*

*Sometimes the analogy is made not between poetry and childbearing proper, but between poetry and an idealized domesticity. Here is the versifier Phyllis McGinley writing in an advertisement for and in *The New York Times:* "I know a remarkable woman who is a true artist, domestic version. She creates an atmosphere in which her children and her husband can move with delight and peace, pouring out all the passion which Emily Dickinson might have spent on perfecting a stanza or—to update the comparison—as Joan Sutherland does on interpreting an aria. Her masterpiece consists of her family, her house, her community duties." But would the gifted McGinley be willing to reverse the metaphor, and compare her witty verses with mopping under the bed? Or match Emily Dickinson's "I Heard a Fly Buzz When I Died" with a good nourishing family breakfast, or a morning on the telephone for the PTA? Or liken rendering an aria to sitting down to an editorial in the *Times?*

All this is, one would think, almost stupefyingly obvious. It is embarrassing, it is humiliating, to be so obvious about the quality either of literature or of woman. She, at any rate, is not a muse, nor is she on the strength of her womb alone an artist. She is—how stupidly obvious—a person. She can be an artist if she was born talented. She can be a muse if she inspires a poet, but she too (if she was born talented) can find her own muse in another person. Madame de Sévigné's muse was her daughter, and what male muse it was who inspired Emily Brontë's Heathcliff, history continues to conjecture. The muse—*pace* Robert Graves—has no settled sex or form, and can appear in the shape of a tree (*Howards End*) or a city (the Paris of *The Ambassadors*) or even—think of Proust—a cookie.

Yet in our culture, in our country, much is not obvious. With respect to woman and with respect to literature (I refer you again to the reviewers), ours is among the most backward areas on earth. It is true that woman has had the vote for fifty years and has begun to enter most professions, though often without an invitation. We are far past the grievances Virginia Woolf grappled with in *A Room of One's Own* and *Three Guineas*—books still sneered at as "feminist."* In 1929, when Virginia Woolf visited Oxford (or was it Cambridge? she is too sly to say which), she was chased off a lawn forbidden to the feet of women. By then, of course, our colleges were already full of coeds, though not so full as now. And yet the question of justification remains. Only a few months ago, in my own college, a startling debate was held—"Should a Woman Receive a College Education?" The audience was immense, but the debaters were only three: an instructor in anthropology (female), a professor of history (male), and a fiercely bearded professor of psychology (ostentatiously male). According to the unironic conventions of chivalry, the anthropologist spoke first. She spoke of opportunities and of problems. She spoke of living wholly and well. She did not ignore the necessities and difficulties of housekeeping and childrearing; she spoke of the relations of parents, children, and work-in-the-world;

---

*The change since this was written is especially striking. These essays are now both the subject and the support of dozens of women's studies courses in many universities. Woolf the feminist has outstripped Woolf the woman of letters. An irony, since—for Virginia Woolf herself—the former was espoused in order to facilitate the latter.

she talked extensively about nursery schools. She took as her premise not merely that woman ought to be fully educated, but that her education should be fully used in society. She was reasoned and reasonable; she had a point of view. Perhaps it was a controversial point of view, perhaps not—her listeners never had the chance of a serious evaluation. Her point of view was never assailed or refuted. It was overlooked. She spoke—against mysterious whispered cackles in the audience—and sat. Then up rose the laughing psychologist, and cracked jokes through his beard. Then up rose the laughing historian, and cracked jokes through his field—I especially remember one about the despotism of Catherine the Great. "That's what happens when a woman gets emancipated." Laughter from all sides. Were the historian and the psychologist laughing at the absurdity of the topic the callow students' committee had selected for debate? An absurd topic—it deserves to be laughed out of court, and surely that is exactly what is happening, since here in the audience are all these coeds, censuring and contradicting by their very presence the outrageous question. Yet look again: the coeds are laughing too. Everyone is laughing the laughter of mockery. They are not laughing at the absurdly callow topic. They are laughing at the buffoonery of the historian and the psychologist, who are themselves laughing at the subject of the topic: the whole huge room, packed to the very doors and beyond with mocking boys and girls, is laughing at the futility of an educated woman. *She* is the absurdity.

The idea of an educated woman is not yet taken seriously in American universities. She is not chased off the campus, she is even welcomed there—but she is not taken seriously as a student, and she will not be welcomed if she hopes to return as a serious lifelong scholar. Nor will she be welcomed afterward in the "world." A law firm may hire her, but it will hide her in its rear research offices, away from the eyes of clients. The lower schools will receive her, as they always have, since she is their bulwark; their bulwark, but not their principal, who is a man. We have seen her crawling like Griselda through the long ordeal of medicine: she is almost always bound to be a pediatrician, since it is in her nature to "work with children."

I will not forget the appalling laughter of the two mocking debaters. But it was not so appalling as the laughter of the young men and the young women in the audience. In the laughter of the historian and the psychologist I heard the fussy cry—a cry of violated venerable decorum, no doubt—of the beadle who chased Virginia Woolf off the grass in 1929. But what of that youthful mockery? Their laughter was hideous; it showed something ugly and self-shaming about the nature of our society and the nature of our education—and by "our education" I do not mean the colleges, I mean the kindergartens, I mean the living rooms at home, I mean the fathers and the mothers, the men and the women.

In this country the women, by and large, are at home. Let us consider that first. Most of the women are at home. Why are they at home? Well, plainly because they belong there. They are there to rear the children, and if they have a whole lot of children (in our country they have an amazing number of children, without regard to the diet of algae they are imposing on their children's children), there will usually be a helpless baby. The mother is at home to take care of the helpless baby. That is right and reasonable. Everyone agrees—Nature agrees, the father agrees, Society agrees. Society agrees? That is very interesting. That too is an idea worth examination. It is very useful for society to have the mother at home. It keeps her out of the way. If, say, she stopped at only two children (but if she stopped at only two she would be in danger of reducing the birth rate, which now rivals India's), those two might be half-grown, and safely shut up in a school building most of the day, by the time she is thirty-five. And if she were thirty-five—a young, healthy, able, educated thirty-five—with no helpless baby to keep her at home, and most of the day free, what would she do? Society shudders at the possibility: she might want to get a job. But that would never do. Why, if you counted up all the young, healthy, able, educated, free women of thirty-five, it might come to nearly half the population! And, as things stand now, there are not even enough jobs for the other half of the population, the truly breadwinning half. And what about all those three-quarters-grown persons we call adolescents? Society shudders at them too: the economy is an inn with no room for adolescents and women. But if it will not allow adolescents and women to share in its work (how can it? so much of the work is done by machines), society must at least provide something else to keep the adolescents and women occupied, if only artificially. So, out of the largesse of its infinitely adaptable lap, it gives women knitting and adolescents transistor radios to dance to. (And for the adolescents of even mediocre capacities—here there is not so much discrimination by sex—it comes up with colleges, and fraudulent debates, and more dancing.) Society provides a complete—and in essence custodial—culture for each group it is forced to keep out of the way. It is a culture of busywork and make-believe and distraction. Society is very clever and always has been. Once upon a time, before machines, women and adolescents *were* needed and used to the last degree in the economy. Women were not educated because an unautomated house requires a work horse to maintain it, and a woman who cannot read or write is somehow better at hauling water in from the pump than one who can. (Why this should be, only the experience of society can explain.) But now society—so long as we fail to renovate it—can furnish work for only a quarter of the population, and so the rest must be lured into thinking it is performing a job when it is really not doing anything beyond breathing.

That is why there are in our society separate minority cultures for adolescents and for women. Each has its own set of opinions, prejudices, tastes, values, and—do not underestimate this last—magazines. You and I are here concerned only with the culture of women. Society, remember, is above men and women; it acts *in* men and women. So you must not make the mistake of thinking that the culture of women is the conspiracy of men. Not in the least. That is an old-fashioned, bluestocking view of the matter, and it is erroneous. The culture of women is believed in by both men and women, and it is the conspiracy of neither, because it is the creature neither of men alone, nor of women alone, but of society itself—that autonomous, cunning, insensitive sibling of history.

The culture of women consists of many, many things—products as well as attitudes, but attitudes mostly. The attitudes generate the products, and the products utilize the attitudes. The most overriding attitude is summed up in a cult word: "Home." (Notice that builders do not sell houses, they sell homes—a case of attitude and product coalescing.) But what does "Home" mean? It means curtains, rugs, furniture, a boiler in the cellar, magazines with dress patterns and recipes and articles full of adulterated Freud, a dog, a box of cereal bones for the dog, a kitchen floor that conscience insists must be periodically waxed, and so forth: but mostly, of course, it means "Children." And "Children" are not regarded as incomplete or new persons, as unformed destinies, as embryo participants in the society; above all, they are not regarded simply as *children:* they are a make-believe entity in themselves, a symbol of need and achievement, just as the dog biscuits (not real bones) are a make-believe entity in themselves (does the dog think they are real?). "Children" as a concept have, in their present incarnation, a definite function, which is to bolster the whole airy system of make-believe. "Children" are there to justify "Home"; and "Home" is there to justify a third phantom entity—the heroine of the fairy tale, also an invention and an abstraction, the "Homemaker."

In this sense, neither "Home" nor "Children" nor "Homemaker" has any reality at all. All are dissemblances, fables, daydreams. All are abstractions designed to give the prestige of sham significance to a fairy tale. Nothing here is in the least related to living persons or to life itself. "Home" and "Children" and "Homemaker" are fabrications in the same sense that a bank is a fabrication: we pretend we are passing something called money, but meanwhile a bookkeeper (that is, a computer) is simply balancing the columns in an account book, more on this side of the line, less on that side. If we should all insist on exchanging metal again, the bank fabrication would dissolve. And when the "Children" grow up a little, refuse to be players in the game of gauze, and insist at last on being real persons, does "Home" dissolve, does "Homemaker" dissolve? Only partially. Because now society steps in and sweeps up the remains under the heading of "Womanhood." The children go away, the dog dies, the house wears out, but "Womanhood" is eternal. Its possessor, the creature in whom "Womanhood" is immanent (divinely, as it were), has her magazines to prove her reality—her reality, mind you, as a concept called "Woman," endowed with another concept called "Womanhood"; she has the benevolent chorus of society to prove it, she has the bearded psychologist and the professor of history to prove it, she has the laughing girls and boys to prove it.

They "prove" it, perhaps—the Ptolemaic system was also in error, and its proofs were magnificent—but they do not justify *her*. No fabrication can be justified. Only a person can be justified. A person is justified by the quality of her life; but a daydream is not a life, no matter how many propose to declare it so.

This is our "problem"—the problem of a majority's giving its credence and its loyalty to a daydream. And it is a bigger problem than any other we know of in this country, for the plain and terrifying reason that we have not even considered it to be a problem. Whenever the cliché-question is put, "What is the number one problem in America today?", the cliché-answer comes: "Civil rights —the Black Revolution." Scarcely. The solution to that problem is there—we have only to catch up to it, with all our might. If the debate at my college had dealt with civil rights it would have been serious, passionate, and argumentative. We had a Vietnam teach-in: *it* was serious and passionate and argumentative. But until now no one has been serious and passionate, and certainly no one has been argumentative, concerning attitudes about woman. Once a problem has been articulated, the answer is implicit; the answer is already fated. But this problem was never articulated; there was no answer, because no one ever asked the question. It was a question that had not yet found its incarnation. Its substance was, on every level, the stuff of primitive buffoonery.

Virginia Woolf is the artist-pioneer, the Margaret-Sanger-as-bard, so to speak, of this social question. Among artists she has no successor. Not until art has seized and possessed and assimilated this question will it begin to interest the scientist-humanists.

But what are the components of the question? Perhaps they can once again crudely be set out, though they are so old and so tiresome, though we have no poet to speak them forth once and for all, though we handle them with the weariness of overuse. Here they are: no great female architects, painters, playwrights, sailors, bridge-builders, jurists, captains, composers, etc., etc. Everyone knows that list; everyone can recite it at length, now and then hesitating to allow for a Saint Joan or an empress or an influential courtesan or a salon wit. But the list of omissions is long, as long almost as history, or, to use a more telling simile, as long almost as the history of the Jews.

And here I think of a curious analogy. Say what you will about the gifted Jews, they have never, up until times so recent that they scarcely begin to count, been plastic artists. Where is the Jewish Michelangelo, the Jewish Rembrandt, the Jewish Rodin? He has never come into being. Why? Have oppression and persecution erased the possibility of his existence? Hardly. Oppression and persecution often tend to reinforce gifts; to proscribe is more effective than to prescribe. Where then *is* the Jewish Michelangelo? Is it possible that a whole people cannot produce a single painter? And not merely a single painter of note, but a single painter at all? Well, there have been artists among the Jews—artisans, we should more likely call them, decorators of trivial ceremonial objects, a wine cup here, a scroll cover there. Talented a bit, but nothing great. They never tried their hand at wood or stone or paint. "Thou shalt have no graven images"—the Second Commandment—prevented them. And it is not until a very, very little while ago, under the influence of a movement called "Emancipation" or "Enlightenment," that we begin to see creeping in a Chagall, a Modigliani, an Epstein, who have ceased to believe that art insults the Unity of God. It will be a long, long time before the Jews have their Michelangelo. Before a "David" can happen, a thousand naked Apollos must be hewn. (And Apollo *did* insult the Unity of God.) There must be a readied ground, a preparation—in short, a relevant living culture to frame the event.

The same, I think, with our problem. Gifts and brains are not transmitted, like hemophilia, from the immune sex to the susceptible sex. Genius is the property of both sexes and all nations alike. That is the humanist view. The Jews have had no artists not because they have had no genius for art, but because their image of themselves as a culture inhibited the exercise of the latent gift. And all those nonexistent female Newtons and Bachs and Leonardos and Shakespeares (all? surely they would be very few indeed, so rare is genius of that degree)—they have had no more chance of leaping from the prison of their societal fates than any Greek slave, or a nomad's child in Yemen today. The emancipation of women is spectacularly new. Emancipation does not instantly result in achievement. Enlightenment must follow. And the enlightenment has, for women, and especially by women, not yet occurred.

It has not yet occurred even at the most expressive point of all— in the universities. It is the function of a liberal university not to give right answers, but to ask right questions. And the ultimate humanist question, as we have seen, has not yet been expressed (my students had never in all their lives heard it put); the components of the unrealized question, as we have seen, are the experiences and needs and omissions and premises of a culture. A culture can have a seemingly unchanging premise, and then suddenly it will change; hence, among the Jews, Chagall and Modigliani and Epstein; hence, in literature, the early epistolary artists—Madame de Sévigné and Lady Mary—and then, close on their heels, the genius novelists, Jane and George. Literature was the first to begin it, since literature could be pursued privately and at home. But here let us listen to Elizabeth Hardwick: "Who is to say that *Remembrance of Things Past* is 'better' than the marvelous *Emma?* *War and Peace* better than *Middlemarch?* *Moby-Dick* superior to *La Princesse de Clèves?* But everybody says so! It is only the whimsical, the cantankerous, the eccentric . . . who would say that any literary work by a woman, marvelous as these may be, is on a level with the very greatest accomplishments of men."* I am not sure it is whimsical, cantankerous, or eccentric not to feel the need to make such distinctions, but even if the distinctions *are* justified—perhaps they are, I cannot tell—who is to say that *Emma* and *Middlemarch* and *La Princesse de Clèves* are not simply forerunners? In England Lady Mary preceded Jane. In France Madame de Sévigné preceded George Sand. Cultivation precedes fruition. Perhaps we cannot have our great women architects, painters, playwrights, sailors, bridge-builders, jurists, captains, composers, and so forth, until we have run-of-the-mill women in these roles, until all that is a commonplace—until, in short, women enter into the central stream of mankind's activities, until woman-as-person becomes as flat and unremarked a tradition as man-as-person. Reproduction, trick it out as you will in this or that myth, is still only reproduction, a natural and necessary biological function, and biol-

---

*A View of One's Own.

ogy, however fancied up with tribal significance and mystical implication, is not enough. Unless you are on the extreme verge of death,
it is never enough just to keep on breathing.

Even woman's differing muscular capacity—much is made of this,
unsurprisingly—is, in the age of the comprehensive machine, an
obstacle to almost no pursuit. It would be difficult to insist that a
woman on board the sort of ship Conrad describes in that remarkable
novella "Youth" would be as efficient as most male members of the
crew; but muscle is no longer an issue anywhere. Evolution has now
become, in Julian Huxley's words, a "psycho-social process"—that
is, man is now able consciously to contribute to his own development. He lives, Huxley writes, "not only in relation with the physico-
chemical and biological environment provided by nature, but with
the psycho-social environment of material and mental habitats which
he has himself created," and those habitats include the muscle-
augmenting machine and its incalculable influences. Might a woman
have written "Youth"? Who would dare to say yes? In Conrad's day
—in the scope of technology a very short time ago—almost no
woman and very few men could have the stamina to wrest out
Conrad's strenuous sea experience. Yet the machine widens experience for everyone and equalizes the physical endurance of men and
women. A long journey is no longer a matter of muscle, but of jet
schedules. Presumably it will become harder and harder to maintain
that novelists who are women are condemned to a narrower focus
than men because their lives are perforce narrower. The cult of
Experience is, more and more, accessible to anyone who wishes to
be lured by it: though it might well be argued that novels and poems
grow out of something other than raw physical experience. "It is not
suggested," Elizabeth Hardwick continues, "that muscles write
books, but there is a certain sense in which, talent and experience
being equal, they may be considered a bit of an advantage. In the end,
it is in the matter of experience that women's disadvantage is catastrophic. It is very difficult to know how this may be extraordinarily
altered." Huxley's self-propelled evolutionary view is more optimis-
tic, though perhaps both views, Hardwick's and Huxley's, are at
bottom equally irrelevant to the making of literature, which is, after
all, as unknown a quantity as mind itself.

The question is, then, I believe, a question touching at least peripherally on art. Not merely literary art, but all the human arts, including those we call science. And I have ventured that the question must be formulated as a humanistic issue, not a sectarian one, not a divisive one. Art must belong to all human beings, not alone to a traditionally privileged segment; every endeavor, every passion must be available to the susceptible adult, without the intervention of myth or canard. Woman will cease solely to be man's muse—an It (as she is, curiously, for writers as disparate as Graves and Mailer, as she was for Freud)—and will acquire muses of her own when she herself ceases to be bemused with gaudy daydreams and romances —with lies reinforcing lies—about her own nature. She limits—she self-limits—her aspirations and her expectations. She joins the general mockery at her possibilities. I have heard her laughing at herself as though she were a dancing dog. You have seen her regard her life as a disease to be constantly tended and pacified. She does not yet really believe that she is herself accessible to poetry or science: she wills these into her sons, but not into her daughters. She surrounds herself with the devices and manipulations of an identity that is not an identity. Without protest she permits the intractable momentum of society to keep her from its worthiness and larger adventures, from its expressive labor. She lives among us like a docile captive; a consuming object; an accomplice; an It. She has even been successfully persuaded to work for and at her own imprisonment. No one can deny that imprisonment offers advantages, especially to the morally lazy. There have been slaves who have rejoiced in their slavery (think of the Children of Israel yearning day and night for the fleshpots of Egypt), and female infantilism is a kind of pleasurable slavishness. Dependency, the absence of decisions and responsibility, the avoidance of risk, the shutting-out of the gigantic toil of art— all these are the comforts of the condoning contented subject, and when these are combined, as they are in this country, with excessive leisure, it would almost seem that woman has a vested interest in her excluded role. If one were to bow to the tempting idea that her role has come about through a conspiracy (as it could not have, since custom is no plot), it would appear as though it were a conspiracy of sluggish women, and never of excluding men. The fervor and

energies of the women who are not lazy, those rare activist personali-
ties who feel the call of a Cause, are thrown pragmatically into the
defense of that easy and comfortable role; the barricades of the
pleasant prison are manned—no, womaned—by the inmates themselves, to prevent the rebels from breaking out.

But the rebels are few.

That is because among us for a long time no one rebelled, no one
protested, no one wanted to renovate or liberate, no one asked any
fundamental question. We have had, alas, and still have, the doubtful
habit of reverence. Above all, we respect things as they are. If we
want to step on the moon, it is not to explore an unknown surface
or to divine a new era, but to bolster ourselves at home, among the
old home rivals; there is more preening than science in that venture,
less boldness than bravado. We are so placid that the smallest tremor
of objection to anything at all is taken as a full-scale revolution.
Should any soul speak up in favor of the obvious, it is taken as a
symptom of the influence of the left, the right, the pink, the black,
the dangerous. An idea for its own sake—especially an obvious idea
—has no respectability.

Among my students—let us come back to *them*, since they are our
societal prototypes—all this was depressingly plain. That is why
they could not write intelligibly—no one had ever mentioned the
relevance of writing to thinking, and thinking had never been encouraged or induced in them. By "thinking" I mean, of course, not
the simple ability to make equations come out right, but the devotion
to speculation on that frail but obsessive distraction known as the
human condition. My students—male and female—did not need to
speculate on what goals are proper to the full life; male and female,
they already knew their goals. And their goals were identical. They
all wanted to settle down into a perpetual and phantom coziness.
They were all at heart sentimentalists—and sentimentalists, Yeats
said, are persons "who believe in money, in position, in a marriage
bell, and whose understanding of happiness is to be so busy whether
at work or play, that all is forgotten but the momentary aim." Accordingly, they had all determined, long ago, to pursue the steady
domestic life, the enclosed life, the restricted life—the life, in brief,

of the daydream, into which the obvious must not be permitted to thrust its scary beams.

By the "obvious" I mean, once again, the gifts and teachings and life-illuminations of art. The methods of art are variegated, flexible, abstruse, and often enough mysterious. But the burden of art is obvious: here is the world, here are human beings, here is childhood, here is struggle, here is hate, here is old age, here is death. None of these is a fantasy, a romance, or a sentiment, none is an imagining; all are obvious. A culture that does not allow itself to look clearly at the obvious through the universal accessibility of art is a culture of tragic delusion, hardly living; it will make room for a system of fantasy Offices on the one hand, and a system of fantasy Homes on the other, but it will forget that the earth lies beneath all. It will turn out role-playing stereotypes (the hideousness of the phrase is appropriate to the concept) instead of human beings. It will shut the children away from half the population. It will shut aspiration away from half the population. It will glut its colleges with young people enduringly maimed by illusions learned early and kept late. It will sup on make-believe. But a humanist society—you and I do not live in one—is one in which a voice is heard: "Come," it says, "here is a world requiring architects, painters, playwrights, sailors, bridge-builders, jurists, captains, composers, discoverers, and a thousand things besides, all real and all obvious. Partake," it says; "live."

Is it a man's voice or a woman's voice? Students, colleagues, listen again; it is two voices. "How obvious," you will one day reply, and if you laugh, it will be at the quaint folly of obsolete custom, which once failed to harness the obvious; it will not be at a dancing dog.

2. *Literature and the Politics of Sex: A Dissent*

Women who write with an overriding consciousness that they write *as women* are engaged not in aspiration toward writing, but chiefly in a politics of sex. A new political term makes its appearance: *woman writer*, not used descriptively—as one would say "a lanky brown-haired writer"—but as part of the language of politics.

Now a politics of sex can be very much to the point. No one would deny that the movement for female suffrage was a politics of sex, and obviously any agitation for equality in employment, in the professions, and in government is a politics of sex.

But the language of politics is not writer's language. Politics begins with premises; imagination goes in search of them. The political term *woman writer* signals in advance a whole set of premises: that, for instance, there are "male" and "female" states of intellect and feeling, hence of prose; that individuality of condition and temperament do not apply, or at least not much, and that all writing women possess—not by virtue of being writers but by virtue of being women—an instantly perceived common ground; that writers who are women can best nourish other writers who are women.

"There is a human component to literature," according to Ellen

Essay published in *Ms.*, December 1977.

Moers, "which a woman writer can more easily discuss with another woman writer, even across an ocean, than she can with the literary man next door."*

I deny this. There is a human component to literature that does not separate writers by sex, but that—on the contrary—engenders sympathies from sex to sex, from condition to condition, from experience to experience, from like to like, and from unlike to unlike. Literature universalizes. Without disparaging particularity or identity, it universalizes; it does not divide.

But what, with respect to particularity or identity, is a "woman writer"? Outside its political uses, "woman writer" has no meaning —not intellectually, not morally, not historically. A writer is a writer.

Does a "woman writer" have a separate psychology—by virtue of being a woman? Does a "woman writer" have a separate body of ideas—by virtue of being a woman? It was these misleading currencies that classical feminism was created to deny.

Does a "woman writer" have a body of separate experience—by virtue of being a woman? It was this myth-fed condition of segregation that classical feminism was created to bring an end to.

Insofar as some women, and some writers who are women, have separate bodies of experience or separate psychologies, to that degree has the feminism of these women not yet asserted itself. In art, feminism is that idea which opposes segregation; which means to abolish mythological divisions; which declares that the imagination cannot be "set" free, because it is already free.

To say "the imagination is free" is, in fact, a tautology. The imagination is by definition, by nature, freedom and autonomy. When I write, I am free. I am, as a writer, whatever I wish to become. I can think myself into a male, or a female, or a stone, or a raindrop, or a block of wood, or a Tibetan, or the spine of a cactus.

In life, I am not free. In life, female or male, no one is free. In life, female or male, I have tasks; I have obligations and responsibilities; I have a toothache, being contingent on nature; I am devoured by drudgery and fragmentation. My freedom is contingent on need. I

**Literary Women.*

am, in short, claimed. Female or male, I am subject to the disciplines of health or disease, of getting and spending, of being someone's child and being someone's parent. Society—which is not yet utopia —tells me to go stand there and do that, or else keep my distance and not do this. In life, I accept those dictums of Society which seem to me to be the same as Civilization, and quarrel with the rest.

But when I write, what do Society and its protocol mean to me? When I write, I am in command of a grand *As If.* I write *As If* I were truly free. And this *As If* is not a myth. As soon as I proclaim it, as soon as my conduct as a writer expresses it, it comes into being.

A writer—I mean now a fiction writer or a poet, an *imagining* writer—is not a sociologist, or a social historian, or a literary critic, or a journalist, or a politician. The newspeak term "woman writer" has the following sociological or political message: "Of course we believe in humanity-as-a-whole. Of course we believe that a writer is a writer, period. But let us for a little while gather together, as women, to become politically strong, strong in morale, a visible, viable social factor; as such, we will separate ourselves only temporarily, during this strengthening period, and then, when we can rejoin the world with power and dignity in our hands, we *will* rejoin it, and declare ourselves for the unity of the human species. This temporary status will be our strategy in our struggle with Society."

That is the voice of the "woman writer." But it is a mistaken voice. Only consider: in intellectual life, a new generation comes of age every four or five years. For those who were not present at the inception of this strategy, it will not seem a strategy at all; it will be the only reality. Writers will very soon find themselves born into one of two categories, "woman writer" or "writer," and all the "writers" will be expected to be male—an uninspiring social and literary atmosphere the world has known before. "Literature cannot be the business of a woman's life, and it ought not to be," the Poet Laureate Robert Southey scolded Charlotte Brontë. But that was the early half of the nineteenth century. Only twenty years ago, an anthologist of Russian literature, speaking of a Russian writer's international influence, remarked that "in the case of certain British lady-writers it may be said to have been nothing short of disastrous." He does not tell us about those British gentleman-writers who were also bad literary imitators. One could raise a mountain of such quotations, all specializing in the disparagement that inevitably emerges out of segregation. The success of feminism inhibited such views, but regression will be made easy once the pure, unqualified, unpolemical, unpoliticized word "writer" begins all over again to refer to only half the writers there are.

And not only this. The strategy is based on a temporary assumption of an untruth. When the strategy's utility passes, we are assured, the natural condition of unity will be resumed. But it is dangerous to accommodate to a falsehood even for a single minute. The so-called temporary has an ineluctable inclination to turn into long-range habit. All politicians know that every "temporary" political initiative promised as a short-term poultice stays on the books forever. *Strategies become institutions.* If writers promise themselves that they will organize as "women writers" only "temporarily," that they will yoke themselves to a misleading self-definition only for the sake of a short-term convenience, it is almost certain that the temporary will become the long-term status quo, and "convenience" will be transmogrified into a new truth.

But worse than that. Belief in a "new truth" nearly always brings authoritarianism in its wake. As the temporary-segregation strategy more and more loses its character both as to "temporary" and as to "strategy," it begins also to lay claim to a full, in fact to the only, definition of feminism. More and more, apartness is perceived as the dominant aim, even the chief quality, of feminism. More and more, women are urged to think of themselves in tribal terms, as if anatomy were the same as culture. More and more, artists who are women are made to feel obliged to deliver a "women's art," as if ten thousand other possibilities, preoccupations, obsessions, were inauthentic for women, or invalid, or, worse yet, lyingly evasive. We grow familiar, currently, with the presumption of a "women's photography";* will

---

*Molly Haskell, *Ms.*, September 1977: "There is a tendency (and this is true of women's films as well) toward a novelistic rather than dramatic organization of material, meaning that character is conveyed evocatively through an accumulation of small gestures, half notes, and ordinary details rather than through the climactic scenes of confrontation and revelation." Since all of this is also an excellent description of the short stories and plays of, say, Chekhov, the attempt to prove female "tendency" through illustration turns out to be just as unimpressive when performed by a female critic as by a male critic.

there eventually arise a women's entomology, or a women's astrophysics? Or will only the sciences, in their objective universalism, retain the freedom of the individual mind, unfettered by *a priori* qualification?

Art formed or even touched by any inflexibility—any topical or social expectation, any extrinsic burden, any axiom or presumption or political nuance, any prior qualification at all—will always make for a debased culture. Sometimes history gives this inflexibility the name of "dogma"; sometimes "party line"; sometimes, alas, "truth."

Classical feminism—i.e., feminism at its origin, when it saw itself as justice and aspiration made universal, as mankind widened to humankind—rejected anatomy not only as destiny, but as any sort of governing force; it rejected the notion of "female sensibility" as a slander designed to shut women off from access to the delights, confusions, achievements, darknesses, and complexities of the great world. Classical feminism was conceived of as the end of false barriers and boundaries; as the end of segregationist fictions and restraints; as the end of the Great Multiple Lie.

What was the Great Multiple Lie? It applied to all women, and its premise was that there is a "female nature" which is made manifest in all art by women. For imaginative writers, its assertions were especially limiting and corrosive. For example:

1. It assumed a psychology and an emotional temper peculiar to women.

2. It assumed a prose or verse style endemic in, and characteristic of, women.

3. It assumed a set of preoccupations appropriate, by nature, to female poets and novelists—e.g., female friendship, female madness, motherhood, love and romance, domestic conflict, duty, religiosity, etc.

4. It assumed a natural social community grounded in biology and reproductive characteristics ("sisters under the skin"), rather than in intellect or temperament or derivation or societal experience.

5. It took for granted the difference (from "male" writing) of "women's" poetry and "women's" novels by assuming a "woman's" separate sensibility.

6. It posited for intellect and imagination a purely sexual base. It

assumed the writer's gender inherently circumscribed and defined and directed the writer's subject matter, perspective, and aspiration.

All this emits a certain melancholy familiarity: the old, old prejudices, after all. Their familiarity in voices hostile to women is melancholy, and usual, enough; but now, more and more, the voices that carry these convictions are women's voices. With some small modifications (for love and romance, substitute sex; for domestic conflict, substitute home-and-career clashes; for female madness, female rage; and omit duty and religiosity altogether), these ideas make up the literary credo of the new feminism. More and more, there are writers and artists and other masters of imagination who declare themselves freed by voluntary circumscription. "Up till now I was mistaken," they will testify; "I was trying to write like a man. Then I began to write about myself as a daughter, as a lover, as a wife, as a mother, as a woman in relation to other women; as a *self*. I learned to follow the contours of my emotional life. I began to write out of my femaleness."

Thurber once wrote a story about a bear who leaned so far backward that he ended up by falling on his face. Now we are enduring a feminism so far advanced into "new truths" that it has arrived at last at a set of notions indistinguishable from the most age-encrusted, unenlightened, and imprisoning antifeminist views.

Occasionally one hears of prisoners who decline parole, preferring fences and cells. Having returned, they still continue, sensibly and sanely, to call their comfortable old cages "prison." Artists who insist on defining themselves as "women" artists may, after a fashion, flourish under that designation, but they should not stumble into the misnomer of calling voluntary circumscription "feminism." Classical feminism, while not denying the body, while not precluding self-image and self-knowledge, never dreamed of engaging these as single-minded objectives. Feminism means, has always meant, access to possibilities beyond self-consciousness. Art, freed of restrictions, grows in any space, even the most confined. But polemical self-knowledge is restricted knowledge. Self-discovery is only partial discovery. Each human being is a particle of a generation, a mote among the revealing permutations of Society. When you know yourself, when you have toiled through "the contours of emotional life," where are you, what is it that you know, how far can it take you? Self-consciousness—narcissism, solipsism—is small nourishment for a writer. Literature is hungrier than that: a writer with an ambitious imagination needs an appetite beyond the self. For writers who are women, the "new truth" of self-regard, of biologically based self-confinement, is the Great Multiple Lie freshly got up in drag.

For writers there *are* no "new truths." There is only one very old truth, as old as Sappho, as old as Homer, as old as the Song of Deborah, as old as the Songs of David—that the imagination is free, that the gift of making literature is accessible to every kind and condition of human being, that when we write we are not women or men but blessèd beings in possession of a Promethean art, an art encumbered by peril and hope and fire and, above all, freedom. What we ought to do, as writers, is not wait for freedom, meanwhile idling in self-analysis; the freedom one waits for, or builds strategies toward, will never come. What we ought to do, as writers, is seize freedom now, immediately, by recognizing that we already have it.

The Lesson of the Master

There was a period in my life—to purloin a famous Jamesian title, "The Middle Years"—when I used to say, with as much ferocity as I could muster, "I hate Henry James and I wish he was dead."

I was not to have my disgruntled way. The dislike did not last and turned once again to adoration, ecstasy, and awe; and no one is more alive than Henry James, or more likely to sustain literary immortality. He is among the angels, as he meant to be.

But in earlier days I felt I had been betrayed by Henry James. I was like the youthful writer in "The Lesson of the Master" who believed in the Master's call to live immaculately, unspoiled by what we mean when we say "life"—relationship, family mess, distraction, exhaustion, anxiety, above all disappointment. Here is the Master, St. George, speaking to his young disciple, Paul Overt:

> "One has no business to have any children," St. George placidly declared. "I mean, of course, if one wants to do anything good."
>
> "But aren't they an inspiration—an incentive?"
>
> "An incentive to damnation, artistically speaking."

Essay published in *The New York Review of Books*, August 12, 1982.

And later Paul inquires:

> "Is it deceptive that I find you living with every appearance of domestic felicity—blest with a devoted, accomplished wife, with children whose acquaintance I haven't yet had the pleasure of making, but who *must* be delightful young people, from what I know of their parents?"
>
> St. George smiled as for the candour of his question. "It's all excellent, my dear fellow—heaven forbid I should deny it. . . . I've got a loaf on the shelf; I've got everything in fact but the great thing."
>
> "And the great thing?" Paul kept echoing.
>
> "The sense of having done the best—the sense which is the real life of the artist and the absence of which is his death, of having drawn from his intellectual instrument the finest music that nature had hidden in it, of having played it as it should be played. He either does that or he doesn't—and if he doesn't he isn't worth speaking of."

Paul pursues:

> "Then what did you mean . . . by saying that children are a curse?"
>
> "My dear youth, on what basis are we talking?" and St. George dropped upon the sofa at a short distance from him. . . . "On the supposition that a certain perfection's possible and even desirable—isn't it so? Well, all I say is that one's children interfere with perfection. One's wife interferes. Marriage interferes."
>
> "You think, then, the artist shouldn't marry?"
>
> "He does so at his peril—he does so at his cost."

Yet the Master who declares all this is himself profoundly, inextricably, married; and when his wife dies, he hastens to marry again, choosing Life over Art. Very properly James sees marriage as symbol and summary of the passion for ordinary human entanglement, as experience of the most commonplace, most fated kind.

But we are also given to understand, in the desolation of this comic tale, that the young artist, the Master's trusting disciple, is left both perplexed and bereft: the Master's second wife is the young artist's first love, and the Master has stolen away his disciple's chance for ordinary human entanglement.

So the Lesson of the Master is a double one: choose ordinary human entanglement, and live; or choose Art, and give up the vitality of life's passions and panics and endurances. What I am going to tell now is a stupidity, a misunderstanding, a great Jamesian life-mistake: an embarrassment and a life-shame. (Imagine that we are in one of those lavishly adorned Jamesian chambers where intimate confessions not accidentally but suspensefully take place.) As I have said, I felt myself betrayed by a Jamesian trickery. Trusting in James, believing, like Paul Overt, in the overtness of the Jamesian lesson, I chose Art, and ended by blaming Henry James. It seemed to me James had left out the one important thing I ought to have known, even though he was saying it again and again. The trouble was that I was listening to the Lesson of the Master at the wrong time, paying powerful and excessive attention at the wrong time; and this cost me my youth.

I suppose a case can be made that it is certainly inappropriate for anyone to moan about the loss of youth and how it is all Henry James's fault. All of us will lose our youth, and some of us, alas, have lost it already; but not all of us will pin the loss on Henry James.

I, however, do. I blame Henry James.

Never mind the sublime position of Henry James in American letters. Never mind the Jamesian prose style—never mind that it too is sublime, nuanced, imbricated with a thousand distinctions and observations (the reason H. G. Wells mocked it), and as idiosyncratically and ecstatically redolent of the spirals of past and future as a garlic clove. Set aside also the Jamesian impatience with idols, the moral seriousness active in both the work and the life. (I am thinking, for example, of Edith Wharton's compliance in the face of their mutual friend Paul Bourget's anti-Semitism, and James's noble and definitive dissent.) Neglect all this, including every other beam that flies out from the stupendous Jamesian lantern to keep generations reading in rapture (which is all right), or else scribbling away at dissertation after dissertation (which is not so good). I myself, after all, committed a Master's thesis, long ago, called "Parable in Henry James," in which I tried to catch up all of James in the net of a single idea. Before that, I lived many months in the black hole of a microfilm cell, transcribing every letter James ever wrote to Mr. Pinker, his London agent, for a professorial book; but the professor drank, and died, and after thirty years the letters still lie in the dark.

All that while I sat cramped in that black bleak microfilm cell, and all that while I was writing that thesis, James was sinking me and despoiling my youth, and I did not know it.

I want, parenthetically, to recommend to the Henry James Society—there is such an assemblage—that membership be limited: no one under age forty-two and three-quarters need apply. Proof of age via birth certificate should be mandatory; otherwise the consequences may be harsh and horrible. I offer myself as an Extreme and Hideous Example of Premature Exposure to Henry James. I was about seventeen, I recall, when my brother brought home from the public library a science-fiction anthology, which, through an odd perspective that perplexes me still, included "The Beast in the Jungle." It was in this anthology, and at that age, that I first read James—fell, I should say, into the jaws of James. I had never heard of him before. I read "The Beast in the Jungle" and creepily thought: Here, here is my autobiography.

From that time forward, gradually but compellingly—and now I yield my scary confession—I became Henry James. Leaving graduate school at the age of twenty-two, disdaining the Ph.D. as an acquisition surely beneath the concerns of literary seriousness, I was already Henry James. When I say I "became" Henry James, you must understand this: though I was a near-sighted twenty-two-year-old young woman infected with the commonplace intention of writing a novel, I was *also* the elderly bald-headed Henry James. Even without close examination, you could see the light glancing off my pate; you could see my heavy chin, my watch chain, my walking stick, my tender paunch.

I had become Henry James, and for years and years I remained Henry James. There was no doubt about it: it was my own clear and faithful truth. Of course, there were some small differences: for one thing, I was not a genius. For another, even in my own insignificant scribbler class, I was not prolific. But I carried the Jamesian idea, I was of his cult, I was a worshiper of literature, literature was my single altar; I was, like the elderly bald-headed James, a priest at that altar; and that altar was all of my life. Like John Marcher in "The Beast in the Jungle," I let everything pass me by for the sake of waiting for the Beast to spring—but unlike John Marcher, I knew what the Beast was, I knew exactly, I even knew the Beast's name: the Beast was literature itself, the sinewy grand undulations of some unraveling fiction, meticulously dreamed out in a language of masterly resplendence, which was to pounce on me and turn me into an enchanted and glorious Being, as enchanted and glorious as the elderly bald-headed Henry James himself.

But though the years spent themselves extravagantly, that ambush never occurred: the ambush of Sacred and Sublime Literature. The great shining Beast of Sacred and Sublime Literature did not pounce. Instead, other beasts, lesser ones, unseemly and misshapen, sprang out—all the beasts of ordinary life: sorrow, disease, death, guilt, responsibility, envy, grievance, grief, disillusionment—the beasts that are chained to human experience, and have nothing to do with Art except to interrupt and impede it, exactly according to the Lesson of the Master.

It was not until I read a certain vast and subtle book that I understood what had happened to me. The book was not by Henry James, but about him. Nowadays we give this sort of work a special name: we call it a nonfiction novel. I am referring, of course, to Leon Edel's ingenious and beautiful biography of Henry James, which is as much the possession of Edel's imagination as it is of the exhilaratingly reported facts of James's life. In Edel's rendering, I learned what I had never before taken in—but the knowledge came, in the Jamesian way, too late. What I learned was that Henry James himself had not always been the elderly bald-headed Henry James!—that he too had once been twenty-two years old.

This terrible and secret knowledge instantly set me against James. From that point forward I was determined to eradicate him. And for a long while I succeeded.

What had happened was this: in early young-womanhood I believed, with all the rigor and force and stunned ardor of religious belief, in the old Henry James, in his scepter and his authority. I believed that what *he* knew at sixty I was to encompass at twenty-two; at twenty-two I lived like the elderly bald-headed Henry James. I thought it was necessary—it was imperative, there was no other path!—to be, all at once, with no progression or evolution, the author of the equivalent of *The Ambassadors* or *The Wings of the Dove*, just as if "A Bundle of Letters," or "Four Meetings," or the golden little "The Europeans" had never preceded the great late Master.

For me, the Lesson of the Master was a horror, a Jamesian tale of a life of mishap and mistake and misconceiving. Though the Master himself was saying, in *The Ambassadors,* in Gloriani's garden, to Little Bilham, through the urgent cry of Strether, "Live, live!"—and though the Master himself was saying, in "The Beast in the Jungle," through May Bartram, how ghastly, how ghostly, it is to eschew, to evade, to turn from, to miss absolutely and irrevocably what is all the time there for you to seize—I mistook him, I misheard him, I missed, absolutely and irrevocably, his essential note. What I heard instead was: *Become a Master.*

Now the truth is it could not have been done, even by a writer of genius; and what a pitiful flicker of the flame of high ambition for a writer who is no more than the ordinary article! No one—not even James himself—springs all at once in early youth into full Mastery, and no writer, whether robustly gifted, or only little and pale, should hope for this implausible fate.

All this, I suppose, is not at all a "secret" knowledge, as I have characterized it, but is, rather, as James named it in the very person of his naïve young artist, most emphatically *overt*—so obvious that it is a mere access of foolishness even to talk about it. Still, I offer the implausible and preposterous model of myself to demonstrate the proposition that the Lesson of the Master is not a lesson about genius, or even about immense ambition; it is a lesson about misreading— about what happens when we misread the great voices of Art, and suppose that, because they speak of Art, they *mean* Art. The great voices of Art never mean *only* Art; they also mean Life, they always mean Life, and Henry James, when he evolved into the Master we revere, finally meant nothing else.

The true Lesson of the Master, then, is, simply, never to venerate what is complete, burnished, whole, in its grand organic flowering or finish—never to look toward the admirable and dazzling end; never to be ravished by the goal; never to worship ripe Art or the ripened artist; but instead to seek to be young while young, primitive while primitive, ungainly when ungainly—to look for crudeness and rudeness, to husband one's own stupidity or ungenius.

There *is* this mix-up most of us have between ourselves and what we admire or triumphantly cherish. We see this mix-up, this mishap, this mishmash, most often in writers: the writer of a new generation ravished by the genius writer of a classical generation, who begins to dream herself, or himself, as powerful, vigorous and original—as if being filled up by the genius writer's images, scenes, and stratagems were the same as having the capacity to pull off the identical magic. To be any sort of competent writer one must keep one's psychological distance from the supreme artists.

If I were twenty-two now, I would not undertake a cannibalistically ambitious Jamesian novel to begin with; I would look into the eyes of Henry James at twenty-two, and see the diffident hope, the uncertainty, the marveling tentativeness, the dream that is still only a dream; the young man still learning to fashion the Scene. Or I would go back still further, to the boy of seventeen, misplaced in a Swiss Polytechnic School, who recalled in old age that "I so feared and abhorred mathematics that the simplest arithmetical operation had always found and kept me helpless and blank." It is not to the Master in his fullness I would give my awed, stricken, desperate fealty, but to the faltering, imperfect, dreaming youth.

If these words should happen to reach the ears of any young writer dumbstruck by the elderly bald-headed Henry James, one who has hungrily heard and ambitiously assimilated the voluptuous cathedral-tones of the developed organ-master, I would say to her or him: put out your lean and clumsy forefinger and strike your paltry, oafish, feeble, simple, skeletal, single note. Try for what Henry James at sixty would scorn—just as he scorned the work of his own earliness, and revised it and revised it in the manner of his later pen in that grand chastisement of youth known as the New York Edition. Trying, in youth, for what the Master in his mastery would condemn—that is the only road to modest mastery. Rapture and homage are not the way. Influence is perdition.

A Drugstore in Winter

This is about reading; a drugstore in winter; the gold leaf on the
dome of the Boston State House; also loss, panic, and dread.

First, the gold leaf. (This part is a little like a turn-of-the-century
pulp tale, though only a little. The ending is a surprise, but there is
no plot.) Thirty years ago I burrowed in the Boston Public Library
one whole afternoon, to find out—not out of curiosity—how the
State House got its gold roof. The answer, like the answer to most
Bostonian questions, was Paul Revere. So I put Paul Revere's gold
dome into an "article," and took it (though I was just as scared by
recklessness then as I am now) to the *Boston Globe*, on Washington
Street. The Features Editor had a bare severe head, a closed paren-
thesis mouth, and silver Dickensian spectacles. He made me wait,
standing, at the side of his desk while he read; there was no bone in
me that did not rattle. Then he opened a drawer and handed me
fifteen dollars. Ah, joy of Homer, joy of Milton! Grub Street bliss!

The very next Sunday, Paul Revere's gold dome saw print. Appetite for more led me to a top-floor chamber in Filene's department
store: Window Dressing. But no one was in the least bit dressed—
it was a dumbstruck nudist colony up there, a mob of naked frozen

---

Essay published in *The New York Times Book Review*, January 21, 1982.

enigmatic manikins, tall enameled skinny ladies with bald breasts and skulls, and legs and wrists and necks that horribly unscrewed. Paul Revere's dome paled beside this gold mine! A sight—mute numb Walpurgisnacht—easily worth another fifteen dollars. I had a Master's degree (thesis topic: "Parable in the Later Novels of Henry James") and a job as an advertising copywriter (9 a.m. to 6 p.m. six days a week, forty dollars per week; if you were male and had no degree at all, sixty dollars). Filene's Sale Days—Crib Bolsters! Lulla-Buys! Jonnie-Mops! Maternity Skirts with Expanding Invisible Trick Waist! And a company show; gold watches to mark the retirement of elderly Irish salesladies; for me the chance to write song lyrics (to the tune of "On Top of Old Smoky") honoring our Store. But "Mute Numb Walpurgisnacht in Secret Downtown Chamber" never reached the *Globe*. Melancholy and meaning business, the Advertising Director forbade it. Grub Street was bad form, and I had to promise never again to sink to another article. Thus ended my life in journalism.

Next: reading, and certain drugstore winter dusks. These come together. It is an aeon before Filene's, years and years before the Later Novels of Henry James. I am scrunched on my knees at a round glass table near a plate glass door on which is inscribed, in gold leaf Paul Revere never put there, letters that must be read backward: PARK VIEW PHARMACY There is an evening smell of late coffee from the fountain, and all the librarians are lined up in a row on the tall stools, sipping and chattering. They have just stepped in from the cold of the Traveling Library, and so have I. The Traveling Library is a big green truck that stops, once every two weeks, on the corner of Continental Avenue, just a little way in from Westchester Avenue, not far from a house that keeps a pig. Other houses fly pigeons from their roofs, other yards have chickens, and down on Mayflower there is even a goat. This is Pelham Bay, the Bronx, in the middle of the Depression, all cattails and weeds, such a lovely place and tender hour! Even though my mother takes me on the subway far, far downtown to buy my winter coat in the frenzy of Klein's on Fourteenth Street, and even though I can recognize the heavy power of a quarter, I don't know it's the Depression. On the trolley on the way to Westchester Square I see the children who live

in the boxcar strangely set down in an empty lot some distance from
Spy Oak (where a Revolutionary traitor was hanged—served him
right for siding with redcoats); the lucky boxcar children dangle
their stick-legs from their train-house maw and wave; how I envy
them! I envy the orphans of the Gould Foundation, who have their
own private swings and seesaws. Sometimes I imagine I am an
orphan, and my father is an impostor pretending to be my father.

My father writes in his prescription book: #*59330 Dr. O'Flaherty
Pow .60/ #59331 Dr. Mulligan Gtt .65/ #59332 Dr. Thron Tab .90.*
Ninety cents! A terrifically expensive medicine; someone is really
sick. When I deliver a prescription around the corner or down the
block, I am offered a nickel tip. I always refuse, out of conscience;
I am, after all, the Park View Pharmacy's own daughter, and it
wouldn't be seemly. My father grinds and mixes powders, weighs
them out in tiny snowy heaps on an apothecary scale, folds them into
delicate translucent papers or meticulously drops them into gelatin
capsules.

In the big front window of the Park View Pharmacy there is a
startling display—goldfish bowls, balanced one on the other in amazing pyramids. A German lady enters, one of my father's cronies—
his cronies are both women and men. My quiet father's eyes are
water-color blue, he wears his small skeptical quiet smile and receives
the neighborhood's life-secrets. My father is discreet and inscrutable.
The German lady pokes a punchboard with a pin, pushes up a bit
of rolled paper, and cries out—she has just won a goldfish bowl, with
two swimming goldfish in it! Mr. Jaffe, the salesman from McKesson
& Robbins, arrives, trailing two mists: winter steaminess and the
animal fog of his cigar,* which melts into the coffee smell, the
tarpaper smell, the eerie honeyed tangled drugstore smell. Mr. Jaffe
and my mother and father are intimates by now, but because it is the
1930s, so long ago, and the old manners still survive, they address one
another gravely as Mr. Jaffe, Mrs. Ozick, Mr. Ozick. My mother calls
my father Mr. O, even at home, as in a Victorian novel. In the street

---

*Mr. Matthew Bruccoli, another Bronx drugstore child, has written to say that he remem-
bers with certainty that Mr. Jaffe did not smoke. In my memory the cigar is somehow
there, so I leave it.

my father tips his hat to ladies. In the winter his hat is a regular fedora; in the summer it is a straw boater with a black ribbon and a jot of blue feather.

What am I doing at this round glass table, both listening and not listening to my mother and father tell Mr. Jaffe about their struggle with "Tessie," the lion-eyed landlady who has just raised, threefold, in the middle of that Depression I have never heard of, the Park View Pharmacy's devouring rent? My mother, not yet forty, wears bandages on her ankles, covering oozing varicose veins; back and forth she strides, dashes, runs, climbing cellar stairs or ladders; she unpacks cartons, she toils behind drug counters and fountain counters. Like my father, she is on her feet until one in the morning, the Park View's closing hour. My mother and father are in trouble, and I don't know it. I am too happy. I feel the secret center of eternity, nothing will ever alter, no one will ever die. Through the window, past the lit goldfish, the gray oval sky deepens over our neighborhood wood, where all the dirt paths lead down to seagull-specked water. I am familiar with every frog-haunted monument: Pelham Bay Park is thronged with WPA art—statuary, fountains, immense rococo staircases cascading down a hillside, Bacchus-faced stelae—stone Roman glories afterward mysteriously razed by an avenging Robert Moses. One year—how distant it seems now, as if even the climate is past returning—the bay froze so hard that whole families, mine among them, crossed back and forth to City Island, strangers saluting and calling out in the ecstasy of the bright trudge over such a sudden wilderness of ice.

In the Park View Pharmacy, in the winter dusk, the heart in my body is revolving like the goldfish fleet-finned in their clear bowls. The librarians are still warming up over their coffee. They do not recognize me, though only half an hour ago I was scrabbling in the mud around the two heavy boxes from the Traveling Library—oafish crates tossed with a thump to the ground. One box contains magazines—*Boy's Life, The American Girl, Popular Mechanix.* But the other, the other! The other transforms me. It is tumbled with storybooks, with clandestine intimations and transfigurations. In school I am a luckless goosegirl, friendless and forlorn. In P.S. 71 I carry, weighty as a cloak, the ineradicable knowledge of my scandal—I am cross-eyed, dumb, an imbecile at arithmetic; in P.S. 71 I am publicly shamed in Assembly because I am caught not singing Christmas carols; in P.S. 71 I am repeatedly accused of deicide. But in the Park View Pharmacy, in the winter dusk, branches blackening in the park across the road, I am driving in rapture through the Violet Fairy Book and the Yellow Fairy Book, insubstantial chariots snatched from the box in the mud. I have never been *inside* the Traveling Library; only grownups are allowed. The boxes are for the children. No more than two books may be borrowed, so I have picked the fattest ones, to last. All the same, the Violet and the Yellow are melting away. Their pages dwindle. I sit at the round glass table, dreaming, dreaming. Mr. Jaffe is murmuring advice. He tells a joke about Wrong-Way Corrigan. The librarians are buttoning up their coats. A princess, captive of an ogre, receives a letter from her swain and hides it in her bosom. I can visualize her bosom exactly—she clutches it against her chest. It is a tall and shapely vase, with a hand-painted flower on it, like the vase on the secondhand piano at home.

I am incognito. No one knows who I truly am. The teachers in P.S. 71 don't know. Rabbi Meskin, my *cheder* teacher, doesn't know. Tessie the lion-eyed landlady doesn't know. Even Hymie the fountain clerk can't know—though he understands other things better than anyone: how to tighten roller skates with a skatekey, for instance, and how to ride a horse. On Friday afternoons, when the new issue is out, Hymie and my brother fight hard over who gets to see *Life* magazine first. My brother is older than I am, and doesn't like me; he builds radios in his bedroom, he is already W2LOM, and operates his transmitter *(da-di-da-dit, da-da-di-da)* so penetratingly on Sunday mornings that Mrs. Eva Brady, across the way, complains. Mrs. Eva Brady has a subscription to *The Writer;* I fill a closet with her old copies. How to Find a Plot. Narrative and Character, the Writer's Tools. Because my brother has his ham license, I say, "I have a license too." "What kind of license?" my brother asks, falling into the trap. "Poetic license," I reply; my brother hates me, but anyhow his birthday presents are transporting: one year *Alice in Wonderland, Pinocchio* the next, then *Tom Sawyer.* I go after Mark Twain, and find *Joan of Arc* and my first satire, *Christian Science.* My mother surprises me with *Pollyanna*, the admiration of her Lower East Side childhood, along with *The Lady of the Lake*. Mrs. Eva Brady's daughter Jeannie has outgrown her Nancy Drews and Judy Boltons, so on rainy afternoons I cross the street and borrow them, trying not to march away with too many—the child of immigrants, I worry that the Bradys, true and virtuous Americans, will judge me greedy or careless. I wrap the Nancy Drews in paper covers to protect them. Old Mrs. Brady, Jeannie's grandmother, invites me back for more. I am so timid I can hardly speak a word, but I love her dark parlor; I love its black bookcases. Old Mrs. Brady sees me off, embracing books under an umbrella; perhaps she divines who I truly am. My brother doesn't care. My father doesn't notice. I think my mother knows. My mother reads the *Saturday Evening Post* and the *Woman's Home Companion;* sometimes the *Ladies' Home Journal,* but never *Good Housekeeping*. I read all my mother's magazines. My father reads *Drug Topics* and *Der Tog,* the Yiddish daily. In Louie Davidowitz's house (waiting our turn for the rabbi's lesson, he teaches me chess in *cheder*) there is a piece of furniture I am in awe of: a shining circular table that is also a revolving bookshelf holding a complete set of Charles Dickens. I borrow *Oliver Twist*. My cousins turn up with *Gulliver's Travels, Just So Stories, Don Quixote,* Oscar Wilde's *Fairy Tales,* uncannily different from the usual kind. Blindfolded, I reach into a Thanksgiving grabbag and pull out *Mrs. Leicester's School,* Mary Lamb's desolate stories of rejected children. Books spill out of rumor, exchange, miracle. In the Park View Pharmacy's lending library I discover, among the nurse romances, a browning, brittle miracle: *Jane Eyre*. Uncle Morris comes to visit (*his* drugstore is on the other side of the Bronx) and leaves behind, just like that, a three-volume Shakespeare. Peggy and Betty Provan, Scottish sisters around the corner, lend me their *Swiss Family Robinson*. Norma Foti, a whole year older, transmits a rumor about Louisa May Alcott; afterward I read *Little Women* a thousand times. Ten thousand! I am no longer incognito, not even to myself. I am Jo in her "vortex"; not Jo exactly, but some Jo-of-the-future. I am under an enchantment: who I truly am must be deferred, waited for and waited for. My father, silently filling capsules, is grieving over his mother in Moscow. I write letters in Yiddish to my Moscow grandmother, whom I will never know. I will never know my Russian aunts, uncles, cousins. In Moscow there is suffering, deprivation, poverty. My mother, threadbare, goes without a new winter coat so that packages can be sent to Moscow. Her fiery justice-eyes are semaphores I cannot decipher.

Some day, when I am free of P.S. 71, I will write stories; meanwhile, in winter dusk, in the Park View, in the secret bliss of the *Violet Fairy Book*, I both see and do not see how these grains of life will stay forever, papa and mama will live forever, Hymie will always turn my skatekey.

Hymie, after Italy, after the Battle of the Bulge, comes back from the war with a present: *From Here to Eternity*. Then he dies, young. Mama reads *Pride and Prejudice* and every single word of Willa Cather. Papa reads, in Yiddish, all of Sholem Aleichem and Peretz. He reads Malamud's *The Assistant* when I ask him to.

Papa and mama, in Staten Island, are under the ground. Some other family sits transfixed in the sun parlor where I read *Jane Eyre* and *Little Women* and, long afterward, *Middlemarch*. The Park View Pharmacy is dismantled, turned into a Hallmark card shop. It doesn't matter! I close my eyes, or else only stare, and everything is in its place again, and everyone.

A writer is dreamed and transfigured into being by spells, wishes, goldfish, silhouettes of trees, boxes of fairy tales dropped in the mud, uncles' and cousins' books, tablets and capsules and powders, papa's Moscow ache, his drugstore jacket with his special fountain pen in the pocket, his beautiful Hebrew paragraphs, his Talmudist's rationalism, his Russian-Gymnasium Latin and German, mama's furnace-heart, her masses of memoirs, her paintings of autumn walks down to the sunny water, her braveries, her reveries, her old, old school hurts.

A writer is buffeted into being by school hurts—Orwell, Forster, Mann!—but after a while other ambushes begin: sorrows, deaths, disappointments, subtle diseases, delays, guilts, the spite of the private haters of the poetry side of life, the snubs of the glamorous, the bitterness of those for whom resentment is a daily gruel, and so on and so on; and then one day you find yourself leaning here, writing at that selfsame round glass table salvaged from the Park View

Pharmacy—writing this, an impossibility, a summary of how you came to be where you are now, and where, God knows, is that? Your hair is whitening, you are a well of tears, what you meant to do (beauty and justice) you have not done, papa and mama are under the earth, you live in panic and dread, the future shrinks and darkens, stories are only vapor, your inmost craving is for nothing but an old scarred pen, and what, God knows, is that?

A NOTE ON THE TYPE

This book was set via computer-driven cathrode-ray tube in Janson, a redrawing of type cast from matrices long thought to have been made by the Dutchman Anton Janson, who was a practicing type founder in Leipzig during the years 1668–87. However, it has been conclusively demonstrated that these types are actually the work of Nicholas Kis (1650–1702), a Hungarian, who most probably learned his trade from the master Dutch type founder Dirk Voskens. The type is an excellent example of the influential and sturdy Dutch types that prevailed in England up to the time William Caslon developed his own incomparable designs from them.

Composed, printed and bound by
The Haddon Craftsmen, Inc., Scranton, Pennsylvania

Typography and binding design
by Dorothy Schmiderer